THE ETHICAL
ARGUMENT
AGAINST
GOVERNMENT

John T. Sanders
Rochester Institute of Technology

D1264518

University Press
of America™

Copyright © 1980 by
John T. Sanders

University Press of America, Inc.
4710 Auth Place, S.E., Washington, D.C. 20023

Library of Congress Catalog Card Number: 80-488

Acknowledgements

My debts to others are too extensive to cata-
logue in a complete way, but some of them are important enough that they ought to be acknowledged
here. First and foremost, I must express my grati-
tude to David B. Suits, who first directed my attention to the issues discussed here, and whose
critical help has been crucial throughout the whole
project. Second, I must acknowledge a special debt
to David Friedman, Ayn Rand, and Murray Rothbard,
whose work provided the foundations upon which the
present essay has been based. It will be clear to
those familiar with these authors that I have been
rather selective regarding the use to which their
thoughts have been put here, but it will be equally
clear that they have had a profound influence upon
me, especially with regard to the arguments of
Chapters VII-IX. Prof. Rothbard, in particular,
must be thanked for his hearty encouragement in the
early stages of this project.

Among other important debts, I must acknowledge the help of P.T. Sagal and Elizabeth Rapaport.
Their criticism was indispensable in developing the
earliest drafts. In addition, I must thank the
faculty and students of the Department of Philosophy at Boston University for providing an environment especially well suited for nurturing a work of
this kind. It was an eclectic environment, which I
always found to be extraordinarily stimulating.
Finally, David Henderson must be thanked for an
extremely careful reading of the manuscript, for a
warmly critical response that led to additions here
and there (especially in Chapter VII), and for many
helpful stylistic suggestions.

Among the many good friends who have had to
listen, for the past six years, to the arguments
that have finally been set down here, I must thank,
in particular, Jane E. Sanders, who has not only
given me all the moral support that I could ever
need, but who has been consistently helpful in
reminding me of my obligation to common sense. I
am also indebted to Cathie Truver for her unreason-
ably cheerful attitude about doing a large part of
the dull work that dominated the late stages of the

- iii -

project, and to the Reason Foundation and Liberty
Fund, Inc., both of which provided time and funds
that helped in my effort to tie up loose ends.

Many of those who have helped me through this
ordeal have been skeptical of my conclusions. I
think this must be, in part at least, because I
have never yet been able to present to them the
whole case. I hope that this work will help to
make the conclusions more plausible.

*   *   *

Chapter X has appeared, in only slightly different form, in *The Journal of Libertarian Studies*, 1,
No. 1 (Winter, 1977), pp. 35-44.

Rochester
October, 1979

Table of Contents

Acknowledgements   iii

Introduction   vii

I: Community or Social Cooperation as
      a Human "Good".   1

II: Government as a "Necessary Evil"   13

III: Transitional Necessity.   41

IV: The Rawlsian Framework   63

V: The Structure of the Counter-Argument . . . 91

VI: Public Goods and the Free Market 97

VII: Peace on the Market 119

VIII: Justice on the Market. 177

IX: Transition on the Market 193

X: Some Proposed Problems of the Model 213

Conclusion 237

Works Cited. 241

Introduction

Mankind is now faced with what may be the most confusing array of crises it has ever confronted. There is a population crisis, an energy crisis, and an economic crisis; there is a "crisis in morals" and there is a crisis of political ideology. For each crisis, there is a battery of thinkers who have argued that failure to resolve the crisis in question may mean the end of "civilization as we know it." The time is ripe for a critical re-examination of the nature of the crises with which the world is faced, and of the ways in which they might be resolved.

It may be thought that this is most appropriately the task of the "experts": of population experts, of resource management experts, of economists, and of, perhaps, politicians. Indeed, the work of specialists is of vital importance, and it is to such experts that contemporary governments have belatedly begun to turn as they have awakened to the several crises.

The problems may go much deeper, however, than the level at which such experts have their special competencies. It may be that the problems are embedded in the traditional process of social decision-making itself.

Throughout most of human history, the task of resolving the most crucial social problems has been consigned to governments. In the contemporary era, for example, governments have been entrusted with responsibility for guiding the economy, with providing aid to the poor, and with making available to their citizens certain valuable services, like education and medical care. These responsibilities are often regarded as at least as important as the more traditional governmental tasks, such as protecting citizens from foreign and domestic aggression. In each case, governments have acquired the responsibility in question because of the widely held belief that only governments are competent to achieve just and efficient solutions to social problems.

The history of political thought records the dominance of this belief, at least over the last few thousand years. But it also records a recurrent theme of dissent.[1] This theme plays an important role in the works of the "classical liberals," and is central to the thought of nineteenth and twentieth century anarchists and libertarians. Such thinkers not only maintain that governmental activity, as such, is often pernicious, they frequently argue that many of the social problems not actually *caused* by governments could have been expected to find their own resolutions if governments had not intervened.

If careful scrutiny of the several contemporary crises leads to similar conclusions, then it seems reasonable to suspect that solutions to these problems may involve the radical limitation of governmental activities in relevant areas. Or perhaps, if the problem appears to be pervasive enough, it will be necessary to suggest the abolition of decision-by-government altogether. Even if the analysis does not lead to agreement with the critics of government, however, there is clearly a place for philosophers--as well as for specialists in the various problem areas--in the dialogue that results once the question has been raised.

As indicated above, however, it is not as if that dialogue has to be initiated from scratch at this late date. Much of the ground that must be covered was explored by the end of the eighteenth century, by thinkers like John Locke, Jean Jacques Rousseau, Anne Robert Jacques Turgot, Adam Smith, Thomas Jefferson, James Madison, and William God-

---

[1]Wilhelm Hennis, in "Ende der Politik? Zur Krisis der Politik in der Neuzeit," [54 (complete references to sources may be found among the numbered listings included under "Works Cited," at the end of this book. Henceforth, all bibliographic reference will be made by citing, in square brackets, the number of a source as it appears under "Works Cited."], demonstrates concern over this situation without clearly aligning himself with those who criticize government. Neither, however, does he propose any other solution. He seems to counsel despair, more than anything else.

win. The critique continued during the nineteenth
and twentieth centuries in the work of writers like
Pierre Joseph Proudhon, Michael Bakunin, Benjamin
Tucker, Peter Kropotkin, Emma Goldman, and Paul
Goodman, from one political perspective, and in the
work of such thinkers as Henry David Thoreau,
Frédéric Bastiat, Lysander Spooner, Eugen von
Böhm-Bawerk, Ludwig von Mises, Friedrich A. Hayek,
and Henry Hazlitt, from another perspective. Currently, authors like Milton Friedman, Ayn Rand,
Murray Rothbard, John Hospers, Robert Paul Wolff,
Richard Taylor, Jerome Tuccille, David Friedman,
and Robert Nozick have further refined the arguments, and have brought them to bear on the characteristic problems of the present.[2] This relatively
long tradition has not yet earned full-fledged
respectability for the idea that governments may be
more trouble than they are worth, but it has certainly improved its status.[3]

It is not the immediate purpose of the present
essay to focus further attention on the possibility
that the activities of governments often cause--but
rarely or never resolve--social problems. That
possibility has been thoroughly discussed by the
authors named above, and their arguments will be
repeated here only where they shed light upon another side of the same issue.

Whether or not governments are the ultimate
social trouble-makers, questions may be raised as
to what positive reasons exist for maintaining
them. If there are none, then the very *possibility*
that they are the causes of the present social ills
may lead to advocating their abolition. Furthermore, it may be that there are significant social
ills inherent in the institution of government
itself, and if these are not ameliorated by greater
social goods, then it is hard to see how the institution can be defended. The question to be addressed

---

[2]For specific works by all these authors, see "Works Cited."

[3]For an extensive twentieth century bibliography, see Robert
Goehlert, "Anarchism: A Bibliography of Articles, 1900-
1975," [37].

in this essay, then, is the old question as to whether government is justified.

Government does require justification. It is a human creation, the product of deliberate human action. Acts are performed in its name. The act of creating--or deliberately maintaining--government, as well as the acts typically performed in the name of government, may and should be evaluated as to morality, and as to appropriateness for achieving intended goals.

This book will challenge the almost universally held belief that creating and maintaining governments is morally acceptable. Its arguments will be guided by three relatively weak postulates, the accuracy (or truth) of which will not here be questioned (although some weak support will be given to each of them, insofar as something like them seems to have been accepted by those defenders of government here to be discussed). For those who accept the three postulates, the line of argument presented in the text of the book should lead to the conclusion that the institution of government should be abandoned. To the extent that the postulates are controversial, however, their explicit enunciation should facilitate criticism.

The three postulates are:

A) An essential character of government is its assumed right to coerce its own "clients" (or "subjects").

B) Where there is no government, there is no state (*qua* state); where there is no state, there is no government (as such).

C) In the absence of good reasons to the contrary, people should not be coerced.

These three postulates will be discussed briefly in this introductory section.

Of the three, the first two postulates are definitional in character. They can be regarded as proposed partial *explications* of the relevant terms (and thus as partially stipulative), and this should soften potential criticisms of their accuracy or truth. The arguments presented here do not rely essentially on these two postulates, except in respect of the way that they (the arguments) are phrased.

The third postulate, although quite weak, seems to be the most likely locus of controversy. It is an ethical postulate, and it is this one of the three that will support most of the weight of the subsequent argument.

A) *An essential character of government*[4] *is its assumed right to coerce its own "clients" (or "subjects").*

An organization or institution that delivered the mails, like United Parcel Service, would not be a government because of this. An organization that provided armed protection, like Pinkerton's, would not yet be a government. An organization, such as a mercenary army, that provided defensive services for a large community, would not, simply because it provided this service, be a government. Finally, even an organization that provided *all* these services would not thereby become a government. *One* of the reasons that such organizations and institutions would not yet be governments is expressed in this first postulate: simply because they provide services of the kinds that governments often provide, they do not necessarily thereby claim for themselves a right to coerce their own clients (i.e., the people they serve), and such a claim is an *essential character* of government; people are not free to avoid supporting the government that rules the territory in which they live.

Another way of expressing the postulate is this: the claim of the right to coerce its own clients is a *necessary condition* of government. It is not, of course, a sufficient condition. It is not

---

[4]In order to avoid unnecessary confusion, the term "government" is used here and in what follows in the sense in which it refers to a certain kind of *institution*, rather than the sense in which it denotes *processes* of a special kind.

the case, that is, that all institutions that claim such a right are (or would be) governments. But if an institution is to be identified as a government, it must claim such a right.

A third way of expressing the postulate is in linguistic terms: "government" is defined in terms of coercion. When viewed in this way, the postulate can be regarded as a *partial explication* of the term "government." This partial explication is offered primarily as a guide to the way the term is used in what follows. Even if the postulate is not accepted, therefore, it should be possible to follow the subsequent argument simply by substituting "coercive government" wherever the term "government" appears. For those who accept the partial explication, of course, the phrase "coercive government" will appear redundant.[5]

B) *Where there is no government, there is no state (qua state); where there is no state, there is no government (as such)*.

This postulate amounts to a partial explication of the term "state." It is an attempt to provide a means of distinguishing between "states," on the one hand, and "communities" or "societies," on the other.

States are not taken to be the *same* as governments, however. They are communities-with-governments. Thus, one of the ways of dissecting the concept of "state" would allow one to view the concept "government" as one of its "parts."

As was the case with the first postulate, this second postulate is intended as a guide to usage in

---

[5]A good source for this kind of characterization of government is Franz Oppenheimer, *The State* [105], especially pp. 24-27, where the author differentiates between "political means" and "economic means" of acquiring things. See also Elizabeth Anscombe, "On the Source of the Authority of the State" [1]. For one of the most concise defenses of this kind of definition of government, see David Friedman, *The Machinery of Freedom* [31], chap. 28.

the present work. It is useful because, in enunciating the relation between states and governments, the postulate clarifies a minor technical problem in dealing with the historical literature: a large number of those writers whose work is relevant to the present discussion have talked more about "the state" than about government. If, however, the second postulate is rejected, then another substitution is called for: wherever the term "state" occurs, insert "community-with-government" (or "community-with-coercive-government," if both postulates are rejected).[6]

    C) *In the absence of good reasons to the contrary, people should not be coerced.*

    A "good reason" for coercing another person is exemplified in the following case: a certain person, Kowalski, is being threatened with murder by another person, Jones. Kowalski is unarmed and Jones has a gun. Suddenly, Kowalski sees an opportunity to grab Jones, and (he hopes) to force him to drop his weapon. This involves coercing Jones, but Kowalski must do so if he is to save his own life. In this case, self-defense seems to be a good reason for coercion.[7]

---

[6]Robert Paul Wolff seems to conceive of the "state" as more or less the same thing as "government" (*In Defense of Anarchism* [158], pp. 3,4). In general, there has been no end of confusion with regard to the relation between states and governments, although the issue doesn't seem to be particularly difficult. For some of the problems engendered by Wolff's conflation of the notions, see Jeffrey H. Reiman, "Anarchism and Nominalism: Wolff's latest Obituary for Political Philosophy" [117].

[7]Under some quite plausible definitions of "coercion," it is inappropriate to use the term to describe Kowalski's behavior toward Jones. Nevertheless, adopting such definitions imposes a significant risk of question-begging in discussions about certain acts which may or may not be described as coercive. The term will therefore be used here in what is perhaps an over-broad sense, in the hope that the present analysis will thereby avoid unnecessary problems. The main potential problem, of course, has to do with the possibil-

As it stands, the third postulate seems to include too much. For example, Jones may be threatening Kowalski in an effort to force Kowalski to give up his money, or perhaps Jones intends to murder Kowalski in order to gain a position of power now held by Kowalski. Jones might thus point out that he would not be able to gain a certain degree of wealth or power if he were to refrain from coercing Kowalski, and that this fact constitutes a "good reason" for the coercion.

To avoid this problem, two comments are in order.

Firstly, the arguments here presented will limit themselves to considerations of (alleged) *morally acceptable* "good reasons." It is here uncritically assumed that moral acceptability affects the "goodness" of reasons, although it is certainly not assumed that *only* moral considerations are relevant.

This proposed limitation is justified because the intent of the book is to challenge the belief that creating and maintaining governments is morally acceptable. Jones-like arguments, since they would probably be rejected by anyone who takes moral considerations to be relevant, will be ignored altogether.

---

ity--or the likelihood--that coercion of one kind or another will be present even in societies which do not institutionalize it through governments. It might be thought, after all, that governmental coercion may be justifiable as a means of minimizing the *total* amount of coercion in society. It might be thought, that is, that it is reasonable to correct certain coercive factors that would prevail in an ungoverned society by administering a controlled dose of coercion via government. As will become clear in what follows, a main contention of the present essay may be understood as a rejection of this view: coercion in society may be controlled without resorting to government. For an interesting discussion of some of the problems involved in trying to get clear on coercion, see Robert Nozick's article, "Coercion" [103].

Secondly, the present arguments will focus only on a special class of alleged (morally acceptable) "good reasons." In the light of the first and third postulates, defenses of government can be viewed as attempts to provide (morally acceptable) good reasons for coercion. This book amounts, then, to a criticism of the adequacy of such attempts. Criticism will be directed, however, only at a few of the many arguments that have been (or might be) made in behalf of government. This second limitation is necessary because of the difficulty of constructing an "impossibility proof" (or a "proof" of any kind) in the field of moral and political philosophy. It cannot be emphasized too often that it is *not* the intent of this book to establish that it is *impossible* to justify government. Rather, the present work is intended as a critical analysis of a few justificatory attempts; the few attempts to be criticized here are singled out because they seem best to reflect the attitudes about government that most people share. It is assumed that if the present arguments succeed in undermining these attitudes, then the thesis that governments should no longer be maintained will have received rather strong support.

In what follows, the first three chapters will be devoted to outlining the *prima facie* case for government, as it has been presented by a few historically influential thinkers. The fourth chapter will pursue this line a bit further, by sketching a methodological framework for comparing such arguments, which seems to be extremely helpful in identifying the points in the *prima facie* case that might be vulnerable to criticism. It will be argued that, with certain qualifications, the framework gives a fair rendering of all of the arguments in defense of government presented in the first three chapters, and provides a valuable perspective on each of them (although it must be filled out in different ways for each of them).

The fifth chapter will mark the beginning of the critical analysis of the received views sketched in the first three chapters. It will be argued that the alleged moral acceptability of government, defended in the arguments of the first

three chapters, relies upon the perceived necessity
of government for achieving certain valued ends.[8]
Since this is the case, a counter-argument to the
effect that government is *not* necessary to achieve
these ends would, if successful, undermine the
belief that government is morally acceptable. Further, it will be argued that careful consideration
of the methodological framework outlined in the
fourth chapter shows just how such a counter-
argument would have to work.

_____

[8]A somewhat weaker version of the same argument might be ventured, to the effect that although government may not be
necessary for achieving the ends in question, it is *unlikely*
that these ends would be reached without government. It
will therefore be crucial to frame the counter-argument in
such a way that it accounts for this alternate version as
well. It will be argued that it is at least as likely that
the ends intended for government would be achieved in an
ungoverned society of a certain kind as it is that they
would be achieved in governed societies. Since this problem
of relative "likelihoods" raises special problems for proposed social systems that have never yet been tried, questions arise as to how one is to evaluate claims that such
systems are likely to perform in a given way. Indeed, this
is a central problem for social science in general: How is
one to extrapolate from data in the social sciences, and
make predictions about what *would* happen under a different
set of circumstances? How does one make reasonably sound
predictions in the social sciences? How does one even
establish canons for evaluating the existing data? These
are rather complicated questions, which require considerable
work. They are certainly too immense to be dealt with adequately in the present discussion. For present purposes, it
will be necessary to appeal to an intuitive notion of what
it is reasonable to expect, given certain background data.
For an extremely provocative discussion of these questions,
however, see Ludwig von Mises' *Human Action* [94], esp. pp.
1-69. The "praxeological" approach recommended by von Mises
has born fruit in the work of such authors as Murray Rothbard and recent Nobel Prize winner Friedrich Hayek (see
"Works Cited" for sources). For quite a different sort of
approach, see Raymond Dacey, "The Role of Economic Theory in
Supporting Counterfactual Arguments" [23], and the works
referred to there.

In the sixth chapter, an important problem for any alternative to government--the "public goods" problem--will be discussed. In the light of this discussion, certain guidelines will appear regarding the kinds of options available to non-coercive alternatives to government, if they are to provide people with "public goods." A general sketch of the particular alternative here to be examined will then be given.

In Chapters Seven through Nine, the non-coercive model will be compared with government, in the light of the defenses of government outlined in the earlier chapters, and in terms of the framework developed and adopted in Chapter Four. It will be argued that the model seems to achieve the ends for which government is intended by the thinkers discussed earlier, but that it avoids the coercion inherent in government. That such a model can be constructed without ignoring any obvious facts of nature seems, it will be argued, to refute the view that government is necessary, and thereby to seriously undermine the belief that government is morally acceptable. The model will be presented in such a way as to illustrate its ability to meet the needs discussed earlier (for which government was thought to be necessary), and to compare it with governmental models as to moral acceptability.

The tenth chapter, finally, will be devoted to answering a pair of recent objections to the model.

Chapter I

Community or Social Cooperation as a Human "Good"

Since the present aim is to criticize the view that creating and maintaining governments is morally acceptable, it is clear that the first step in the argument must be to spell out the characteristic features of that view, as fully as possible.

To argue against government is to support anarchy, and most people have such a strong aversion to the idea of anarchy, that it will be fruitful to begin the discussion with an attempt to discover the reasons for this antipathy. Doing so will begin to yield an understanding of people's general acceptance of government, and will allow attention to be focused upon a small set of core arguments that can be handled in the present analysis.

According to one popular usage of the term, "anarchy" simply *means* "social chaos." Prominent New York City officials, for example, have been from time to time quoted as expressing fears that, if the city were to go bankrupt, life there would "degenerate" to anarchy. What they fear is that there would, under such circumstances, be rioting in the streets, looting of stores, widespread hunger, more mugging than usual, and, in general, a Hobbesian war "of every man, against every man."[1] It is this sort of situation that many people think of when they hear the term "anarchy." Here it is necessary only to point out that the term is not, in this discussion, being used in this particular sense. The arguments about to be outlined are not designed as a defense of rioting, looting, mugging, or social chaos in general. An appeal is made, rather, to the sense of "anarchy" in which it means no more than society without government.[2] It will

---

[1]See Thomas Hobbes, *Leviathan* [55], p. 185.

[2]I do not, therefore, understand anarchism as recommending a "total absence of any rules whatsoever." It is certainly

- 1 -

(later) be contended that social chaos is not even
a likely *consequence* of anarchy in the present sense.

A *somewhat* more sympathetic reading of the term
"anarchy" may still lead to the conclusion that
governments are not only acceptable, but necessary.
On this second reading (also a fairly popular one),
anarchy implies a sort of "hermitism," in which
people are regarded as more self-sufficient than
they really are. "No man is an island," the criticism goes, and since anarchism implies (on the
second reading) that people do not need to cooperate with one another, it is false.

In a moment, a typical argument, brought in
behalf of the thesis that human beings need to work
cooperatively, will be explored, since that need
plays a prominent role in the version of anarchism
that will later be presented as an alternative to
governments. Exploring these arguments will also
expose the "core arguments" in behalf of government that will be the focus of later criticism.
But the notion that anarchy implies hermitism is
here to be rejected; the term "anarchy" is to
mean no more than society without a government. It
is *not* here contended that people ought to break
their social ties, any more than it is argued that
people ought to go to war with one another.

Finally, it may be concluded that anarchy is
unacceptable even if "anarchy" is understood in the
sense in which it is here being used. Arguments to
this effect will be isolated in the second and
third chapters, and dealt with in later chapters.
Prior to that, first steps must be taken toward
isolating these arguments by inspecting typical
arguments adduced in behalf of social cooperation
or community--arguments often utilized in refuta-
tions of anarchy on the second meaning of the term.

---

true that some anarchists have advocated rulelessness, but
it hardly seems reasonable to grant them exclusive use of
the name "anarchism." It is this "no-rules" branch of the
anarchist family that has received the most attention, however; see, for example, Richard H.S. Tur, "Anarchy versus
Authority: Towards a Democratic Theory of Law" [152].

The *locus classicus* for discussions of the
values of community is Aristotle's *Politics* [2]. Not
only does the book contain arguments of the kind
needed, it purports to show that the state (and
government, therefore) is a natural phenomenon,
"needed by man in order to fulfil his nature."[3] It
is packed with valuable historical data about the
various kinds of state apparati that had been tried
by different peoples in Aristotle's day, and
includes such tidbits as Aristotle's own somewhat
Machiavellian advice about how various forms of
government might be adjusted to increase their stability. Most importantly, it handles, in a relatively small volume, an incredibly large number of
political issues that are still being debated,
including most of the issues that will be discussed
in the present essay.

All that will be attempted here, however, will
be the extraction from the *Politics* of a fairly typical argument in support of the value of community.
Since Aristotle is primarily concerned with the
state, or with city-states, it will be necessary to
do more than merely report what he says. His argument will be reconstructed, and then compared with
the idea of the "state" as it is explicated in postulate (B) of the Introduction. Given certain
remarks of Aristotle's, it will be argued that the
Politics contains precisely what is presently being
sought: a defense of the values of community which
raises all the questions that need here to be
raised about whether the human need for community
requires that people have governments.

For Aristotle, the state is "an association of
persons" ([2], p. 25)--a "partnership" (p. 29).
This association has its foundation in the fact
that human beings cannot, in general, even *survive*
without some form of cooperation. It is the simple
desire to survive which leads people to take the
first steps toward forming a state: " . . . every
state is an association of persons formed with a
view to some good purpose" (p. 25); " . . . [the
state] started as a means of securing life itself"
(pp. 27-28).

---

[3]T.A. Sinclair, [2], p. 12.

This is only the first step, however; a step which could be made by non-intelligent animals. Merely to form an "association" for mutual preservation does not yet make a state. It is a necessary step, but not a sufficient one:

> a state is something more than an investment; its purpose is not merely to provide a living but to make a life that is worth while. (p. 119)

So the state has two basic functions: first, it is supposed to provide for the survival of its members. The goal is the self-sufficiency of the community: " . . . a state is not a chance agglomeration but, we repeat, a body of men aiming at a self-sufficient life" (p. 272).

Second, the state is supposed to provide for a *life that is worth while* for its members. Aristotle explains what this means in the following passages:

> When we speak of city or state, we mean a community of like persons whose end or aim is the best life possible. The best is happiness and this consists in the exercise of all good qualities and their fullest possible use. (p. 271)

> The state is intended to enable all, in their households and their kinships, to live *well*, meaning by that a full and satisfying life. (p. 120)

> . . . it is our love of others that causes us to prefer life in a society; and they all contribute towards that good life which is the purpose of the state; and that, we hold, means living happily and nobly. So we must lay it down that the political association which we call a state exists not simply for the purpose of living together but for the sake of noble actions. (p. 121)

The argument seems to go something like this: individuals are not (normally) endowed with the capacity to survive completely alone. No man is an island. People enter into various arrangements with others to facilitate survival, and this is the

first step toward the state. But as people form
these cooperative associations, they place themselves " . . . in a position to secure the good
life" (p. 28). This becomes an end in itself, born
of the capacity, unique in human beings, to perceive good and evil, right and wrong, just and
unjust (pp. 28-29). The good life is the life dedicated to virtue, both in the classical sense in
which the "virtue" of man is his rationality, and
in the narrower sense in which helping others is
"virtuous." Having accomplished the task that it
was initially devised for--the achieving of self-
sufficiency with respect to the survival of its
"members"--the state focuses its attention on the
pursuit of virtue and the good life. This becomes
its primary function.

The cooperative association, which began as a
means to survival, has become more than merely a
means to some other, higher, end. There is a sense
in which it seems to have become an end in itself,
to which individual interests seem, at least, to
have become subordinate:

> . . . the city or state has priority over . . .
> any individual among us. For the whole must be
> prior to the parts (p. 29)

> It is clear . . . that the state is both natural
> and prior to the individual. For as an individ-
> ual is not fully self-sufficient after separa-
> tion, he will stand in the same relationship to
> the whole as the other parts. (p. 29)

> . . . it is not right . . . that any of the
> citizens should think that he belongs just to
> himself; all citizens belong to the state, for
> each is a part of the state; and the care
> bestowed on each part naturally looks also
> towards the care of the whole. (p. 300)

Cooperation *itself* is part of virtue, and anyone who would isolate himself from the community is
treated by Aristotle far more roughly than would be
appropriate if such a person were merely risking
his own survival, or his own virtue:

He who by his nature and not simply by ill-luck
has no city, no state, is either too bad or too
good, either sub-human or super-human--sub-human
like the war-mad man condemned in Homer's words
'having no family, no morals, no home;' for
such a person is by his nature mad on war, he is
a non-cooperator like an isolated piece in a
game of draughts. (p. 28)

The non-cooperator, if not super-human, is *immoral*.

If this much was known about the Aristotelian
argument, and no more, it would appear that he is
only a step or two away from declaring the state--
in the sense of "state" outlined in postulate (B)
of the Introduction--as justified. For the postulate's explication of "state" suggested that states
were communities with governments, and postulate
(A) suggested that governments were institutions
that claimed the right to coerce their own clients
(or subjects). Aristotle's assertion that the
state is "prior" to the individual, and that all
citizens belong to the state, comes very close to
the kind of claim that was there envisioned. If
one adds to this the Aristotelian argument for a
natural distinction between ruler and ruled (pp.
26, 33-35), then the argument may appear to have
been completed: it is the function of the state to
pursue goodness, it is a duty of the citizen to
subordinate his own more immediate interests to the
state in making this pursuit, and " . . . the superior in goodness shall rule and be master" (p. 35).
It is not so clear, however, that this sketch provides an accurate portrayal of what Aristotle is
doing.

There are, in particular, several remarks, all
to a similar effect, that appear throughout the
Politics , and which seem to make rather serious
trouble for the kind of analysis so far proposed.
Here are some examples:

. . . which life is one to choose, the life of a
citizen, fully participating in the work of the
city, or that of a foreign resident, cutting
oneself adrift from the political nexus? . . .
[this] question [is] a matter of an individual's
choice. (pp. 258-59)

Just as one way of setting a kingdom on the road
to destruction is to make its rule more tyrannical, so conversely it protects a tyranny to make
it more kingly, always preserving one thing--the
power of the ruler, power enabling him to govern
*not only those who consent but also those who do
not*. For if he abandons that, *he abandons his
whole position as tyrant*. (p. 228; stress
added)

Yet surely, if we will but examine carefully, we
shall see how completely unreasonable it would
be if the work of a statesman were to be reduced
to seeing how he could rule and dominate others
with or without their consent. How could that
be regarded as part of statecraft or lawgiving
which is not even lawful in itself? To rule at
all costs, not only justly but unjustly, that is
simply non-legal, and merely to have the power
is not to have the right. One does not find
this insistence on power in any of the other
professions; it is not the job of a doctor or a
ship's captain to *persuade* or to *force* patients
or passengers. Certainly most people seem to
think that domination and government are one and
the same thing; they have no compunction about
inflicting upon others what as individuals they
regard as neither just nor beneficial to themselves. For themselves and among themselves
they ask for just government but in the treatment of others they do not worry about what
things are just (p. 260; stress added)

The first passage seems to suggest that Aristotle leaves to the individual the choice as to
whether to enlist in the cooperative state project.
The second passage implies that rulers who govern
not only those who consent but also those who do
not consent are tyrants, and Aristotle does not
approve of tyrants. The third passage, finally,
suggests that ruling others, without their consent,
is unjust. The tone of all three taken together
seems to thoroughly undo the tentative conclusion
that Aristotle is defending the state in the present sense. Indeed, he seems, in the third passage, to reject the idea proposed in postulates (A)
and (B). It may be that *most* people think that domination and government are "one and the same thing,"

- 7 -

says Aristotle, but surely this can't be right.

That's one difficulty.

A second difficulty arises in connection with the idea that it is the "superior" people--the wise or the good--who should rule the state. The idea seems itself to be perfectly reasonable, but the second difficulty is a practical one. As Bertrand Russell has put it,

> is there any form of constitution which will give the government to the wise? It is clear that majorities, like general councils, may err, and in fact have erred. Aristocracies are not always wise; kings are often foolish; Popes, in spite of infallibility, have committed grievous errors. Would anybody advocate entrusting the government to university graduates, or even to doctors of divinity? Or to men who, having been born poor, have made great fortunes? It is clear that no legally definable selection of citizens is likely to be wiser, in practice, than the whole body.
>
> It might be suggested that men could be given political wisdom by a suitable training. But the question would arise: what is a suitable training? And this would turn out to be a party question.[4]

Saying that the "wise" or the "good" should rule does not answer the most important questions--the questions that press hard when people set out actually to construct a social arrangement for themselves. Aristotle seems to realize the difficulty of this problem too, for in the portion of the *Politics* where he is discussing the importance of training people both to rule and to be ruled, he notes that

> it is not certain whether training should be directed at things useful in life, or at those

---

[4]Bertrand Russell, *History of Western Philosophy* [124], p. 124.

conducive to virtue, or at non-essentials. (All
these answers have been given.) And there is no
agreement as to what in fact does tend towards
virtue. Men do not all prize most highly the
same virtue, so naturally they differ also about
the proper training for it. (*Politics*, p. 300)

There are two difficulties, then, involved
with assessing the conclusion that Aristotle argues
in behalf of the state as it is characterized in
the initial postulates sketched in the introduction
to this book: first, there is evidence that he
does not regard the state as coercive; second, he
seems to be aware of an important practical problem
that plagues attempts to form states. It would
seem that some sort of reevaluation of the Aristotelian position is called for, and clues as to
which form the reevaluation should take may be present in a final pair of Aristotle's characteriza-
tions of the state:

> Our own observation tells us that every state is
> an association of persons formed with a view to
> some good purpose. I say 'good' because in
> their actions all men do in fact aim at what
> they think good. Clearly then, as all associa-
> tions aim at some good, that one which is supreme
> and embraces all others will have also as its
> aim the supreme good. That is the association
> which we call the State, and that type of assoc-
> iation we call political. (p. 25)
>
> . . . it is the sharing of a common view in . .
> . . matters [of good and evil, right and wrong,
> just and unjust] that makes . . . a city. (p.
> 29)

It is clear what the "supreme good" is: it is
the good life--the life of happiness, which ". . .
. .consists in the exercise of all good qualities
and their fullest possible use" (p. 271)--the life
dedicated to virtue.

If the two passages quoted here are taken as
definitive, then it may be that they provide a key
to understanding the apparently conflicting ideas
that seem to comprise the Aristotelian view of the

state. That is, if the state is, for Aristotle, to
be defined as nothing more than that kind of "association of persons" that aims at the good life,
then it may be that a somewhat different picture of
the Aristotelian position emerges--a picture that
takes into account more of the divergent strains of
Aristotle's thought than did the earlier, rather
superficial sketch. If a city (or state) is no
more than a group of persons who share a common
view in matters of good and evil, right and wrong,
just and unjust, and who therefore have the same
"aim," then the earlier difficulties may become
resolved.

One might be led to differentiate between two
things that Aristotle is doing in the *Politics*. On
the one hand, it seems that he wants to identify
what the state is, and having done that, to show
that the state is (in some sense) natural. On the
other hand, he gives some rather vague, general
advice about how states should be formed, and once
formed, how they may be maintained.[5]

Toward identifying the state, and toward
showing that the state is natural, Aristotle argues
as follows: people need to cooperate in order to
survive, and they need to cooperate in order to
achieve the good life. Both survival and the good
life ought to be striven for. Therefore people
ought to cooperate. The state is nothing more than
an association of people striving for the life of
virtue. The state is *not* to be coercive, and it is
therefore not a state in the sense of the initial
postulates. It is more like a *community* of like-
minded individuals, seeking a common goal in a common way.

This cooperation is itself part of the good
life. Community becomes an end in itself. Once
involved in a community, it is perverse to resist
its efforts, although the choice as to whether to
become involved in any particular community in the

_____

[5]For a somewhat similar analysis of the Aristotelian argument, see Fred D. Miller, Jr., "The State and the Community
in Aristotle's *Politics*," [92].

first place remains with the individual. The
"non-cooperator" condemned by Aristotle is that
individual who rejects *all* communities--the
non-cooperator-on-principle. The hermit.

But in any case, to rule those who do not consent to be ruled is unjust. The proper place for
government is within a community of people, who
share a common view of justice and injustice, and
who thus consent to be commanded by the ruler. To
govern otherwise is to be a tyrant. A just ruler
will not force his subjects, individually or collectively, any more than a doctor or a ship's captain will force patients or passengers.[6]

Toward answering questions on how communities
of this kind may best be formed and maintained in
practice, Aristotle notes that people differ as to
which "virtues" are to be striven for, and as to
what sort of training is conducive to virtue. This
implies, first of all, that there will be different
communities which tend to correspond to the broader
differences among people. But secondly, practical-
ity may require that compromises be made *within* such
communities. Compromises, that is, both among the
members of the community and with the ideal of community, as outlined above.

Now the *ideal* of community, as expressed in
Aristotle's sketch of the nature of his "state,"
excludes coercion of citizens by the government.
It is not absolutely clear that Aristotle would
find any compromise which included such coercion of
citizens morally acceptable, but for present purposes, the possibility must be considered that some
coercion of citizens is necessary if the community
life envisioned by Aristotle is even to be approach-
able, and that if this were the case, such coercion
would be justified.[7] Here it need only be empha-

---

[6]For a slightly different approach to the same conclusion
regarding Aristotle's position, see Hennis [54], esp. p.
513. He suggests that *coercive* rule would have been
regarded by Aristotle as a collapse of political order.

[7]See below, Chapter VI, for a more complete analysis of this
question.

sized that if government in the *present* sense--
coercive government--has any place in the Aristotelian scheme, it can enter only at this point. It
is not part of the ideal "state," and could only be
acceptable as a *means* for achieving something close
to it. If it did enter the Aristotelian scheme, it
would do so only because it would be practically
necessary for achieving community.

It would appear, then, that the Aristotelian
analysis of the state provides the kind of argument
that is needed to begin the present discussion.

It seems clear that Aristotle's argument in
behalf of the "state" revolves around the *value of
community* , and that coercive government would be
acceptable *only* if it were a necessary means to
achieving community. Furthermore, the argument
contains, at least in rough form, the suggestion
that to rule those who do not consent to be ruled
is unjust; it takes note of the kinds of problems
that are raised once the fact that people differ
over what "virtues" should be pursued is recognized; and it acknowledges, at least, the problems
involved with choosing the ruler of a state. These
are the kinds of issues that will demand attention
throughout the present essay.

What is needed now, however, is an elaboration
of the possibility suggested in this chapter: that
government may be practically necessary for achieving certain basic communal values. This elaboration needs to provide a bit more precision than has
been presented so far, and it is therefore necessary to leave Aristotle, and to turn to a few core
arguments to the effect that government is a necessary evil.

Chapter II

Government as a "Necessary Evil"

If it weren't for governments, people would be forever threatened with violence. Or so runs what must be the most prevalent objection to anarchism. At the beginning of the last chapter, the sense in which the term "anarchy," or the term "anarchism," is being used here, was distinguished from the sense in which "anarchy" simply *means* social chaos. But the view that a state of anarchy would *amount* to a state of social chaos, due to certain facts about people, must still be discussed.

In the present chapter, this view will be outlined, in the form in which it has been persuasively defended by Thomas Hobbes. After the view has been sketched, attention will be directed to another position, equally influential in classical and contemporary thought, which reflects a second common reason people give for accepting government, and therefore for rejecting anarchism. The next chapter will discuss a third such position. No criticisms of the three positions will be ventured in these two chapters, since the present purpose is to do no more than to outline the core arguments in defense of government that will be responded to later.

Attention is first directed, then, to the argument that government is necessary to make or preserve peace. As was the case in the last chapter, it will be convenient to select a single source for this argument, and there is probably no source more powerful or influential than Thomas Hobbes's *Leviathan* [55].

Hobbes begins with an analysis of human action:

> . . . because *going*, *speaking*, and the like Voluntary motions, depend always upon a precedent thought of *whither*, *which way*, and *what*; it is evident, that the imagination is the first internall beginning of all Voluntary Motion. (*Leviathan* [55], p. 118)

- 13 -

> These small beginnings of Motion, within the body
> of Man, before they appear in walking, speaking,
> striking, and other visible actions, are commonly
> called ENDEAVOUR. (p. 119)
>
> This Endeavour, when it is toward something which
> causes it, is called APPETITE, or DESIRE; the
> later, being the generall name; and the other,
> oftentimes restrayned to signifie the Desire of
> Food, namely *Hunger* and *Thirst*. And when the
> Endeavour is fromward something, it is generally
> called AVERSION. (p. 119)

So according to Hobbes, the internal beginning of
all voluntary motion--all human action--is desire
or aversion.

It is true, of course, that Hobbes's theory of
man elaborates a still more remote basis for
desires and aversions. For as is apparent in the
passages cited here, desire and aversion are, for
Hobbes, kinds of human endeavor, and he classifies
endeavor as falling under what he calls "imagination." Now of imagination, Hobbes says that it
" . . . is nothing but *decaying sense*" (p. 88),
rather like the after-image that remains when one
closes one's eyes after looking directly at a
bright light. Imagination, therefore, is to be
analyzed in terms of sensation, and sensation, for
Hobbes, is caused by various pressures exerted upon
the sense organs by external objects (pp. 85-86).
" . . . Sense in all cases, is nothing els but originall fancy, caused . . . by the pressure, that
is, by the motion, of externall things upon our
Eyes, Eares, and other organs thereunto ordained"
(p. 86).

It is not necessary to be overly concerned,
however, with the Hobbesian analysis of the basis
of desires and aversions. What is important is the
much less controversial assertion that the source
of voluntary human action is to be found in human
desire and aversion.

Of the particular desires and aversions that
motivate human action, some are innate, but *most* of
them are acquired:

- 14 -

> Of Appetites, and Aversions, some are born with
> men; as Appetite of food, Appetite of excretion,
> and exoneration, (which may also and more pro-
> perly be called Aversions, from somewhat they
> feele in their Bodies;) and some other Appetites,
> not many. The rest, which are Appetites of par-
> ticular things, proceed from Experience, and
> triall of their effects upon themselves, or
> other men. (pp. 119-20)

Hobbes does not raise the question as to whether
the acquired appetites and aversions are themselves
related in some way to those that are innate, but
he does not seem to exclude this possibility,
either. Present purposes do not require that a
decision be made on this matter, however. It need
only be seen that Hobbes is arguing that human
action arises out of desires and aversions, and
that these desires and aversions are, for the most
part, acquired in the course of people's lives.
These are "Appetites of particular things," such as
a desire for this house or that field, or even for
this *kind* of house or that *kind* of field (since such
appetites "proceed from Experience, and triall of
their effects upon themselves, or other men").

Now, it is obvious that desires and aversions
are not merely acquired and stored away. Tastes
change constantly throughout a person's life, and
what an individual desires today he may loathe
tomorrow. So what a person desires changes with
time.

This being the case, it is clearly unlikely
that any *two* people, asked for a list of the things
they desire and dislike, will list all the same
things. Unlikely, that is, unless patterns of
changing desires were a great deal more constant
and the range of possible desires a great deal more
restricted than they are known to be. As it happens, there are certainly some things that each
person desires that others would regard as quite
worthless. There is thus a difference in desires
between different individuals at any given time,
and between different times in any given individual's life.

> . . . because the constitution of a mans Body,
> is in continuall mutation; it is impossible
> that all the same things should always cause in
> him the same Appetites, and Aversions: much
> lesse can all men consent, in the Desire of
> almost any one and the same Object. (p. 120)

Hobbes argues that people never really come to a stopping place in this flux of desires and aversions:

> . . . there is no such thing as perpetuall Tran-
> quility of mind, while we live here; because
> Life it selfe is but Motion, and can never be
> without Desire, nor without Feare, no more than
> without Sense. What kind of Felicity God hath
> ordained to them that devoutly honour him, a man
> shall no sooner know, than enjoy; being joyes,
> that now are as incomprehensible, as the word of
> School-men *Beatificall Vision* is unintelligible.
> (pp. 129-30)

And that's pretty unintelligible.

Human action, then, is determined by desires and aversions that differ from person to person, change in the course of each person's life, and go on changing *throughout* each person's life:

> . . . the Felicity of this life, consisteth not
> in the repose of a mind satisfied. For there is
> no such *Finis ultimus*, (utmost ayme,) nor *Summum
> Bonum*, (greatest Good,) as is spoken of in the
> Books of the old Morall Philosophers.[1] Nor can
> a man any more live, whose Desires are at an
> end, than he, whose Senses and Imaginations are
> at a stand. Felicity is a continuall progresse
> of the desire, from one object to another; the
> attaining of the former, being still but the way
> to the later. The cause whereof is, That the
> object of mans desire, is not to enjoy once

---

[1]As Hennis observes, this line of argument against the existence of a "summum bonum" does not prevent Hobbes from believing in a "summum malum," as will shortly become apparent. See Hennis [54], p. 523.

onely, and for one instant of time; but to
assure for ever, the way of his future desire.
And Therefore the voluntary actions, and inclinations of all men, tend, not only to the procur-
ing, but also to the assuring of a contented
life; and differ onely in the way: which aris-
eth partly from the diversity of passions, in
divers men; and partly from the difference of
the knowledge, or opinion each one has of the
causes, which produce the effect desired. (pp.
160-61)

Now, the "diversity of passions" among people
amounts to more than just a difference as to the
objects of desire or aversion. There is also a difference in the intensity with which different people desire or hate various things. Joe likes Max's
new Edsel much more than Eddy does, and has never
been able to understand Eddy's love of old potato
whistle recordings.[2] Evil Knievel may desire the
applause of a stadium full of people more than most
of us, but he surely doesn't enjoy getting a philosophical point right as much as some others do.

The causes of . . . the difference of Passions,
proceedeth partly from the different Constitution of the body, and partly from different Education. (pp. 138-39)

Difference of education, along with differences
in natural capacities and differences in desire for
a particular end, lead to differences in "the knowledge, or opinion each one has of the causes, which
produce the effect desired." But knowledge of the
correct causes is power, since power, for Hobbes, is
the " . . . present means, to obtain some future
apparent Good" (p. 150).

So within any large group of people, there
will be differences among members of the group as
regards the actions they are prepared to undertake.
This may be because of their differences in nat-

---

[2]There is also a difference in how much Joe and Eddy *desire*.
 Period. Some people just don't get as excited over things
 as do other people. ([55], p. 139)

ural capacities, or because of differences in education (or in "customes" (p. 139)), or simply because of different " . . . Desire of Power, of Riches, of Knowledge, and of Honour. All which may be reduced to the first, that is Desire of Power. For Riches, Knowledge and Honour are but severall sorts of Power" (p. 139).

One of the most crucial steps in Hobbes's argument is his contention that, in the state of nature, people would constantly be making attacks upon one another.

Since the "continuall progresse of the desire, from one object to another" never stops during people's lives, people will be forever striving toward satisfaction. Each person's *power* is his present means to obtain particular satisfactions in the future. So each person must at least either have some power now, or be trying to obtain some. It is not necessary that everyone have the same power, since people differ in what they desire, in how much they desire given things, and in how intensely they desire at all. It could be that some people would be content with what power they have, since power, by definition, assures future satisfaction. People will always go on wanting new things, never completely satisfied with what they have. But power is what allows them to go on getting those new things, and of that it is possible that they could have enough. Or, rather, it would be possible, if it weren't for a pair of factors that seriously complicate matters.

In spite of the wide variety of desires and aversions that different people have, and in spite of the differing intensities with which different people desire or hate different things, there are some things that most people want a great deal, and a great many things that most people want at least a little. The first complicating factor is this: many of the things that are desired by many people at once are in short supply. This being the case, people come into conflict with one another. And if the desired scarce item is important enough--that is, if it is desired intensely enough--then people will begin to struggle with one another to get it.

> . . . if any two men desire the same thing,
> which neverthelesse they cannot both enjoy, they
> become enemies; and in the way to their End,
> (which is principally their owne conservation,
> and sometimes their delectation only,) endeavour
> to destroy, or subdue one an other. (p. 184)

This leads to a very unpleasant state of
affairs. For if a person has managed to provide
himself and his family with things that make life
more pleasant for them, he has to consider the possibility that there are others out there who want
those same things. And if the things that person
has are of the kind that he and they cannot both
enjoy, he is faced with the prospect that he will
be invaded.

> And from hence it comes to passe, that where an
> Invader hath no more to feare, than an other
> mans single power; if one plant, sow, build, or
> possesse a convenient Seat, others may probably
> be expected to come prepared with forces united,
> to dispossesse, and deprive him, not only of the
> fruit of his labour, but also of his life, or
> liberty. And the Invader again is in the like
> danger of another. (p. 184)

Everyone, therefore, has to concern himself
with the possibility that others will come and
seize what he has managed to provide for himself.
Everyone fears everyone else, in such a situation.

> . . . from this diffidence of one another, there
> is no way for any man to secure himselfe, so
> reasonable, as Anticipation; that is, by force,
> or wiles, to master the persons of all men he
> can, so long, till he see no other power great
> enough to endanger him: And this is no more
> than his own conservation requireth . . . .
> (p. 184)

Everyone goes about making "pre-emptive attacks" on
his neighbors, in the hope of making it impossible
for others to attack first.

That's the first complicating factor.

The second factor is this: Hobbes has argued
that people differ in what they desire. They also
differ as regards the intensities with which they
desire various things. It is possible that some
people might be so difficult to satisfy that they
try to grab everything in sight. And of course it
is possible that some people might desire power for
its own sake, in which case power becomes more like
the "particular things" that people will never stop
striving for.[3] But in either case--whether some
people are so difficult to satisfy that they try to
grab everything, or whether some people merely are
out after power for its own sake--the same effect
arises here as arose above: everyone will have to
become concerned that others will try to snatch
what they have provided for themselves, and
pre-emptive attacks will be in order.

> So . . . I put for a generall inclination of all
> mankind, a perpetuall and restlesse desire of
> Power after power, that ceaseth onely in Death.
> And the cause of this, is not alwayes that a man
> hopes for a more intensive delight, than he has
> already attained to; or that he cannot be con-
> tent with a moderate power: but because he can-
> not assure the power and means to live well,
> which he hath present, without the acquisition
> of more. (p. 161)

Self-defense requires that people aggress against
one another.

> . . . they are in that condition which is called
> Warre; and such a warre, as is of every man,
> against every man. For WARRE, consisteth not in
> Battell onely, or the act of fighting; but in a
> tract of time, wherein the Will to contend by
> Battell is sufficiently known: and therefore
> the notion of *Time*, is to be considered in the

---

[3]Since power is, by definition, " . . . the present means, to
obtain some future apparent Good," it is possible in such
cases to talk about the power to get power, the power to get
power to get power, etc. Lest the discussion become too
confused, every effort will here be made to avoid talking
about such things.

nature of Warre; . . . the nature of War, con-
sisteth not in actuall fighting; but in the
known disposition thereto, during all the time
there is no assurance to the contrary. (pp.
185-86)

As might be suspected, social conditions in
this state of war of all against all are not particularly pleasant:

In such condition, there is no place for Industry; because the fruit thereof is uncertain:
and consequently no Culture of the Earth; no
Navigation, nor use of the commodities that may
be imported by Sea; no commodious Building; no
Instruments of moving, and removing such things
as require much force; no Knowledge of the face
of the Earth; no account of Time; no Arts; no
Letters; no Society; and which is worst of all,
continuall feare, and danger of violent death;
And the life of man, solitary, poore, nasty,
brutish, and short. (p. 186)

All this stems from Hobbes's analysis of human
nature.

The obvious question is: what accounts for
the fact that things are somewhat better in the
world than would be expected, given this analysis?
The answer: government.

Earlier, it was noted that Hobbes argues that
"from this diffidence of one another, there is no
way for any man to secure himselfe, so reasonable,
as Anticipation." That is, the most rational way
of defending one's life and property is, in the
state of war, to attack first. This turns out to
be not quite true, even for Hobbes. For him, the
most rational thing to do is to form a state.[4]

Given the evils of the state of nature, it is

---

[4]For an interpretation of Hobbes that yields the conclusion
that, for him, formation of a state is *morally obligatory*,
see George Schedler, "Hobbes on the Basis of Political Obligation" [128].

reasonable that people make every effort to end universal war. As long as the struggle goes on, no one can be at all secure. It is a "precept, or generall rule of Reason"

> *That every man, ought to endeavour Peace, as*
> *farre as he has hope of obtaining it; and when*
> *he cannot obtain it, that he may seek, and use,*
> *all helps, and advantages of Warre.* (p. 190)

It is reason, therefore, which suggests a remedy to the ills of the state of nature. If universal war is to be avoided at all, it is to be avoided by adhering to the rule of reason.

Hobbes calls it the first and "Fundamentall Law of Nature" that people "seek Peace, and follow it" (p. 190). But how is peace to be achieved? Hobbes argues that, in the state of nature, each person has the liberty--as a "Right of Nature"--

> to use his own power, as he will himselfe, for
> the preservation of . . . his own Life; and
> consequently, of doing any thing, which in his
> own Judgement, and Reason, hee shall conceive to
> be the aptest means thereunto. (p. 189)

Because of the insecurities in the state of nature, the aptest means for the preservation of a person's life may seem to be pre-emptive attack upon others. Indeed, Hobbes acknowledges that "It followeth, that in such a condition, every man has a Right to every thing; even to one anothers body" (p. 190).

The contribution made by reason, in considering this problem, is a conditional one: *if* a peace pact were secure, it would resolve the problems of the state of nature. It is therefore essential that people make every effort to find a way of making such pacts, even though it may mean giving up some natural liberty. The second law of nature commands

> *That a man be willing, when others are so too,*
> *as farre-forth, as for Peace, and defence of*
> *himselfe he shall think it necessary, to lay*
> *down [his] right to all things; and be con-*

> *tented with so much liberty against other men,*
> *as he would allow other men against himselfe.*
> (p. 190)

Reason dictates that people seek peace through covenant, where this is possible.[5]

It would be foolish, of course, for a person in a state of universal war simply to lay down his arms. It would be equally foolish for someone simply to take the word of his fellows that they will do the same. The condition attached to the law of nature just cited is that others be actually willing to lay down their rights to all things if a person is to lay down his own. How does someone determine another's willingness in this matter?

> . . . he that should be modest, and tractable, and performe all he promises, in such time, and place, where no man els should do so, should but make himselfe a prey to others, and procure his own certain ruine, contrary to the ground of all Lawes of Nature, which tend to Natures preservation. (p. 215)

> . . . Covenants, without the Sword, are but Words, and of no strength to secure a man at all. (p. 223)

What is required is a sword--a power great enough that nobody would dare violate his word. A common power is needed, which would assume the defense of each individual and levy punishment on those who attempt to take up the sword against others. And there is only one way to establish this common

---

[5]See Steve Beackon and Andrew Reeve, "The Benefits of Reasonable Conduct: The *Leviathan* Theory of Obligation" [7], for a suggestive analysis of the relations between promises, covenants and contracts in Hobbes. Making distinctions among these three notions and following up the consequences promises to yield an extremely rich and provocative view of the logical structure of *Leviathan*. The Beackon/Reeve analysis does not, however, seem to have much bearing on the sketch of Hobbes presented here. See also M.T. Dalgarno, "Analysing Hobbes's Contract" [24].

power, says Hobbes:

> The only way to erect . . . a Common Power, as
> may be able to defend [people] from the invasion
> of Forraigners, and the injuries of one another,
> and thereby to secure them in such sort, as that
> by their owne industrie, and by the fruites of
> the Earth, they may nourish themselves and live
> contentedly; is, to conferre all their power
> and strength upon one Man, or upon one Assembly
> of men, that may reduce all their Wills, by plu-
> rality of voices, unto one Will: which is as
> much as to say, to appoint one man, or Assembly
> of men, to beare their Person; and every one to
> owne, and acknowledge himselfe to be Author of
> whatsoever he that so beareth their Person,
> shall Act, or cause to be Acted, in those things
> which concerne the Common Peace and Safetie;
> and therein to submit their Wills, every one to
> his Will, and their Judgements, to his Judgment.
> This is more than Consent, or Concord; it is a
> reall Unitie of them all, in one and the same
> Person, made by Covenant of every man with every
> man, in such manner, as if every man should say
> to every man, *I Authorise and give up my Right*
> *of Governing my selfe, to this Man, or to this*
> *Assembly of men, on this condition, that thou*
> *give up thy Right to him, and Authorise all his*
> *Actions in like manner.* This done, the Multi-
> tude so united in one Person, is called a
> COMMON-WEALTH, in latine CIVITAS. This is the
> Generation of that great LEVIATHAN, or rather
> (to speake more reverently) of that *Mortall God*,
> to which wee owe under the *Immortall God*, our
> peace and defence. For by this Authoritie,
> given him by every particular man in the
> Common-Wealth, he hath the use of so much Power
> and Strength conferred on him, that by terror
> thereof, he is inabled to forme the wills of
> them all, to Peace at home, and mutuall ayd
> against their enemies abroad. And in him con-
> sisteth the Essence of the Common-wealth; which
> (to define it,) is *One Person, of whose Acts a*
> *great Multitude, by mutuall Covenants one with*
> *another, have made themselves every one the*
> *Author, to the end he may use the strength and*
> *means of them all, as he shall think expedient,*

for their Peace and Common Defence. (pp. 227-28)

That, then, is the first argument in behalf of the state. Without a powerful, coercive government, there would be universal war, of everyone against everyone. And Hobbes makes it clear that the kind of government that is needed would be coercive in the present sense:

> . . . because the major part hath by consenting voices declared a Soveraigne; he that dissented must now consent with the rest; that is, be contented to avow all the actions he shall do, or else justly be destroyed by the rest. For if he voluntarily entered into the Congregation of them that were assembled, he sufficiently declared thereby his will (and therefore tacitely covenanted) to stand to what the major part should ordayne: and therefore if he refuse to stand thereto, or make Protestation against any of their Decrees, he does contrary to his Covenant, and therfore unjustly. And whether he be of the Congregation, or not; and whether his consent be asked, or not, he must either submit to their decrees, or be left in the condition of warre he was in before; wherein he might without injustice be destroyed by any man whatsoever. (pp. 231-32)

And just to insure that his talk of consent and covenant has not been misunderstood, Hobbes clarifies his position somewhat by distinguishing between Commonwealth by Institution and Commonwealth by Acquisition:

> A *Common-wealth by Acquisition*, is that, where the soveraign Power is acquired by Force; And it is acquired by force, when men singly, or many together by plurality of voyces, for fear of death, or bonds, do authorise all the actions of that Man, or Assembly, that hath their lives and liberty in his Power. (pp. 251-52)

> And this kind of Dominion, or Soveraignty, differeth from Soveraignty by Institution, onely in this, That men who choose their Soveraign, do

it for fear of one another, and not of him whom
they Institute: But in this case, they subject
themselves, to him they are afraid of. In both
cases they do it for fear . . .

But the Rights, and Consequences of Sover-
aignty, are the same in both. His Power cannot,
without his consent, be Transferred to another:
He cannot Forfeit it: He cannot be Accused by
any of his Subjects, of Injury: He cannot be
Punished by them: He is Judge of what is necessary for Peace; and Judge of Doctrines: He is
Sole Legislator; and Supreme Judge of Controversies; and of the Times, and Occasions of
Warre, and Peace . . .   (p. 252)

So says Hobbes. But it is not necessary to
dwell on the extraordinary power that Hobbes is
willing to grant his sovereign. The major concern
of this discussion will be his main argument, that
government is necessary to preserve peace.

*   *   *

The second argument in behalf of government
suggests that the state is necessary if certain
fundamental human rights are to be preserved.
Arguments of this kind may be brought forward in
conjunction with an argument that government is
necessary to preserve peace, but they seem to have
a special force of their own that is slightly different. After all, even if universal war were not
an immediate consequence of the lack of government,
there may be some human rights that would be jeop-
ardized without it. This argument will be presented
separately, therefore, in this chapter, and dealt
with separately later.

John Locke's argument, from his *Two Treatises of
Government* [73], to the effect that government is
necessary to preserve and enhance freedom, is certainly the most influential of its kind. Since the
present purpose is to find those arguments for
government that are most widely held, it is reasonable to turn to Locke.

For Locke, the key to understanding social and political philosophy is *reason*. It is not just that reason and understanding are inextricably linked, for if that were all he had in mind, it would not be particularly enlightening to say that reason is the key to understanding human social relationships. Much more is at stake, for Locke. For

> [the] Rule . . . of *reason* . . . is that measure God has set to the actions of Men, for their mutual security . . . (*Second Treatise*, p. 312)

> God hath given [reason] to be the Rule betwixt Man and Man, and the common bond whereby humane kind is united into one fellowship and societie . . . (pp. 429-30)

Thus reason plays a central role in the Lockeian argument, just as it did for Hobbes.[6] Reason is more than just a tool for the cool evaluation of explanations and arguments. Reason is a *rule* that is given to people in order that they may live together in harmony. It dictates to a person what he may do, much in the same way that conscience does (p. 312), and places definite constraints upon legitimate activity. In so far as reason plays this important role in human affairs, one may speak not simply of the Rule of Reason, but more strongly, of the *Law* of Reason. And since Locke holds that this law was given to people as part of their natural equipment, that they may be "united into one fellowship and societie," one may reasonably call this law the Law of Nature, as well. " . . . the Law of Nature . . . is the Law of Reason . . . " (*First Treatise* , p. 253).[7]

---

[6]Reason enters the two arguments at different points, however. For Hobbes, reason is a remedy for a rather perverse "natural" human condition. For Locke, reason informs the state of nature from the outset. It is difficult to make too much of this difference, though. Here, the important distinction to be kept in mind is the difference between Hobbes's defense of government as a peace-maker, and Locke's defense of government as a rights-protector.

[7]There is evidence, especially from Locke's *Essay Concerning Human Understanding* [72], that he may have conceived the

Now everyone (with the exception of lunatics, idiots and children) is equipped with the power of reason. Thus everyone has had the law of nature "promulgated" to him. Each individual is thus ". . . capable . . . to provide for his own Support and Preservation, and govern his Actions according to the Dictates of the Law of Reason which God had implanted in him" (*Second Treatise*, p. 347). This implies, Locke argues, that people are born free; not free from the constraints of the Law of Nature, but free from one another:

> . . . God having given Man an Understanding to direct his actions, has allowed him a freedom of Will, and liberty of Acting, as properly belonging thereunto, within the bounds of that Law he is under. (pp. 348-49)

> The *Freedom* then of Man and Liberty of acting according to his own Will, is *grounded on* his having *Reason*, which is able to instruct him in that Law he is to govern himself by, and make him know how far he is left to the freedom of his own will. (p. 352)

> [the] State all Men are naturally in . . . is, a *State of perfect Freedom* to order their Actions, and dispose of their Possessions, and Persons as they think fit, within the bounds of the Law of Nature, without asking leave, or depending upon the Will of any other Man. (p. 309)

People are, by their very natures, politically free. And this implies that they are politically equal, for

> [there is] nothing more evident, than that Creatures of the same species and rank promiscuously

---

relation between reason and Law of Nature to be more complex than is suggested by these passages from the *Two Treatises*. See James O. Hancey, "John Locke and the Law of Nature" [46] for citation of this evidence. It is not clear to me whether this yields an interpretation inconsistent with the present one, however, and even if it did, I am not sure that this would imply that my interpretation of the *Two Treatises* is incorrect.

born to all the same advantages of Nature, and
the use of the same faculties [the faculty of
reason being what Locke has most in mind],
should also be equal one amongst another without
Subordination or Subjection, unless the Lord and
Master of them all, should by any manifest Declaration of his Will set one above another, and
confer on him by an evident and clear appointment an undoubted Right to Dominion and Sover-
eignty. (p. 309)

There has been no such "manifest Declaration," says
Locke; so people are naturally free and equal, as
regards their political relationships. The natural
state of human freedom and equality is one in which
" . . . all the Power and Jurisdiction is recipro-
cal, no one having more than another . . . "   (p.
309).

It is clear that Locke sets great store by the
constraints placed upon human behavior by the Law
of Nature. People are free, but if they violate
the dictates of reason in their behavior toward
others, the consequences are fairly grave;

> In transgressing the Law of Nature, the Offender
> declares himself to live by another Rule, than
> that of *reason* and common Equity, which is that
> measure God has set to the actions of Men, for
> their mutual security: and so he becomes dan-
> gerous to Mankind, the tye, which is to secure
> them from injury and violence, being slighted
> and broken by him. Which being a trespass
> against the whole Species, and the Peace and
> Safety of it, provided for by the Law of Nature,
> every man upon this score, by the Right he hath
> to preserve Mankind in general, may restrain, or
> where it is necessary, destroy things noxious to
> them, and so may bring such evil on any one, who
> hath transgressed that Law, as may make him
> repent the doing of it, and thereby deter him,
> and by his Example others, from doing the like
> mischief. (pp. 312-13)

> . . . having quitted Reason, which God hath
> given to be the Rule betwixt Man and Man, and
> the common bond whereby humane kind is united

into one fellowship and societie; and having
renounced the way of peace, which that teaches,
and made use of the Force of War to compasse his
unjust ends upon an other, where he has no right,
and so revolting from his own kind to that of
Beasts by making Force which is theirs, to be his
rule of right, he renders himself liable to be
destroied by the injur'd person and the rest of
mankind, that will joyn with him in the execution
of Justice, as any other wild beast, or noxious
brute with whom Mankind can have neither Society
nor Security. (pp. 429-30)

Any violation of the Law of Nature implies a rejection of reason, and the offender may be treated
like an animal, in the sense that everyone else has
the right to do what is necessary to stop his
offense, and to prevent future offenses. In the
passages just cited, Locke mentions a new right
that people have--the right to "preserve Mankind in
general." This right follows from God's intent
that reason be given to people that they might live
together in society. Everyone has received the
gift of reason from God, that he might be secure in
his individual life and at the same time unite with
his fellows in "fellowship and societie." When
this security and this fellowship becomes threatened, the Law of Reason itself shows that people
may (or perhaps it is the case that they must) protect themselves and society from destruction. And
since each individual has this right, it follows
that "every *Man hath a Right to punish the Offender, and
be Executioner of the Law of Nature*" (p. 313).

> . . . the *Execution* of the Law of Nature is in
> that [natural] State, put into every Mans hands,
> whereby every one has a right to punish the
> transgressors of that Law to such a Degree, as
> may hinder its Violation. (p. 312)

> . . . in the *State of Nature, every one has the
> Executive Power* of the Law of Nature . . . (p.
> 316)

To summarize Locke's argument up to this point,
it is possible to list several facts about human
beings that Locke says are learned by attending to

reason. People are naturally free from the obligation to ask others for permission to dispose of
themselves and their possessions as they themselves
think fit. People are, by their very natures,
politically equal; no one has a natural right to
rule. Finally, each person has a natural right to
preserve mankind in general, and this implies a
natural right to punish transgressors of the law of
nature--that is, it implies that everyone has the
"Executive Power" of the law of nature. All this
is true, says Locke, even if there were no governments.

The view that everyone has a natural right to
dispose of himself and his possessions as he thinks
fit deserves a bit more comment. Locke's argument
for a natural human freedom from coercion at the
hands of others was fairly clear. People who are
capable of governing themselves (as all people are,
with the exception of lunatics, idiots and children),
by virtue of the same Rule of Reason that is promulgated to all rational creatures, ought to be free
of "Subordination or Subjection," unless God should
make it manifest that He had something else in mind.
But what of this freedom to dispose of "possessions"? The same argument does not seem to work,
without some additions.

The additions are these:

> Though the Earth, and all inferior Creatures be
> common to all Men, yet every Man has a *Property*
> in his own *Person*. This no Body has any Right
> to but himself. The *Labour* of his Body, and the
> *Work* of his Hands, we may say, are properly his.
> Whatsoever then he removes out of the State that
> Nature hath provided, and left it in, he hath
> mixed his *Labour* with, and joyned to it some-
> thing that is his own, and thereby makes it his
> *Property*. It being by him removed from the com-
> mon state Nature placed it in, hath by this
> *labour* something annexed to it, that excludes
> the common right of other Men. For this *Labour*
> being the unquestionable Property of the
> Labourer, no Man but he can have a right to what
> that is once joyned to . . . (pp. 328-29)

- 31 -

People have a right to property, therefore, and property arises when people mix their labor with things provided by nature.[8]

There are limits, of course, to what may be acquired in the way of property. The first qualification is that people may only go on acquiring more property of a specific kind if they leave some for others:

> . . . this *Labour* being the unquestionable Property of the Labourer, no Man but he can have a right to what that is once joyned to, at least where there is enough, and as good left in common for others. (p. 329)

> God the Lord and Father of all, has given no one of his Children such a Property, in his peculiar Portion of the things of this World, but that he has given his needy Brother a Right to the Surplusage of his Goods; so that it cannot justly be denied him, when his pressing Wants call for it. And therefore no Man could ever have a just Power over the Life of another, by Right of property in Land or Possessions; since 'twould always be a Sin in any Man of Estate, to let his Brother perish for want of affording him Relief out of his Plenty. (*First Treatise*, pp. 205-06)

---

[8]Robert Nozick wonders why mixing one's labor with the land isn't just a good way of losing one's labor, rather than a way of acquiring land (*Anarchy, State, and Utopia* [102], pp. 174-75). Actually, Nozick discusses tomato juice, rather than labor, and the ocean, rather than land. But his question is originally raised with regard to the Lockeian theory of property. It's a good question. See Lawrence C. Becker, "The Labor Theory of Property Acquisition" [8], for a recent attempt to deal with this problem. See also Becker's *Property Rights: Philosophic Foundations* [9] for a more general treatment. For "libertarian" arguments in behalf of private property which do not proceed from a "natural rights" position, and for which Nozick's particular question does not arise, see Adam Smith, *The Wealth of Nations* [133], esp. II, pp. 27-30, 290, 371; Ludwig von Mises, *Human Action* [94], esp. pp. 682-84, 698-715; Friedrich A. Hayek, *The Constitution of Liberty* [49], esp. pp. 140-42, 220-33.

The second qualification on property rights is to be found in the second passage. Not only may no one exhaust the stock of natural goods by mixing his labor with it, no one may ignore the plight of the needy, or use his property to subject others:

> . . . a Man can no more justly make use of another's necessity, to force him to become his Vassal, by with-holding that Relief, God requires him to afford to the wants of his Brother, than he that has more strength can seize upon a weaker, master him to his Obedience, and with a Dagger at his Throat offer him Death or Slavery. (p. 206)

The limits to how much property a person may justly acquire are social: they are set by the needs of others.

Yet Locke also says that each person may acquire as much as he needs for the "Conveniency of Life" (*Second Treatise*, p. 334). This is the "measure" of property, set by nature. Locke does not think that there is any conflict between the measure and limitations of property; at least, he felt there was no conflict in his day:

> . . . the same *measure* may be allowed still, without prejudice to any Body, as full as the World seems. For supposing a Man, or Family, in the state they were, at first peopling of the World by the Children of *Adam*, or *Noah*; let him plant in some in-land, vacant places of *America*, we shall find that the *Possessions* he could make himself upon the *measures* we have given, would not be very large, nor, even to this day, prejudice the rest of Mankind, or give them reason to complain, or think themselves injured by this man's Incroachment, though the Race of Men have now spread themselves to all the corners of the World, and do infinitely exceed the small number [which] was at the beginning. (p. 335)

The invention of money has seriously complicated matters, says Locke, but the basic measuring principle is sound:

This I dare boldly affirm, That the same *Rule of Propriety*, (*viz.*) that every Man should have as much as he could make use of, would hold still in the World, without straitning any body, since there is Land enough in the World to suffice double the Inhabitants had not the *Invention of Money*, and the tacit Agreement of Men to put a value on it, introduced (by Consent) larger Possessions, and a Right to them . . . (p. 335)

It is likely that Locke would want to reconsider the empirical statements made in these passages, regarding the sufficiency of land available for the world's inhabitants, in the present day. There are considerably more inhabitants now, and America--Locke's example of wide open spaces--may shortly be pretty fully occupied.[9] But these matters are not the present concern. What is important is that, in addition to natural freedom and equality, and a natural right to preserve mankind in general, with its concomitant right to be executioner of the law of nature, people have property rights, although they are limited by the needs of their fellows.

Attention has been directed, in the last several pages, to Locke's "State of Nature," which is the state mankind would be in even without government. It is important to note that for Locke, the state of nature is not at all a state of universal war, as it was for Hobbes:

. . . the *State of Nature, and the State of War* . . . however some Men have confounded [them], are as far distant, as a State of Peace, Good Will, Mutual Assistance, and Preservation, and a State of Enmity, Malice, Violence, and Mutual Destruction are one from another. (p. 321)

---

[9]Judith Jarvis Thomson has made the interesting suggestion that the "enough and as good . . . for others" proviso really is a sufficient condition for property acquisition, but not a necessary condition. See her "Property Acquisition" [143].

It is true, of course, as Hobbes suggested, that
"Covenants [and laws, presumably], without the
Sword, are but Words, and of no strength to secure
a man at all":

> . . . the Law of Nature would, as all other Laws
> that concern Men in this World, be in vain, if
> there were no body that in the State of Nature,
> had a Power to Execute that Law, and thereby
> preserve the innocent and restrain offenders
> . . . (p. 312)

But people do have such a sword in Locke's state of
nature: it consists in the right each person has
to be the executioner of the law of nature. Those
who make reason their rule may gang up and punish--
or destroy, if necessary--those who don't.

So it is not the case that the state of nature
would amount to a state of war of all against all.
Indeed, Locke equates it with a state of "Peace,
Good Will, Mutual Assistance, and Preservation."
The question obviously arises as to why people would
ever want to leave this state, and establish governments.

The answer is that there are, notwithstanding
the various pleasant features, several disadvantages to life in the state of nature. For one
thing, the fact that each person may execute the
law of nature is likely to lead to problems:

> . . . it is unreasonable for Men to be Judges in
> their own Cases . . . . Self-love will make Men
> partial to themselves and their Friends. And on
> the other side, . . . Ill Nature, Passion and
> Revenge will carry them too far in punishing
> others. (p. 316)

> . . . the Law of Nature being unwritten, and so
> no where to be found but in the minds of Men,
> they who through Passion or Interest shall mis-
> cite, or misapply it, cannot so easily be con-
> vinced of their mistake where there is no estab-
> lish'd Judge: And so it serves not, as it
> ought, to determine the Rights, and fence the
> Properties of those that live under it, espec-

ially where every one is Judge, Interpreter, and
Executioner of it too, and that in his own
Case . . . (p. 404)

There is nothing wrong with the law of nature
itself; it is just that people will interpret it
incorrectly when judging in their own cases, and
the administration of justice within the state of
nature will be, at least, inconsistant.

The second problem is, of course, that not
everyone will be content to make reason their rule,
and *ad hoc* punishment of transgressors may not suffice to make life secure:

> . . . though in the state of Nature [everyone
> has the right to complete freedom regarding him-
> self and his possessions], yet the Enjoyment of
> it is very uncertain, and constantly exposed to
> the Invasion of others. For all being Kings as
> much as he, every Man his Equal, and the greater
> part no strict Observers of Equity and Justice,
> the enjoyment of the property he has in this
> state is very unsafe, very unsecure. This makes
> him willing to quit a Condition, which however
> free, is full of fears and continual dangers:
> And 'tis not without reason, that he seeks out,
> and is willing to joyn in Society with others
> who are already united, or have a mind to unite
> for the mutual *Preservation* of their Lives, Lib-
> erties and Estates, which I call by the general
> Name, *Property*. (p. 395)

So although people have a sword in the state of
nature--the right of everyone to execute the law of
nature--it is insufficient. There is more of a
chance that the bad guys will gang up on the good
guys, than vice versa, since the former comprise
"the greater part" of humanity. Everyone has certain natural rights, but these rights are "very
insecure" in the state of nature:

> . . . were it not for the corruption, and vit-
> iousness of degenerate Men, there would be
> no . . . necessity that Men should separate from
> [the] great and natural Community, and by posi-
> tive agreements combine into smaller and div-

- 36 -

ided associations. (p. 397)

The great and *chief end* therefore, of Mens unit-
ing into Commonwealths, and putting themselves
under Government, *is the Preservation of their
Property* [i.e., their Lives, Liberties and
Estates]. (p. 395)

More particularly, the state of nature lacks
three important things:

First, There wants an *establish'd*, settled,
known *Law*, received and allowed by common consent to be the Standard of Right and Wrong, and
the common measure to decide all Controversies
between them. For though the Law of Nature be
plain and intelligible to all rational Creatures;
yet Men being biassed by their Interest, as well
as ignorant for want of study of it, are not apt
to allow of it as a Law binding to them in the
application of it to their particular Cases.
(p. 396)

Secondly, In the State of Nature there wants a
known and indifferent Judge, with Authority to
determine all differences according to the
established Law. For every one in that state
being both Judge and Executioner of the Law of
Nature, Men being partial to themselves, Passion
and Revenge is very apt to carry them too far,
and with too much heat, in their own Cases; as
well as negligence, and unconcernedness, to make
them too remiss, in other Mens. (p. 396)

Thirdly, In the state of Nature there often
wants *Power* to back and support the Sentence
when right, and to *give* it due *Execution*. They
who by any Injustice offended, will seldom fail,
where they are able, by force to make good their
Injustice: such resistance many times makes the
punishment dangerous, and frequently destruc-
tive, to those who attempt it. (pp. 396-97)

Thus the state of nature is not so pleasant
after all. Considered by itself, it is the ideal
condition of mankind. The problem, however, is in
maintaining it in the face of human foibles.

Thus Mankind, notwithstanding all the Privi-
ledges of the state of Nature, being but in an
ill condition, while they remain in it, are
quickly driven into Society. Hence it comes to
pass, that we seldom find any number of Men live
any time together in this State. The inconven-
iencies, that they are therein exposed to, by
the irregular and uncertain exercise of the
Power every Man has of punishing the transgres-
sions of others, make them take Sanctuary under
the establish'd Laws of Government, and therein
seek *the preservation of their Property*. 'Tis
this makes them so willingly give up every one
his single power of punishing to be exercised by
such alone as shall be appointed to it amongst
them; and by such Rules as the Community, or
those authorised by them to that purpose, shall
agree on. And in this we have the original
right and rise of both *the Legislative and Executive Power*, as well as of the Governments and
Societies themselves. (p. 397)

The establishment of government, therefore, is
nothing more nor less than the setting up of "a
Judge on Earth, with Authority to determine all the
Controversies, and redress the Injuries, that may
happen to any Member of the Commonwealth" (p. 369).
In order that this judge may be able to do the
intended job effectively, it is necessary that each
person entering the commonwealth give up, first,
the "*Power* . . . *of doing whatsoever he thought fit for
the Preservation of himself* , and the rest of Mankind"
(pp. 397-98), and submit himself to laws made by
society; and second, the "*Power of punishing*" (p.
398), and commit his own strength to supporting the
executive power in punishing transgressors according to society's law. Having given up these powers
or natural rights, a person is no longer in the
state of nature, but a member of a commonwealth.

It may be objected that the Lockeian government is not a government in the present sense,
since Locke argues that each person's *consent* is
necessary to justify government's taking power over
him:

Men being, as has been said, by Nature, all
free, equal and independent, no one can be put

- 38 -

out of this Estate, and subjected to the Political Power of another, without his own *Consent*.
The only way whereby any one devests himself of
his Natural Liberty, and *puts on the bonds of
Civil Society* is by agreeing with other Men to
joyn and unite into a Community, for their comfortable, safe, and peaceable living one amongst
another, in a secure Enjoyment of their Properties, and a greater Security against any that are
not of it. (pp. 374-75)

Can government really be said to be *coercive* under
such a condition?

It will later be argued that it is, and that
Locke can plausibly add his consent condition only
by virtue of his rather liberal reading of "consent." It is not appropriate immediately to elaborate upon the argument that Lockeian government is
coercive, since the present task is to do no more
than to get Locke's defense of government straight.
There will be occasion, in a later chapter, to
reinforce the view that Locke's commonwealth is
coercive. For the moment, it will be fruitful
merely to note the ground that "consent" is
intended to cover in the *Second Treatise*:

Every *Man* being, as has been shewed, *naturally
free*, and nothing being able to put him into
subjection to any Earthly Power, but only his
own Consent; it is to be considered, what shall
be understood to be *a sufficient Declaration of*
a Mans *Consent, to make him subject* to the Laws
of any Government. There is a common distinction of an express and a tacit consent, which
will concern our present Case. No body doubts
but an *express Consent*, of any Man, entring into
any Society, makes him a perfect Member of that
Society, a Subject of that Government. The difficulty is, what ought to be look'd upon as a
tacit Consent, and how far it binds, *i.e.* how
far any one shall be looked on to have consented,
and thereby submitted to any Government, where
he has made no Expressions of it at all. And to
this I say, that every Man, that hath any Possession, or Enjoyment, of any part of the Dominions of any Government, doth thereby give his

> *tacit Consent,* and is as far forth obliged to
> Obedience to the Laws of that Government, during
> such Enjoyment, as any one under it; whether
> this his Possession be of Land, to him and his
> Heirs for ever, or a Lodging only for a Week;
> or whether it be barely travelling freely on the
> Highway; and in Effect, it reaches as far as
> the very being of any one within the Territories
> of that Government. (p. 392)

It is not a simple matter to avoid consenting to
government, according to Locke.

At any rate, Locke's *Two Treatises* provides the
kind of argument that was here being sought: an
argument for government, based on the contention
that government is necessary to preserve or protect
certain fundamental human rights. " . . . *where
there is no Law, there is no Freedom"* (p. 348); and
where there is no government, the law will not be
properly observed. " . . . *Civil Government* is the
proper Remedy for the Inconveniences of the State
of Nature" (p. 316). Its role, like that of law
itself, is to *"preserve and enlarge Freedom "* (p. 348),
and for that it is indispensable.

Chapter III

Transitional Necessity

The first argument in behalf of government suggested that, because of certain facts about human nature, the absence of state power would lead to war of all against all. Government is necessary, that argument concluded, if peace is to be preserved. The second argument held that, although the absence of government would not lead to universal war, there are nevertheless certain fundamental human rights that would be very insecure without the state. Government was held to be necessary, in the second argument, to preserve and protect these fundamental rights. Both arguments implied that government is likely always to be necessary in human social arrangements.

The last argument in defense of government differs from the first two in that it concedes that government is, in the long run, undesirable. It defends government only as a temporary instrument for making certain crucial social changes; changes that are necessary to prepare people for the ultimate abolition of government.

A modified form of this argument might be brought forward in support of the thesis that government ought always to be maintained as a standing instrument for achieving valuable social changes. This sort of variation will not be of major concern here, however. Consonant with the present effort to isolate the most widely held arguments in behalf of government, attention will be focused only upon the purest formulation of this third type of argument: and for that formulation, it is best to turn to the thought of Karl Marx:

> . . . we do not set out from what men say, imagine, conceive, nor from men as narrated, thought of, imagined, conceived, in order to arrive at men in the flesh. We set out from real, active men, and on the basis of their real life-process we demonstrate the development of the ideological reflexes and echoes of this life-process . . .

men, developing their material production and
their material intercourse, alter, along with
this their real existence, their thinking and
the products of their thinking. Life is not
determined by consciousness, but consciousness
by life. In the first method of approach the
starting-point is consciousness taken as the
living individual; in the second method, which
conforms to real life, it is the real living
individuals themselves . . . [1]

Marx is committed to a method of analysis that
takes as its data the things that people *do* ; the
things that fill out their "life-processes." Furthermore, the distinguishing characteristics of
human activity are the major factors that set mankind apart from the rest of the animal world:

The animal is one with its life activity.
It does not distinguish the activity from
itself. It is *its activity*. But man makes his
life activity itself an object of his will and
consciousness. He has a conscious life activity.
It is not a determination with which he is completely identified. Conscious life activity
distinguishes man from the life activity of animals . . . Only for this reason is his activity
free activity . . .

The practical construction of an *objective
world*, the *manipulation* of inorganic nature, is
the confirmation of man as a conscious species-
being, i.e. a being who treats the species as
his own being or himself as a species-being. Of
course, animals also produce. They construct
nests, dwellings, as in the case of bees, bea-
vers, ants, etc. But they only produce what is
strictly necessary for themselves or their
young. They produce only in a single direction,
while man produces universally. They produce
only under the compulsion of direct physical
needs, while man produces when he is free from
physical need and only truly produces in freedom

---

[1]Karl Marx and Frederick Engels, *The German Ideology* [87],
p. 47.

from such need . . . . [2]

So, first, Marx proposes to begin his analysis from human activity. And *human* activity is conscious activity. It is production.

But what people are conscious of is itself altered in the course of the development of human activity. " . . . men, developing their material production and their material intercourse, alter, along with this their real existence, their thinking and the products of their thinking." So, second, what people are depends upon what they produce:

> The way in which men produce their means of subsistence depends first of all on the nature of the actual means of subsistence they find in existence and have to reproduce. This mode of production must not be considered simply as being the production of the physical existence of the individuals. Rather it is a definite form of expressing their life, a definite *mode of life* on their part. As individuals express their life, so they are. What they are, therefore, coincides with their production, both with *what* they produce and with *how* they produce. The nature of individuals thus depends on the material conditions determining their production. (*German Ideology*, p. 42)

Finally, in so far as each individual's activity contributes to the change and development of the total environment in which people live and work, human activity is social activity:

> Even when I carry out *scientific* work, etc., an activity which I can seldom conduct in direct association with other men, I perform a *social*, because *human*, act. It is not only the material of my activity--such as the language itself which the thinker uses--which is given to me as a social product. My *own existence* is a social

---

[2]"Economic and Philosophical Manuscripts," in *Karl Marx: Early Writings* [84], pp. 127-28.

- 43 -

activity. For this reason, what I myself produce I produce for society, and with the consciousness of acting as a social being. ("Economic and Philosophical Manuscripts," pp. 157-
58)

In summary, then, the proper analysis of both
the individual person and his society proceeds from
human activity. Human activity is conscious activity; it is activity for the sake of *producing*, not
just for the satisfaction of some physical need.
So what an individual is coincides with what he
produces and with how he produces. But the conditions of production are themselves dependent upon
what other, earlier individuals have produced. In
the same way, what a person now produces will contribute to the conditions of production for later
people. All human activity is profoundly social,
therefore, both because it begins in an environment
which has been created by earlier generations, and
because it contributes to the environment which
will inform the activity of later generations. And
in so far as individual human activity has this
doubly social character, so has individual human
nature, since what people *are* is determined by, and
determines, the conditions of human production.

In the social production of their existence, men
inevitably enter into definite relations, which
are independent of their will, namely relations
of production appropriate to a given stage in
the development of their material forces of production. The totality of these relations of
production constitutes the economic structure of
society, the real foundation, on which arises a
legal and political superstructure and to which
correspond definite forms of social consciousness. The mode of production of material life
conditions the general process of social, political and intellectual life. It is not the consciousness of men that determines their existence, but their social existence that determines
their consciousness.[3]

---

[3]*A Contribution to the Critique of Political Economy* [83],
pp. 20-21.

It is not, of course, merely the links between generations of producers that make human activity social. At any given time, people will find that producing requires that they enter into special kinds of relationships with others. The pattern of social relations that people enter into in the process of production will reflect the stage in the development of these processes that has been attained.

The Marxian argument suggests that the conditions of production evolve through time, and now Marx is saying that this evolution is reflected in changing patterns of social relations. The total array of relationships that people must enter into in their life activity at any given time--relationships both with things and with other people--constitutes the economic and political superstructure at that stage of development.

It is within the context of changing conditions of production, and concomittant changing social relations, that the concept of "social class" is best understood. It will be most illuminating to look at one of Marx's historical examples, to see how this works:

> In the Middle Ages the citizens in each town
> were compelled to unite against the landed nobil-
> ity to save their skins. The extension of trade,
> the establishment of communications, led the
> separate towns to get to know other towns, which
> had asserted the same interests in the struggle
> with the same antagonist. Out of the many local
> corporations of burghers there arose only grad-
> ually the burgher *class*. The conditions of life
> of the individual burghers became, on account of
> their contradiction to the existing relation-
> ships and of the mode of labour determined by
> these, conditions which were common to them all
> and independent of each individual. The bur-
> ghers had created the conditions insofar as they
> had torn themselves free from feudal ties, and
> were created by them insofar as they were deter-
> mined by their antagonism to the feudal system
> which they found in existence. When the individ-
> ual towns began to enter into associations,

these common conditions developed into class
conditions. The same conditions, the same con-
tradiction, the same interests necessarily
called forth on the whole similar customs every-
where. (*German Ideology*, p. 82)

Classes arise, therefore, in reaction to pressure within the pattern of productive relationships. Oppressed by the landed nobility, the burghers took what steps they could in self-defense.
To the extent that the steps taken were similar, it
is possible to identify the emergence of the burgher class.

The success of the burghers did not mean, however, total individual freedom within the pattern
of social relationships:

The separate individuals form a class only insofar as they have to carry on a common battle
against another class; otherwise they are on
hostile terms with each other as competitors.
On the other hand, the class in its turn
achieves an independent existence over against
the individuals, so that the latter find their
conditions of existence predestined, and hence
have their position in life and their personal
development assigned to them by their class,
become subsumed under it. (p. 82)

The class itself gives new structure to social
relationships, to the relations of production. The
emergence of a class is the hallmark of a new stage
in social development, but it does not free people
from material conditions. They have simply traded
the old patterned relationship for a new one, with
different terms.

At a certain stage of development, the material
productive forces of society come into conflict
with the existing relations of production or--
this merely expresses the same thing in legal
terms--with the property relations within the
framework of which they have operated hitherto.
From forms of development of the productive forces these relations turn into their fetters.
Then begins an era of social revolution. The

changes in the economic foundation lead sooner
or later to the transformation of the whole
immense superstructure. (*Contribution*, p. 21)

Social revolution is not merely contingent
upon conflict within society. People cannot expect
a successful overthrow of the "superstructure"
merely because they are unhappy. Again, a necessary pre-condition of social transformation is that
the material conditions of production be suited to
that transformation:

> No social order is ever destroyed before all the
> productive forces for which it is sufficient
> have been developed, and new superior relations
> of production never replace older ones before
> the material conditions for their existence have
> matured within the framework of the old society.
> (p. 21)

The "old society" is the source not only of the
pressures and antagonisms that lead to class formation and revolution, but also of the resolution of
those pressures and antagonisms. Particular pressures lead to particular social fissures, which the
oppressed see as a means of escape. Classes arise
because the steps similar people take in their
self-defense *must* be similar, since the possibility
for self-defense arises only when the old social
pattern yields a way out. And classes arise when,
and only when, they are possible.

Now, this whole dynamic is the result of antagonisms within the social order. Classes struggle
against classes for dominance. It is this struggle
that has been the story of social relationships to
date. Indeed, politics itself is merely the business of domination, in the context of the development process of the conditions of material production: " . . . political power is precisely the
official expression of antagonism in civil society."[4]

The centralised State power, with its ubiquitous

---

[4]*The Poverty of Philosophy* [85], p. 174.

organs of standing army, police, bureaucracy,
clergy, and judicature--organs wrought after the
plan of a systematic and hierarchic division of
labour,--originates from the days of absolute
monarchy, serving nascent middle-class society
as a mighty weapon in its struggles against
feudalism. Still, its development remained
clogged by all manner of mediaeval rubbish,
seignorial rights, local privileges, municipal
and guild monopolies and provincial constitu-
tions. The gigantic broom of the French Revolution of the eighteenth century swept away all
these relics of bygone times, thus clearing
simultaneously the social soil of its last hind-
rances to the superstructure of the modern State
edifice raised under the First Empire, itself
the offspring of the coalition wars of old
semi-feudal Europe against modern France.
During the subsequent *régimes* the Government,
placed under parliamentary control--that is,
under the direct control of the propertied
classes--became not only a hotbed of huge
national debts and crushing taxes; with its
irresistible allurements of place, pelf, and
patronage, it became not only the bone of contention between the rival factions and adventur-
ers of the ruling classes; but its political
character changed simultaneously with the economic changes of society. At the same pace at
which the progress of modern industry developed,
widened, intensified the class antagonism
between capital and labour, the State power
assumed more and more the character of the
national power of capital over labour, of a public force organised for social enslavement, of
an engine of class despotism. After every revolution marking a progressive phase in the class
struggle, the purely repressive character of the
State power stands out in bolder and bolder
relief.[5]

For Marx, the rise of the burgher class was
ultimately to be traced to certain tensions in

---

[5]"The Civil War in France," in Karl Marx and Frederick
Engels, *Selected Works* [88], vol. II, pp. 217-18.

feudal society. Similarly, tensions in the subsequent middle-class society gave rise to the proletariat:

> In proportion as the bourgeoisie, *i.e.* capital,
> is developed, in the same proportion is the pro-
> letariat, the modern working class, developed--
> a class of labourers, who live only so long as
> they find work, and who find work only so long
> as their labour increases capital.[6]

> . . . not only has the bourgeoisie forged the
> weapons that bring death to itself; it has also
> called into existence the men who are to wield
> those weapons--the modern working class--the
> proletarians. (*Communist Manifesto*, p. 87)

The tensions have widened and deepened to such an
extent that the state, whose "repressive character . . . stands out in bolder and bolder relief"
with each successive progressive step in the development of the material conditions of production,
has "assumed . . . the character of the national
power of capital over labour."

  The laborer is on the short end of economic
development under capitalism:

> Labour certainly produces marvels for the rich
> but it produces privation for the worker. It
> produces beauty, but deformity for the worker.
> It replaces labour by machinery, but it casts
> some of the workers back into a barbarous kind
> of work and turns the others into machines. It
> produces intelligence, but also stupidity and
> cretinism for the workers. (*Economic and Philo-
> sophical Manuscripts*, p. 124)

It is not just that workers don't get compensated
sufficiently for what they do; the very conditions
of work under capitalism are *alienating* :

> What constitutes the alienation of labour? First,

---

[6]Karl Marx and Fredrick Engels, *The Communist Manifesto* [86],
p. 87.

that the work is *external* to the worker, that it
is not part of his nature; and that, consequently, he does not fulfil himself in his work but
denies himself, has a feeling of misery rather
than well-being, does not develop freely his
mental and physical energies but is physically
exhausted and mentally debased. The worker,
therefore, feels himself at home only during his
leisure time, whereas at work he feels homeless.
His work is not voluntary but imposed, *forced
labour*. It is not the satisfaction of a need,
but only a *means* for satisfying other needs.
Its alien character is clearly shown by the fact
that as soon as there is no physical or other
compulsion it is avoided like the plague.
External labour, labour in which man alienates
himself, is a labour of self-sacrifice, of mor-
tification. Finally, the external character of
work for the worker is shown by the fact that it
is not his own work but work for someone else,
that in work he does not belong to himself but
to another person. (pp. 124-25)

The *alienation* of the worker in his product
means not only that his labour becomes an
object, assumes an *external* existence, but that
it exists independently, *outside himself*, and
alien to him, and that it stands opposed to him
as an autonomous power. The life which he has
given to the object sets itself against him as
an alien and hostile force. (pp. 122-23)

It is important to understand that, for Marx,
the dynamic development of society, proceeding in
terms of changing material conditions of production, does have a definite direction, or tendency.
Indeed, he felt that the whole process would ultimately lead to the " . . . emancipation and rehabilitation of man" (p. 167)--to the " . . . fully
constituted society" (p. 162):

. . . the fully constituted society produces man
in all the plenitude of his being, the wealthy
man endowed with all the senses, as an enduring
reality. (p. 162)

A new social order is possible in which the pre-

sent class differences will have disappeared and
in which--perhaps after a short transitional
period involving some privation, but at any rate
of great value morally--through enormous productive forces of all members of society, and with
uniform obligation to work, the means for existence, for enjoying life, for the development
and employment of all bodily and mental faculties will be available in an equal measure and
in ever-increasing fulness.[7]

. . . things have now come to such a pass,
that the individuals must appropriate the existing totality of productive forces . . .

The appropriation of these forces is itself
nothing more than the development of the individual capacities corresponding to the material
instruments of production. The appropriation of
a totality of instruments of production is, for
this very reason, the development of a totality
of capacities in the individuals themselves.[8]

Frederick Engels, discussing the fully constituted society in a work written in 1847, a work
which amounted to a preliminary draft of the *Communist Manifesto*, wrote that

society will produce sufficient products to
arrange a distribution that will satisfy the
requirements of all its members. The division
of society into various antagonistic classes
will thereby become superfluous. Not only will
it become superfluous, but it will even be incom-
patible with the new social order. Classes came
into existence through the division of labour
and the division of labour in its hitherto
existing form will entirely disappear . . . Education will enable young people quickly to
acquaint themselves with the whole system of

---

[7]"Wage Labour and Capital," in *Selected Works* [88], vol. I,
p. 149.

[8]"Feuerbach. Opposition of the Materialistic and Idealistic
Outlook," in *Selected Works* [88], vol. I, pp. 74-75.

production, it will enable them to pass in turn
from one branch of industry to another according
to social needs or the bidding of their own
inclinations. It will therefore abolish the
one-sidedness in development imposed on all by
the present division of labour.[9]

Thus it is clear that although the conditions
of labor under the capitalist or bourgeois system
were dismal, Marx foresaw yet another revolution
arising from the conflict between the classes. The
end result of the whole historical process would be
the abolition, not only of the particular griefs
now afflicting the working class, but of the class
system itself. And with the abolition of classes,
the tensions in society that produce constant conflicts between people would also come to an end,
for the two were of a piece.

The most important thing to know about Marx's
view of the final stage of social development is
that he was convinced that the time had come when
it was possible to take deliberate steps toward its
achievement. It is clear that Marx thought that
the requisite tensions existed in society, between
capital and labor, to motivate social revolution.
But it is just as clear that, for Marx, these alone
would not be sufficient: the material conditions
of production must be such that a transformation
from the old order to the new could be made. Marx
thought that those conditions had been met with the
advent of modern industry:

The essential condition for the existence, and
for the sway of the bourgeois class, is the formation and augmentation of capital; the condition for capital is wage labour. Wage labour
rests exclusively on competition between the
labourers. The advance of industry, whose
involuntary promoter is the bourgeoisie,
replaces the isolation of the labourers, due to
competition, by their revolutionary combination,
due to association. The development of Modern

_____

[9]"Principles of Communism," in *Selected Works* [88], vol. I,
pp. 92-93.

Industry, therefore, cuts from under its feet
the very foundation on which the bourgeoisie
produces and appropriates products. What the
bourgeoisie, therefore, produces, above all, is
its own grave-diggers. Its fall and the victory
of the proletariat are equally inevitable.
(*Communist Manifesto*, pp. 93-94)

What is more, the reign of the bourgeoisie has
produced such material abundance that the conditions are now at hand for resolving the age-old
antagonism that has brought about the constant
struggle among classes for social dominance:

The bourgeoisie, during its rule of scarce one
hundred years, has created more massive and more
colossal productive forces than have all preceding generations together. Subjection of
Nature's forces to man, machinery, application
of chemistry to industry and agriculture,
steam-navigation, railways, electric telegraphs,
clearing of whole continents for cultivation,
canalization of rivers, whole populations con-
jured out of the ground--what earlier century
had even a presentiment that such productive
forces slumbered in the lap of social labour?
(p. 85)

The bourgeois mode of production is the last
antagonistic form of the social process of pro-
duction--antagonistic not in the sense of individual antagonism but of an antagonism that ema-
nates from the individuals' social conditions of
existence--but the productive forces developing
within bourgeois society create also the material conditions for a solution of this antagonism. The prehistory of human society accord-
ingly closes with this social formation. (*Contribution*, pp. 21-22)

The end of class struggle, as well as the emancipation and rehabilitation of man, is in sight;
"things have now come to such a pass, that the
individuals must appropriate the existing totality
of productive forces," and thus take the first
necessary steps toward achieving the "fully constituted society."

The first step, of course, is the abolition of the bourgeois state: " . . . the violent overthrow of the bourgeoisie lays the foundation for the sway of the proletariat" (*Communist Manifesto*, p. 93).

> . . . the proletarians, if they are to assert themselves as individuals, will have to abolish the very condition of their existence hitherto (which has, moreover, been that of all society up to the present), namely, labour. Thus they find themselves directly opposed to the form in which, hitherto, the individuals, of which society consists, have given themselves collective expression, that is, the State. In order, therefore, to assert themselves as individuals, they must overthrow the State. (*German Ideology*, p. 85)

Once the state is overthrown, steps can be taken to build society along the lines suggested by Marx's analysis of the end result of the long historical process:

> The working class, in the course of its development, will substitute for the old civil society an association which will exclude classes and their antagonism, and there will be no more political power properly so-called, since political power is precisely the official expression of antagonism in civil society. (*Poverty of Philosophy*, p. 174)

> . . . after the enslaving subordination of the individual to the division of labour, and therewith also the antithesis between mental and physical labour, has vanished; after labour has become not only a means of life but life's prime want; after the productive forces have also increased with the all-round development of the individual, and all the springs of co-operative wealth flow more abundantly--only then can the narrow horizon of bourgeois right be crossed in its entirety and society inscribe on its banners: from each according to his ability, to each according to his needs![10]

---

[10]"Critique of the Gotha Programme," in [88], III, p. 19.

. . . the realm of freedom actually begins only
where labour which is determined by necessity
and mundane considerations ceases; thus in the
very nature of things it lies beyond the sphere
of actual material production. Just as the
savage must wrestle with Nature to satisfy his
wants, to maintain and reproduce life, so must
civilised man, and he must do so in all social
formations and under all possible modes of production. With his development this realm of
physical necessity expands as a result of his
wants; but, at the same time, the forces of
production which satisfy these wants also
increase. Freedom in this field can only con-
sist in socialised man, the associated producers, rationally regulating their interchange
with Nature, bringing it under their common control, instead of being ruled by it as by the
blind forces of Nature; and achieving this with
the least expenditure of energy and under conditions most favourable to, and worthy of, their
human nature. But it nonetheless still remains
a realm of necessity. Beyond it begins that
development of human energy which is an end in
itself, the true realm of freedom, which, however, can blossom forth only with this realm of
necessity as its basis.[11]

Political domination, and therefore government, will come to an end in the new society. The
division of community functions becomes a business
matter, and no longer a matter of dominance. This
change will take place because classes and their
antagonism will have been brought to a halt, and
this will amount to an abolition of political
power; the "governing" functions will cease to be
political:

. . . sobald die [Regierungs-] Funktionen auf-
gehört haben, politisch zu sein, existiert
1. keine Regierungsfunktion; 2. die Verteilung
der allgemeinen Funktionen ist Geschäftssache

---

[11]*Capital: A Critique of Political Economy* [82], vol. III,
p. 820.

geworden, die keine Herrschaft gibt . . .[12]

. . . mit [dem] völligen Sieg [des Proletariats] ist daher auch seine Herrschaft zu Ende, weil sein Klassencharakter [verschwunden]. ("Konspekt," p. 634)

In most of the passages just cited, Marx sounds very much like an anarchist. One reads that the proletarians must overthrow the state; they find themselves directly opposed to the state as a form of collective expression; finally, upon the complete victory of the proletariat, there will be an end to political dominance, and thus to government as such. But the last passage hints at a crucial reservation of Marx's: the complete victory of the proletariat will come only after a period in which it *does* dominate according to the old forms. Marx felt very strongly that the change from political society to bold new stateless society could not be made abruptly; a transitional state was necessary. And in this transitional state, the proletariat would have to continue to use the old, discredited political mechanism, if only to secure its gains and make possible the final stage of the revolution:

> What we have to deal with here is a communist society, not as it has *developed* on its own foundations, but, on the contrary, just as it *emerges* from capitalist society; which is thus in every respect, economically, morally and intellectually, still stamped with the birth marks of the old society from whose womb it emerges. (*Gotha Programme*, p. 17)

> . . . [in the transitional state] one [worker] will in fact receive more than another, one will be richer than another, and so on . . . But these defects are inevitable in the first phase of communist society as it is when it has just emerged after prolonged birth pangs from capi-

---

[12]"Konspekt von Bakunins 'Staatlichkeit und Anarchie'," in Karl Marx and Friedrich Engels, *Werke* [89], vol. XVIII, p. 635.

talist society. Right can never be higher than
the economic structure of society and its cul-
tural development conditioned thereby. (p. 19)

During the period of the fight to defeat the
old society, the proletariat is, of necessity,
still working on the basis of societal forms created in that old society. Therefore it must continue to work in the context of political power.
It has not, during this period, reached its final
goal. To *achieve* liberation, the proletariat uses
means that fall away *upon* liberation:

. . . das Proletariat während der Periode des
Kampfs zum Umsturz der alten Gesellschaft noch
auf der Basis der alten Gesellschaft agiert und
daher auch noch in politischen Formen sich be-
wegt, die ihr mehr oder minder angehörten, hat
es seine schliessliche Konstitution noch nicht
erreicht während dieser Kampfperiode und wendet
Mittel zur Befreiung an, die nach der Befreiung
wegfallen . . . ("Konspekt," p. 636)

The role of the proletariat in history, however, is quite different from the role of other
classes that have conquered the "state machine"
that had been the source of their oppression:

All [previous] revolutions perfected this
machine instead of smashing it. The parties
that contended in turn for domination regarded
the possession of this huge state edifice as the
principal spoils of the victor.[13]

. . . the working class cannot simply lay hold
of the ready-made state machinery, and wield it
for its own purposes. (*Civil War in France*,
p. 217)

The proletariat conquers the bourgeois state only
as a *part* of historical class conflict. Classes,
and class conflict, do not simply disappear upon
that conquest. The social and material conditions

---

[13]"Eighteenth Brumaire of Louis Bonaparte," in *Selected Works*
[88], vol. I, p. 477.

that bring about class warfare in the first place
still exist. The special role of the working class
is to put an end to class warfare, and to do this
it must change the material conditions of production. But so long as its job remains unfin-
ished--so long as classes still exist--the proletariat must hold onto political power while it goes
about its work:

> . . . solange die andren Klassen, speziell die
> kapitalistische noch existiert, solange das Pro-
> letariat mit ihr kämpft (denn mit seiner Regie-
> rungsmacht sind seine Feinde und ist die alte
> Organisation der Gesellschaft noch nicht ver-
> schwunden), muss es *gewaltsame* Mittel anwenden,
> daher Regierungsmittel; ist es selbst noch
> Klasse, und sind die ökonomischen Bedingungen,
> worauf der Klassenkampf beruht und die Existenz
> der Klassen, noch nicht verschwunden und müssen
> gewaltsam aus dem Weg geräumt oder umgewandelt
> werden, ihr Umwandlungsprozess gewaltsam
> beschleunigt werden. ("Konspekt," p. 630)

> Between capitalist and communist society lies
> the period of the revolutionary transformation
> of the one into the other. Corresponding to
> this is also a political transition period in
> which the state can be nothing but *the revolu-
> tionary dictatorship of the proletariat*. (*Gotha
> Programme*, p. 26)

It is necessary that the institution of government be maintained, in the hands of the proletariat, until the conditions that give government its
historical role as oppressive force of the ruling
class are changed. Government is, in the long run,
a perverse factor in human affairs; but it is only
a symptom of deeper social ills. Curing the symptom alone would be futile. Thus the working class
must for the time being ignore the symptom, and go
to work on the things that cause it. Once they are
successful in treating these original causes, the
symptom will simply disappear.

A bit more light can be shed upon Marx's conception of the transition from the old social situation to the new through attention to the debate

between Marx and Michael Bakunin.[14] Bakunin advocated immediate abolition of all state machinery.
The Marxian "dictatorship of the proletariat" looked
to him just like every other dictatorship: an
instrument for the oppression of the people by a
small ruling clique.

In criticising Marx's program, Bakunin had
pointed out that the only conceivable way of manag-
ing the transitional state would involve some sort
of representational body, whose assignment it would
be to make the day-to-day decisions necessary for
accomplishing the transition (quoted in "Konspekt,"
pp. 635-36). But handing this kind of power over
to *anyone* --even if they be workers--is fatal, Bakunin argued. The "dictatorship of the proletariat"
would merely lead to a "despotism of the ruling
minority." Marx and his followers soothe themselves with the claim that this transitional state
will only last a brief time, but what reason do
they have for believing this? It is much more
likely, Bakunin thought, that the workers would
merely find themselves enchained anew, by an aris-
tocracy of their own making. To doubt this is to
reveal an unfamiliarity with human nature (pp. 635-
36).

Marx's replies in "Konspekt" are not awfully
helpful. In response to the criticism that the
transitional state would amount to no more than a
new set of chains for the workers, Marx notes only
that upon the establishment of collective ownership, the conditions would be set for expression of
"the real will of the collective" (p. 635). To the
complaint that there is no reason to expect the
"dictatorship of the proletariat" to be short-lived,
Marx answers that " . . . the class dominance of
the workers over those levels of the old world with
which they are in conflict can last only so long as
the economic basis of class existence is not abolished" (p. 636). Where Bakunin implies that Marx
is just unfamiliar with human nature, Marx notes

---

[14]References to Bakunin's argument will, in what follows, be
taken from Marx's copious notes to "Staatlichkeit und Anarchie" (*Werke* [89], vol. XVIII).

only that Bakunin is apparently unfamiliar with the
way a managerial position works in a collectively
run factory (p. 635). He suggests that Bakunin
should have given more thought to the different
forms that administrative jobs could be expected to
take in a workers' state. These responses are
unhelpful, since Bakunin's basic question is this:
What reason is there for thinking that those in
charge of the workers' state will remain faithful
to their trust? Once in power, won't they simply
work to consolidate their own positions, even if
that means acting contrary to the real interests of
the proletariat?

The best answers to these questions are to be
found in other places in the works of Marx. Human
nature, for Marx, is itself conditioned by the
existing status of the productive forces in society.
Furthermore, the class an individual comes from
determines, at least in part, the things he will
think and the things he will do. The conclusion to
be drawn is that the complaint about human nature
is not well founded. Human nature in a proletarian
society will be different, even at the outset, from
human nature in a society dominated by the bourgeoisie. And as the conditions of production change
human nature can be expected to change with it.

To the other objections, that the new society
would be no more than a new set of chains for the
workers, and that it may not be at all short-lived,
Marx can be understood to be at least moderately
sympathetic: he is aware of the dangers. But he
is also fairly confident that the problem is easily
solvable. In *The Civil War in France* , Marx endorses
the Paris Commune of 1871 as the sort of proletarian state he has in mind for the transitional period (*Civil War in France*, p. 223). What is most important about the Commune for present purposes is that
every appointment to an administrative position was
"at all times revocable" (p. 220). Under such a
system, Marx thought, the eye of the community
would always be on its office-holders; it would
not be possible for things to get out of hand in
the way Bakunin foresaw.

So the state was at least necessary for the

duration of the transitional period, and problems of the kind Bakunin raised, if they had not been already solved in the two-month tenure of the Paris Commune, were not fundamental. Governmental power was necessary for making the fundamental changes in society that would presage the final abolition of government. It was in this spirit that Marx endorsed[15] the resolution of the London Conference, which had been adopted at the General Congress at the Hague in 1872. That resolution read, in part, as follows:

> As the landlords and capitalists always use their political privileges in order to defend and perpetuate their economic monopolies and to subjugate labor,--so the conquest of political power becomes the great duty and task of the proletariat.[16]

Marx felt that he had proved

> 1) that the *existence of classes* is only bound up with *particular historical phases in the development of production*, 2) that the class struggle necessarily leads to *the dictatorship of the proletariat*, 3) that this dictatorship itself only constitutes the transition to the *abolition of all classes* and to a *classless society* . . .[17]

It is clear that Marx felt that government was necessary to achieve certain fundamental social changes, even though it was, in the long run, a perverse institution. This is the Marxian argument in behalf of government, which takes its place beside the Hobbesian and Lockeian arguments, and becomes the last of the three arguments in defense

---

[15]For the endorsement, see G.M. Stekloff, *History of the First International* [136], p. 240.

[16]*The First International: Minutes of the Hague Congress of 1872* [35], p. 217.

[17]Letter to J. Weydemeyer, 5 March 1852, in *Selected Works* [88], vol. I, p. 528.

of government that will be considered in this book.
It is now possible to begin setting up the three
arguments for critical analysis.

- 62 -

Chapter IV

The Rawlsian Framework

Three arguments, in support of the thesis that government is necessary, have been sketched in preceeding chapters. It will be recalled that this task was embarked upon in the hope of fleshing out the suggestion, raised in the course of a review of Aristotle's *Politics*, that government may be practically necessary for achieving certain basic communal values.

In the Introduction, where the three postulates guiding the present arguments were listed and briefly discussed, particular attention was directed to the third postulate: a rather broad, and relatively weak, ethical claim. That postulate was presented in the form of a conditional proposition: "In the absence of good reasons to the contrary, people should not be coerced."

This form gives implicit acknowledgment to the possibility that coercion may, in some cases, be justified.[1] As the third postulate is being used in this essay, attention is directed solely to a certain class of potential good reasons for coercion--the class of morally acceptable good rea-

---

[1] It is possible, of course, to define 'coerce' in such a way as to rule out arguments to the effect that coercion is sometimes justified. Self-defense, according to such a definition, would simply not qualify as coercion. In spite of the plausibility of this way of approaching the present problem, it must be emphasized that the present policy will be to use 'coerce' wherever someone is being physically compelled by one or more other people to do something that he or she does not want to do. Thus where reference is here made to someone's attempting to justify coercion by giving morally acceptable good reasons for it, others may choose to describe the same situation as someone's attempting to show that his act was not coercion. This policy is adopted because taking this stand on one somewhat controversial issue may help to avoid several other *more* controversial issues which need not arise here.

sons--and to certain institutional means of insti-
tuting such coercion--namely, governments.

The three arguments in defense of government
outlined in Chapters II and III may be regarded as
attempts to provide morally acceptable good reasons
for government, within the constraints provided by
the third postulate. Each argument, as outlined so
far, may thus be thought of as supporting the thesis that the relatively weak third postulate does
not rule out government. The postulate does seem,
however, at least to impose certain limitations
upon government, and these have not yet been discussed. It is the intent of the present chapter to
deal with this aspect of the issue.

For each of the three arguments, government is
regarded as a means for accomplishing certain ends;
government is portrayed as a "tool" of the governed.
The tool metaphor is useful, because it makes it
possible to view government in the light of certain
general principles of tool design. In particular,
the design of tools is strongly influenced by consideration of such factors as the intended end of
the tool, relevant characteristics of the tool
user, and the necessity of minimizing potential
dangers of tool use. All these factors must be
considered if the tool is to be a good one.

It will be argued here that an especially valuable framework for discussing the powers and limitations to be included in the "design" of government as a social tool is provided by the methodological framework of John Rawls's *Theory of Justice*
[116]. The first task of the present chapter,
then, will be to sketch Rawls's version of the contract theory, and to show how this version (which
is, as it stands, a theory of social justice in
general) is useful in discussing the proper role
(the "design") of government, if there is to be
one, in society. The Rawlsian theory will be analyzed in terms of two "components": a methodological framework--which includes Rawls's notions of
the "initial situation," the "veil of ignorance,"
and the "constitutional convention"--for making
social decisions (of designing social "tools"), on
the one hand, and an ideological content--informed

largely by Rawls's own liberal views--on the other hand. Attention will be focused on the methodological framework as abstracted from the Rawlsian theory (abstracted, that is, from the liberal content).

The second task of the chapter will be to show how the methodological framework provided by Rawls's version of the social contract theory can be used to recast the defenses of government outlined in Chapters II and III. This recasting will provide a valuable perspective upon the ways in which the three defenses are similar, and upon the ways in which they differ from one another. The most important differences will be seen to stem from controversy regarding the way in which the methodological framework is to be fleshed out. The three defenses of government will be recast in terms of Rawls's framework.

It is best to begin, then, with a sketch of the framework. Attention will be focused upon Rawls's notion of an "initial situation," which serves as a forum for arguments regarding proper principles of justice for society as a whole, of a "veil of ignorance," which serves as a device for excluding considerations deemed inappropriate for such arguments, and of a "constitutional convention," which serves as a locus for arguments informed by the principles of justice chosen in the initial situation, regarding appropriate modes of social organization.

Rawls's theory is based upon a sophisticated version of the traditional contract theory. In its best known forms, the contract theory functions as follows: from the sorts of things that more or less ideal people did or would decide upon as the social conditions of their lives, under a set of real or hypothetical constraining circumstances, conclusions are drawn as to how society *should* be arranged. Although the contract theory has been used most often in philosophical arguments about the political structure of society, it seems to function reasonably well with regard to ethical structure.

Now, it has not always been completely clear, in the works of social contractarians, why the contract argument should be at all convincing. It has virtually no merit as an historical argument, since 1) it is extremely unlikely that existing societies have contractual agreements of the kind envisioned as their foundations, and 2) even if they did, it is difficult to see why that should influence conclusions about what society *should* be like. More importantly, since the historical claim has never really been made or taken very seriously, the contract argument has been troublesome because it has not always been clear why normative conclusions about society should be warranted by decisions made collectively in even a hypothetical contract: no matter how the parties to the contract are viewed-- no matter what constraints they are placed under-- why should their decision influence anyone else's? One of the primary virtues of the Rawlsian version of contract theory is that it clears up some of these problems.

Not only is contract theory not to be interpreted as making any historical claims about how societies came to be, but, for Rawls's version anyway, it is not even important for the contractarian argument that separate individuals be involved in making the social decision. Although Rawls characterizes his "original position" as involving several "representative" persons, this aspect of the theory appears not to be essential. Since the hypothetical parties to the social contract are viewed as being equally rational, and as being unaware of individual differences that would cause them to make use of their rationality in different ways (i.e., in pursuit of different ends), each of them will come to the same conclusion about the proper social arrangements. Since this is the case, it is possible to ignore the fact that there are several parties to the hypothetical contract, and to concentrate upon the considerations of any one of them, as he deliberates upon the problem of how society should be arranged. Normative conclusions in Rawls's theory are held to follow *not* from the fact that several people in a certain situation would draw them, but from the fact that they are the conclusions that *reason itself* would yield, when suitably constrained (Rawls [116], esp. p. 139).

The contractarian terminology is useful for
Rawls's framework because it highlights some of the
problems that must be faced in developing a "rational" ethical or political theory, and because it
suggests solutions to these problems. It emphasizes the fact that real people, rational though
they may be, may have interests that are different
enough that their common rationality alone will not
suffice to tell them how, collectively, they should
arrange their social lives. But it also emphasizes
the fact that individual differences need not be
irreconcileable, and lays the groundwork for taking
first steps toward understanding which constraints
it is appropriate to place upon reason in attempting to arrive at the best social arrangements (pp.
16, 140, 185).

So the Rawlsian theory relies, for its argument, not upon agreement or contract between different people, but upon reason. Reason is thus the
foundation upon which the methodological framework
is to be built, and it is not likely that this
choice will instigate much controversy, so long as
it be stipulated that no *particular* conception of
reason is envisioned. Particular conceptions of
reason will comprise part of the content of a
fleshed-out theory.[2]

The problem of how society should be organized
is therefore, for Rawls, a problem of rational
choice. Now, such problems have unique solutions
only in case the circumstances in which the choice
is to be made can be spelled out in some detail.
In general, one must know the beliefs and interests
(the goals) of the party or parties making the
choice, one must know the alternatives from which

---

[2]It is true, as Kai Nielsen reminds us, that we cannot stand
outside our concept of rationality "to see what rationality
really is." What we can do, however, is to try to arrange a
completely general format, within which various understand-
ings of reason may be *displayed* and contrasted. It seems to
me that this is one of the virtues of the Rawlsian methodological framework. See Nielsen, "Distrusting Reason" [100].

the choice is to be made, and so on (pp. 17-18). One must, that is, be able to give content to what Rawls refers to as the "initial situation." With a reasonably filled out initial situation, one should be able to determine the sorts of organizational principles that reason dictates be chosen for society.

Now, it should be clear that giving content to the initial situation is itself a problem of rationa choice. The problem is to list the restrictions that it seems reasonable to impose on arguments for one or another set of social principles. Once any such choice of restrictions is made, the initial situation will have been given a certain content, and will thus amount to a choice among the many possible initial situations.

To choose one situation is to choose what Rawls calls an "original position," but since original positions have to do with some decision as to what is rational in the initial situation, they *fill out* the framework. The present task requires an understanding of the methodological framework itself, rather than of various ways in which it might be given content. Attention is focused, therefore, more upon the initial situation than upon *any* original position, whether it be Rawls's or anyone else's. For now, it need only be noted that the *first* choice in the initial situation will be of some set of restrictions on the choice problem that will yield an original position (pp. 18, 121, 126, 145-47, 189).

Once having characterized the initial situation--having listed the restrictions that reason dictates be imposed upon arguments for social principles--the next choice is that of a set of just principles for the "basic structure of society" (p. 11). Choosing such a set of "principles of justice" may be relatively easy, if the initial situation has been narrowly restricted, or it may be impossible, if the earlier restrictions have been too loose. It may fall anywhere between these two extremes. A great deal depends upon how the initial situation has been characterized.

In any case, any rational argument for a set
of principles of justice will necessarily have
made--even if only tacitly--a move corresponding to
the choice of an original position in the Rawlsian
framework. Agreeing to this proposition will be
enough for present purposes, since the present concern is only with positions that reflect rational
arguments for various sets of principles of justice.

What may *differ* from argument to argument is
the degree to which restrictions are placed upon
the choice problem, or, to speak in Rawlsian terms,
the choice of which considerations to place behind
the "veil of ignorance" (p. 12). Once an original
position is settled upon in the initial situation,
a veil of ignorance is in place; and it is from
behind the veil that principles of justice are to
be chosen.

The last feature of the Rawlsian framework
that will be considered here is what Rawls calls
the "constitutional convention." Given some choice
of principles of justice, it may be that these
principles are such that they would have different
practical applications in different social circumstances. If, for example, the veil of ignorance
were placed in such a way in the original position
that it obscured information about the differing
natural resources, and the various levels of economic advance and political culture to be found in
particular societies, then it may be that decisions
about which specific social institutions should be
established could not effectively be made there.
In such a situation, the institutional decision
could only be made by re-positioning the veil of
ignorance. Doing so amounts to establishing a
revised choice situation, and this is what Rawls
calls the "constitutional convention" (pp. 196-97).

It is in the constitutional convention of
Rawls's own liberal theory that the decision to
establish the "coercive agency" of government is
made (p. 241).[3] In general, it will not be obvious

---

[3]The name 'constitutional convention' almost implies that

that such a decision might not be made in the original position, given different restrictions on placement of the veil of ignorance. But the framework provides for a constitutional convention, even if some choices of original positions make it unnecessary. For the sake of clearer exposition, therefore, it will be the present policy to refer to the constitutional convention as the situation in which decisions about government are to be made. For any theory that would not require more than its original position to make such decisions, one can simply speak as if the theory *does* make use of a constitutional convention, but does not require that the veil of ignorance be re-positioned in establishing it.

It is clear, then, that the methodological framework to be found in *A Theory of Justice* is no more than an extremely suggestive device for portraying ethical and social arguments.

The framework includes the idea of the "initial situation," in which some constraints are placed on the procedure of deciding upon principles of justice that should guide society; it includes the idea of the "veil of ignorance," which serves to separate appropriate from inappropriate considerations; and it includes the idea of the "constitutional convention," in which the decision as to whether to adopt government is made, again under constraints provided by some positioning of the veil of ignorance. The framework may be filled out in a variety of ways, depending upon the decisions made as to which constraints to place on the decision procedure, as to which considerations are to be obscured by the veil of ignorance, and as to which adjustments are to be made for the constitu-

---

some government will be adopted, as is the case for Rawls's own interpretation of it. If government *is* adopted, then the parties will go on to consider what *kind* of government would be best. Rawls does make it clear, however, that one option available to the parties to the constitutional convention will be the rejection of government. The name of this decision situation, while somewhat inapt for present purposes, will therefore be retained here.

tional convention. As such, it is truly neutral
with respect to particular ethical and political
theories. It offers " . . . a general analytic
method for the comparative study of conceptions of
justice" (p. 121).[4]

   But Rawls's book does more than merely set up

---

[4]Robert Nozick argues that "Rawls' construction is incapable
of yielding an entitlement or historical conception of distributive justice," although it "might be used in an attempt
to *derive*, when conjoined with factual information, historical-entitlement principles, as derivative principles falling under a nonentitlement conception of justice." Even if
it *is* used in this way, Nozick thinks that the derived
historical-entitlement principles can, at best, be only
approximations of the principles of acquisition, transfer,
and rectification that he favors. Thus Nozick thinks that
his theory of justice could not be adequately reconstructed
using the Rawlsian framework: " . . . it will produce the
wrong sorts of reasons for them [the Nozickean principles],
and its derived results sometimes will conflict with the
precisely correct principles" (*Anarchy, State, and Utopia*
[102], p. 202). But what are the *right* sorts of reasons for
Nozick's principles? He tells us (p. 51) that he hopes to
grapple with this issue on another occasion. But all of his
clues seem to amount either to factual considerations or to
notions which, Nozick thinks, might "straddle" the is-ought
gap (pp. 49-51). From what Nozick tells us about candidates
for the latter category, it is not easy to see why they,
along with other "factual information," could not be used in
an original position to derive Nozickean principles. Why
couldn't these highly idealized rational persons do what
Nozick hopes to do? If there are any reasons *at all* for
Nozick's theory of justice, they would surely be considered
by the parties to the original position, the only qualification being that these reasons may not themselves rely upon
Nozickean justice. If there are *no* reasons, then either the
theory is not rationally defensible or the principles of
justice are just brute facts. But even in the latter case,
it is hard to see why such facts couldn't be considered in
an original position (they aren't just brute facts for Rawls,
of course). It is hard to see how Nozick can be so circum-
spect about the basis of the constraints he recommends, and
yet so confident that Rawls's framework couldn't be used to
exhibit that basis.

a "general analytic method." The great bulk of *A Theory of Justice* is devoted to presenting a specific theory, as the title suggests. It is the liberal theory, rather than the methodological framework, that has been the target of Rawls's critics.

For example, Rawls imagines that the rational choice of an original position from among the many possible initial situations will be guided, in part, by existing "considered judgments" as to what constitutes justice. Once "reflective equilibrium" has been established between what seem to be reasonable restrictions on the initial situation, on the one hand, and considered judgments, on the other, the best original position has been established (pp. 20-21).

Although it has been suggested by some authors that Rawls's liberalism infects even the idea of reflective equilibrium,[5] most critics have accepted this notion and have objected only to Rawls's specific use of it.

For example, where Rawls concludes that balancing restrictions and considered judgments would yield an original position in which the "parties" desire more, rather than less, liberty, opportunity, and wealth (p. 93), Adina Schwartz argues that this conclusion is not warranted.[6] Particularly as regards wealth, Schwartz argues, it is not at all clear that rational individuals would choose to maximize what they have. It may be that real peo-

---

[5]See Edward F. McClennan [75]; also Peter Singer, "Philosophers are Back on the Job" [131]. Singer's concern may not be quite the same as McClennan's, but it is clear that he is uncomfortable about the idea of "reflective equilibrium" as a tool for discovering or revealing principles of justice. For a response to such suspicions about "reflective equilibrium," see Marcus G. Singer, "Justice, Theory, and a Theory of Justice" [130], especially pp. 608-09. For an extremely suggestive general defense of the "method" of "wide reflective equilibrium," see Norman Daniels, "Wide Reflective Equilibrium and Theory Acceptance in Ethics" [25].

[6]"Moral Neutrality and Primary Goods" [126].

ple have always been inclined in this way, but that
does not mean that ideal people would be, or even
that real people always will be (Schwartz [126], p.
307).

Rawls allows the general facts about human
society to be considered behind the veil of ignorance (Rawls [116], pp. 137-38). Richard Miller
argues that if Karl Marx was right in contending
that people's needs and wants are relative to their
social classes, and that in capitalist society (for
example), people *need* wealth in ever increasing
abundance, then this *fact* will be considered in the
original position, in the course of deciding upon
the principles of justice. But one of the principles Rawls derives from his version of the original
position is the "difference principle," according
to which the advantages that some people have are
to be allowed only if allowing them leads to a net
advantage to the least favored among those who are
affected at all by it. Miller argues that it would
not be rational for the parties to accept this
principle in the original position, if Marx is correct about needs, since they would be aware that if
any one of them were to be stuck in the position of
the capitalist upon lifting the veil of ignorance,
his life would be inexpressably miserable.[7] He
would not be able to fulfill his needs.

David Gauthier has argued, more generally,
that it is not clear that the "maximizing conception of rationality," which Rawls makes use of, is
the one that would be utilized in the initial situation.[8] He contends that there are other interesting alternatives, ignored by Rawls, which might be
better candidates. One might be especially inclined to choose one of the alternatives, Gauthier
argues, when it becomes apparent that Rawls's own
original position, with its maximizing conception
of rationality, would *not* lead to the adoption of

---

[7]Richard Miller, "Rawls and Marxism" [93].

[8]"Justice and Natural Endowment: Toward A Critique of Rawls'
Ideological Framework" [33]. See also David Gauthier,
"Rational Cooperation" [34].

Rawls's two principles. Gauthier suggests that
rational people would agree to apply the difference
principle only to the products of social cooperation, and not to all advantages. It would be irrational for the parties to agree to a principle that
leaves some people worse off than if no agreement
had been reached ([33], p. 20).

Kenneth J. Arrow observes that the derivation
of Rawls's two principles implies rejection of the
"productivity principle"--the principle that a person has a right to what he creates[9]--and Douglas B.
Rasmussen contends that since this principle is a
"considered moral judgment of some force," the
plausibility of Rawls's position is considerably
reduced, relying as it does upon considered moral
judgments.[10] In a similar vein, David Lewis Schaefer argues that Rawls's use of the thesis that no
one deserves his natural assets is unjustified,
since "From the Kantian principle that 'no one
deserves his natural assets,' it does not follow
that other men 'deserve' the fruits of these assets
more than he does."[11]

The tone of all of these criticisms is neatly
captured by Joseph Margolis:

> In a word, what Rawls has provided is an impres-
> sively articulated statement of which 'equili-
> brium' best suits certain intuitions about man's
> condition and the nature of justice: it is a
> philosophically informed ideology, not a demon-
> stration of the validity of the thesis of jus-
> tice as fairness against the claims of its com-
> petitors.[12]

All of the criticisms--whatever their merit--seem

---

[9]"Some Ordinalist-Utilitarian Notes on Rawls' Theory of Justice" [3], p. 248.

[10]"A Critique of Rawls' Theory of Justice" [115], p. 304.

[11]"The 'Sense' and Non-sense of Justice" [127], p. 24.

[12]"Justice as Fairness" [79], p. 37.

actually to be directed at the content of Rawls's theory, and not at the framework. As a matter of fact, each of them is formulated from within the framework. There seems to be no good reason to contend that the framework itself is ideologically tainted (unless, of course, one *identifies* as part of the framework some of Rawls's liberal filler), and this is all that is needed in order to go on. For it is the framework which will here be appealed to, and not the content.[13]

How, then, is advantage to be taken of the "general analytic method" embodied in Rawls's methodological framework? Rawls conjectures that " . . . for each traditional conception of justice there exists an interpretation of the initial situation in which its principles are the preferred solution" (p. 121). It is clear that choosing different interpretations of the initial situation might very well make significant differences in the

---

[13]It seems to me that the Rawls-literature is burdened by confusions over what is framework and what is content. See, for example, Kai Nielsen's "On Philosophic Method" [101], especially pp. 358-68, for some typical confusion. The distinction is, admittedly, difficult to sort out. One of the best critiques of the framework, however, seems to be David Keyt's "The Social Contract as an Analytic, Justificatory, and Polemic Device" [62]. Keyt argues that the "analytic" use of the framework may not expose derived principles of justice to refutation, since there would be, for any set of such principles, an indefinite number of initial situations from which they might be derived. Keyt cites evidence that Rawls would want special attention directed to the "most reasonable" initial situation for any conception of justice, and he argues persuasively that there is no such animal, short of an initial situation that is specified in such a way as to be *logically equivalent* to the principles to be derived. If Keyt is right, then the methodological framework cannot refute "isms" in one fell swoop. Whether Rawls thought it could is, I think, open to question. Whatever the answer may be to this question, though, the Rawlsian framework is still helpful in criticizing *particular* attempts to elaborate a "conception of justice" or a social philosophy. This is the use to which the framework will be put here.

ways in which all other parts of the framework are filled out. In general, portraying any reasonably complex social theory in terms of the Rawlsian framework, if the portrayal is to be complete, will amount to a mammoth translational task, subject to all kinds of controversy. Such quagmires ought to be avoided wherever possible, if the present line of argument is to be reasonably clear.

The framework is terribly inviting, however. Not only does it offer a compelling perspective on the problem situation in which social and political theories are formulated, it has at least two other distinct advantages as well: in the first place, it isolates the initial situation (or, interpreted, the original position) from the constitutional convention, thus focusing attention on the proper locus for controversies regarding the acceptability of government; in the second place, it provides a single format for comparing and contrasting various theories. If it were possible to make use of the framework in evaluating the three arguments in defense of government, it might be that the present task would be considerably simplified.

As it happens, the framework can profitably be used for present purposes. Since the concern of this book is limited to arguments in defense of the thesis that government is necessary, it will not be necessary to give an entire re-casting of the three conceptions of justice associated with the three arguments. Some part of these conceptions of justice will, of course, be needed, since all of the arguments rely, in various degrees, upon at least a tacit ethical assumption. What is necessary is to insure that enough of each of the three arguments gets re-cast in Rawlsian terms to allow conclusions to be drawn about how considerations of justice affect deliberation about government in the constitutional convention. It will turn out that this task is far more manageable than the task of giving a complete translation.

Attention is directed, therefore, to the job of rendering each of the three arguments in defense of government--the argument that government is necessary to preserve peace, the argument that govern-

ment is necessary to protect certain fundamental
human rights, and the argument that government is
necessary for making the transition between present
society and stateless society--in terms of Rawls's
framework.

An initial situation constructed on the basis
of the Hobbesian argument that government is necessary to preserve peace would require that all those
claims made by Hobbes regarding the physics of sensation, the sensory basis of imagination, and the
origins of human action in desire and aversion, be
considered there. These are all alleged "general
facts" about people, and they play the role, in the
framework, of the first principles of constraint in
the specification of the problem situation. The
party or parties to the initial situation consider
that appetites and aversions are, for the most
part, acquired during an individual's life, and
that they are different from person to person and
subject to change within any person's life. These
facts are suggestive of one way of positioning the
veil of ignorance for the Hobbesian argument: the
particular desires and aversions that particular
people have at particular times are to be obscured
by the veil of ignorance. They will not be considered in the initial situation.

Also taken into consideration is the fact that
different people's desires and aversions are felt
with different intensities. The parties consider
this fact, but place the particular intensities
felt on the other side of the veil.

So far, then, the initial situation for the
Hobbesian argument will include consideration of
the idea that human action is motivated by desires
and aversions, the idea that desires and aversions
differ from person to person and from time to time
in any person's life, and the idea that desires and
aversions are felt with different intensities among
people. Taken together, these three considerations
lead to the conclusion that there are differences
among people with respect to the kinds of actions
they are prepared to undertake.

For Hobbes, the fact that desires and aversions are constantly changing implies that people will be forever striving for satisfaction, never completely satisfied with what they have. Further, *power* is present means to future satisfaction. So everyone must either have some power now, or be trying to get some. These things will be considered in the initial situation.

Now, there are some things that are desired by many people at the same time, but which cannot be had by all of them. People will struggle with one another to get such things, and struggle to obtain the power to get them. In such cases, the power to get the objects in question--the power to satisfy these desires--will amount, in part at least, to the power to prevent others from getting them. This includes both the power to retain those things that an individual now has that others may want, and the power to continue to satisfy his desires. Thus the fact that human action is determined in a certain way and the fact that human nature has certain characteristics leads to the conclusion, in the initial situation, that people are naturally motivated to try to acquire power over one another.

This motivation extends not only to those situations in which people are particularly acquisitive, but also to situations where people are concerned with no more than preserving what they already have. Since this is the case, the parties must consider, in the initial situation, that, unless some accomodation between persons is arrived at, people will resort to pre-emptive attacks upon one another, in the hope of making it impossible for others to attack first. The parties must consider that, without some communal arrangement, there is every likelihood that the human condition will be one of universal war.

This, then, is what will be referred to in what follows as the Hobbesian initial situation. It is from the perspective of this initial situation that the party or parties decide upon "principles of justice" which make social accomodation possible. For Hobbes, these principles are the directives that reason dictates be observed, given the miserable condition of mankind in their absence.

They are the Hobbesian "Laws of Nature."[14]

What has been achieved, then, is a characterization of both the initial situation and the principles of justice that would be arrived at from
that situation once the Hobbesian argument is translated into Rawlsian terms. Before the deliberations
in a Hobbesian constitutional convention are considered, however, it will be fruitful to compare
the framework interpretations of the other two
arguments as they would look up to this point.

An initial situation constructed on the basis
of the Lockeian argument that government is necessary to protect certain fundamental human rights
would require that those claims made by Locke
regarding the nature of man as a reasoning animal
be considered there. The parties must consider
that everyone, with the exception of lunatics, idiots and children, is equipped with the power of
reason, and is therefore capable of providing for
his own support and preservation. Exceptions to
this rule--lunatics, idiots, and children--are
obscured by the veil of ignorance.

The Lockeian initial situation will include
consideration of the alleged fact that God has
given people their power to reason and thus to pro-

---

[14]It may be objected that, for Hobbes, " . . . before the
names of Just, and Unjust can have place, there must be
some coercive Power, to compel men equally to the performance of their Covenants, by the terrour of some punishment . . . " (*Leviathan* [55], p. 202). That is, it might
be thought that principles of justice cannot be thought to
enter the Hobbesian argument until government is in place.
As will become evident, such an objection would be mis-
placed. The Rawlsian framework carries no implication that
principles of justice must be established temporally prior
to the decision regarding governments. It is clear that
Hobbes regarded the laws of nature as " . . . the Fountain
and Originall of Justice" (p. 202), and this fits perfectly
into the framework. The argument that laws and other com-
pacts are just words without a coercive enforcing power
will prove to be part of Hobbes's justification of government in the constitutional convention.

vide for their own support and preservation, and of
the implication drawn from this that God must have
intended that people be free to use these powers.
The parties therefore consider that people are
rational in equal measure and that they are free,
by nature. Ignored in the initial situation are
the ways in which real people differ from one another in intelligence and in advantages; such differences are placed on the other side of the veil
of ignorance. People are considered to be naturally free and equal.

Taken together, these considerations lead to
the conclusion that people have a right to protect
themselves and their God-given freedom. That is,
no one has the right to rule others. In addition,
the parties are to consider that since God gave
reason to people in order that they might live
together in society (a second function of reason),
He must have intended that society be preserved.
Therefore people have a right to preserve mankind
in general.

It would seem that this is as far as it is
necessary to go in characterizing the Lockeian initial situation. There is a definite asymmetry
between the structure of Locke's argument and that
of Hobbes's argument, which receives emphasis
through the framework. Where Hobbesian "principles
of justice" are arrived at as a means of alleviat-
ing a miserable human condition, Lockeian principles, as will become apparent, *express* a *benign* human
condition.

Given the nature of man and the intent of God
in creating man as He did, the Lockeian principles
of justice simply fall out of the initial situation. Although Locke does not explicitly spell out
the "Law of Nature" in the way that Hobbes did, it
is clear that this Law plays the role of principles
of justice once Locke's argument is translated into
the Rawlsian framework. For now, it is necessary
only to note that Lockeian principles of justice
would presumably include such notions as "thou
shalt not hinder another person's exercize of his
freedom to act," "no man shall endeavor to rule
another," "every person hath the executive power of

the law of nature," and the like. Having identified the initial situation and the principles of
justice to be associated with the Lockeian argument,
it is possible to turn to the last argument in
defense of government.

The Marxian initial situation[15]--setting the
problem situation for Marx's argument that government is necessary as a temporary instrument for
preparing people for the abolition of government--
requires that the parties consider Marx's claims
about how people's "life-processes" actually proceed, how these are determined, and the implications these claims have upon analyses of "human
nature." The parties must consider that man is,
first and foremost, a *producer*, and that it is the
conditions of material production that determine
the ways in which people express their lives. As
such conditions change, human nature changes.

Thus, in the initial situation, the parties
will consider these facts about people and about
the ways in which they develop, and information
about who the parties are, and about the particular
stage of the development of conditions of material
production in which they will find themselves, must
be obscured by the veil of ignorance.

---

[15]As will become apparent shortly, fitting Marx into the
"Rawlsian framework" is a great deal more problematic than
is the case for Hobbes and Locke. Nevertheless, I think it
can be done (as will also become apparent). Indeed, it
seems to me that there may be special advantages won by
using the framework to contrast Marx with the others. As
J. Murphy has argued, Marx's critiques of "bourgeois" justice include, at least as a tacit charge, the claim that
"justification" of bourgeois principles relies upon ignorance regarding basic empirical facts about society (see J.
Murphy, "Marxism and Retribution" [99]). It seems to me
that one virtue of the Rawlsian "initial situation" is that
it points up the empirical assumptions that support principles of justice, and it thereby provides to Marxians (for
example) a plausible forum in which to make their case. On
the basic issue involved here, see Michael Slote, "Morality
and Ignorance" [132]. I am indebted to Allen Buchanan for
calling my attention to the papers cited in this note.

The initial situation will include, of course, the Marxian claim that human activity, because of its close ties with production, is profoundly social. The parties note that present material conditions have evolved through the efforts of predecessors, and partially determine future changes. And, of course, there are complex links among people at any given stage in the developmental process.

In particular, the parties will note the evolution of class divisions as a product of changing material conditions of production, in circumstances of relative scarcity. They will take into consideration the claim that it is class divisions that lead to antagonisms in the social order, and thus to the phenomenon of political power. In addition, the parties will consider that as material conditio change, and thus create conflicting social classes, the evolution continues, erupting from time to time in social revolutions.

Finally, the parties will consider, in the initial situation, the Marxian claim that the bourgeois mode of production is the last antagonistic form of the social process of production, the claim that the proletarian revolution, born of bourgeois dominance, can ultimately do away with scarcity, and thus with class divisions and political dominance, and the claim that what will result will be the "fully constituted society," the era of the whole man.

This, then, is the Marxian initial situation. There is a special problem, however, in deciding what to choose as Marxian principles of justice.

There is one sense in which the Marxian initial situation seems to exclude consideration of principles of justice. Such principles may be thought of (and Marx's writings give good reason so to think of them) as part of the ways in which people "express their lives." But Marx argued that the ways in which people express their lives depend upon the material conditions of production under which they live. If this is so, then principles of justice will differ from time to time and from place to place, varying with the material condi-

tions. But information about particular stages in
the development of these conditions has been
obscured by the veil of ignorance. It may be that
no principles of justice can be derived from the
Marxian initial situation.

On the other hand, however, there is the curi-
ous feeling that there are very powerful principles
of justice to be found in Marx's works. Marx not
only analyzes the progress of social evolution, he
advocates helping it along. He says not only that
the workers of the world will unite, but also "Workers of the World, Unite!!" The portrayal of the
conditions of the working class under capitalism
can in no way be read without getting the distinct
impression that people of good will and intelligence ought to help to alleviate these conditions.[16]

Perhaps it will not risk too much controversy
to say that at least some relatively weak principles of justice can be arrived at through the Marx-

---

[16]It seems to me that by far the best treatment of these
issues to date is to be found in a paper that came to my
attention only as this manuscript was about to go to press.
The paper is "The Marxian Critique of Justice and Rights,"
by Allen Buchanan [18]. It seems to me that my treatment of
Marx, in the present chapter and in Chapter IX, below, is
consistent, anyway, with Buchanan's analysis of Marx. My
aim, of course, is to meet Marx in argument on his own
ground, as nearly as I can. For further discussion of Marx
and justice, see also Buchanan's "Exploitation, Alienation,
and Injustice" [17]; R. Tucker, *The Marxian Revolutionary
Idea* [151], pp. 37-53; Allen Wood, "The Marxian Critique
of Justice" [159]; William McBride, "The Concept of Justice in Marx, Engels, and Others" [74]; and Nancy Holmstrom, "Exploitation" [56]. For a rather interesting
defense of the way one "Marxist-Leninist" *state* defends
human "rights," see V.M. Chkhikvadze, "Human Rights and the
Ideological Struggle" [21]. Chkhikvadze's article is
interesting, I think, because of its at least partially
successful attempt to highlight similarities between Soviet
law (and practice) and western law (and practice). In
addition, there is some lovely obscuring of the human
rights issue at the beginning of the paper. Marx, I think,
would have laughed aloud.

ian initial situation: principles like "the social progression toward the classless society, toward the era of the whole man, should be assisted wherever possible," or "do what is necessary to accomplish the abolition of class conflict as soon as possible." If these are plausible candidates for Marxian principles of justice, then it will be possible to proceed.[17]

The three arguments in defense of government, cast in terms of the Rawlsian framework, yield three initial situations, and three corresponding sets of principles of justice. The next step in the present argument will be to see how the third postulate fits into the framework. In the Introduction, it was noted that no attempt would be made to give an elaborate defense of any of the three postulates. Instead, they were simply to be treated as basic assumptions. It will be helpful, however, to lend some plausibility to the third postulate by trying to show that it would be agreed to in the initial situation by the three defenders of government.

The third postulate says: "In the absence of good reasons to the contrary, people should not be coerced." It is not too difficult to show that this postulate would be accepted in the Hobbesian initial situation, as a principle of justice. For the postulate seems to follow from Hobbes's Laws of Nature. The first law tells people to seek peace and follow it;   the second law tells people to be content with only those liberties with respect to others that they would allow others against themselves, to the extent that keeping the peace makes this necessary. The fundamental "right of nature" is to defend oneself by whatever means one can. The implication from all of this seems to be that the laws of nature dictate that people refrain from

---

[17]Charles Wei-Hsun Fu tries to work out the details of a "proletarian ethic" in his "Marxism-Leninism-Maoism as an Ethical Theory" [156]. I find it interesting that his formulations of "categorical imperatives of proletarian morality" seem to be roughly equivalent to the suggestions that I offer in the text.

putting others in positions in which they feel that
self-defense is necessary; the laws say that people should place such restraints on their activities unless they are defending themselves, or
unless their action somehow serves to enhance the
prospects of peace. That is, unless there are good
reasons to the contrary, people should not (for
example) coerce others.

It is even easier to show that the third postulate would be accepted in the Lockeian initial
position. For one of the principles of justice
accepted there was "thou shalt not hinder another
person's exercize of his freedom to act." That's a
near enough equivalent to the third postulate to
serve present purposes. That Locke's position
allows for self-defense, considered along with the
remark made in the footnote at the very beginning
of this chapter, suggests that, according to the
way in which the term "coerce" is being used here,
Locke would readily accept the third postulate.

Once again, it is not quite so easy to deal
with the Marxian initial situation. But if the
earlier suggestions as to plausible candidates for
Marxian principles of justice are accepted, then it
would seem that the third postulate would be accepted
here too. For the accepted principles of justice
refer to facilitating the building of a particular
conception of society, a conception in which people
are to be free of political domination and coercion. It is hardly likely, with that goal in mind,
that the third postulate would be rejected. It
seems to embody the goal, while at the same time
allowing for the possibility that some coercion may
be necessary to achieve it.

These are just plausibility arguments, however.
It is hoped that the third postulate seems somewhat
less arbitrary than it might otherwise seem, in the
light of these arguments. But, as was stated in
the Introduction, no strict defense of the postulate will be offered here. It just seems hard to
believe that anyone would object to anything as
weak as "In the absence of good reasons to the contrary, people should not be coerced."

It will here be contended, anyway, that the
third postulate would be accepted in the three initial situations. The final task of this chapter is
to show how accepting this postulate would affect
deliberations in the "constitutional conventions"
corresponding to the three arguments.

The party or parties in the initial situation,
once they have agreed to at least the third postulate as a principle of justice, are ready to move
on to the constitutional convention, where the
decision as to whether a government should be
established will be made. Government is to be
regarded as an institutional device for achieving
certain ends--as a tool of sorts. The task proposed for this chapter can be completed by quickly
outlining the effect of the three principles of
tool design upon this decision, both as regards
what kind of tool government is thought to be, and
as regards the way in which the three principles
are balanced.

For Hobbes, no re-positioning of the veil of
ignorance is necessary in establishing a constitutional convention. Conclusions about government
follow from what is already known in the initial
situation. The intended end of government is
enforcement of the Laws of Nature, which have been
chosen as principles of justice. For achieving this
end, Hobbes argues, there is no other effective
tool. The characteristics of the tool user are
known: they are the characteristics considered in
the initial situation. The dangers of tool use are
acknowledged, but Hobbes argues that these dangers
of government are nothing compared to the miserable
condition of mankind in the absence of government.
The third postulate is agreed to in the initial
situation, but Hobbes argues that the coercive
agency of government ought nevertheless to be
established. This is because without government,
there would be universal war. Government is the
only tool competent to avoid such conflict, and it
is better to accept a lesser evil than be stuck
with a greater.

For Locke, the circumstances are somewhat different. The conditions of the initial situation
alone, it seems, would lead to the conclusion not

only that government is not necessary, but that
government ought not to be established. But the
veil of ignorance in the Lockeian initial situation obscured too much. The veil of ignorance must
be re-positioned in establishing an adequate constitutional convention. Consideration must be
taken of the fact that some people, although
endowed by their Creator with the same powers of
reason that all men have, choose a different principle with which to guide their lives. Some people,
that is, are perverse. This fact must be considered
in the constitutional convention. Government is
viewed as a single institution which people commission to exercize the right that each of them has to
execute the law of nature. Such an institution has
the added advantage of protecting people not only
from those who reject the law of nature, but also
from those who misuse it, whether because of care-
lessness or because of self-interest. Government
is designed to enforce the law of nature, in the
name of its constituents. But these constituents
need not have given explicit consent to the government in order to be subject to its laws. So government is coercive in the present sense. The characteristics of the tool user encompass all those
characteristics of people discussed in the initial
situation, plus all those added when the veil of
ignorance is re-positioned for the constitutional
convention. Thus there are significant dangers of
tool use, if it gets into the wrong hands. Such
cases are avoidable, but should they occur, everyone
still has the right to be executor of the law of
nature. That is, people can revolt if one of the
bad guys gains power. The third postulate is
accepted in the initial situation as a principle of
justice, but it does not rule out government. Government is necessary as a remedy of the social ills
discussed in the constitutional convention. The
dangers of tool use are not severe enough to rule
out government.

For Marx, as for Locke, the veil of ignorance
must be re-positioned in establishing the constitutional convention. The parties have not known
which stage in the development of the material conditions of production they are in during the deliberations in the initial situation. If they find

- 87 -

that they are in the final classless society, upon
removing the veil, then they will not need government. But if the parties find that they are at any
stage between "primitive communism" and the end
stage, then their decision will be different. The
Marxian argument in behalf of government is
directed toward the proletariat, during the decaying period of bourgeois capitalism. It will be
assumed here that the re-positioning of the veil of
ignorance will reveal to the parties that it is
just this era that will define the Marxian constitutional convention. The proletariat is fast gaining strength *vis a vis* the bourgeoisie. Government
is to be viewed, in the Marxian constitutional convention, as a tool to be adopted only temporarily.
The end of the tool is the consolidation of gains
made by the proletariat, and the provision of a
framework from within which conditions of scarcity
may be eliminated, and class divisions abolished.
Characteristics of the tool user are changing, but
in a relatively predictable fashion. As conditions
of production change, human character will change,
in the direction of becoming less inclined to dominate. This is because there will be increasingly
less reason to dominate. This fact helps to ameli-
orate, somewhat, concern about the dangers of tool
use. But it is still possible that, during the
transition, the wrong people will gain control of
power. Such possibilities are rendered less omin-
ous by controls placed upon government, along the
lines suggested by the Paris Commune. The third
postulate would be accepted in the Marxian initial
situation as a principle of justice, but it would
not rule out government. For without government,
progress toward the classless society will at least
be delayed. Government is necessary for the transitional period.

    Each of these arguments will be dealt with
separately in subsequent chapters. For now, it is
important to summarize what has been argued here.
Now that the three arguments have been cast in
terms of the Rawlsian framework, it is easier to
see what was meant earlier by the contention that
all three arguments would agree on the third postulate as a principle of justice, and by the contention that the three arguments can be viewed as

attempts to give good reasons for government within the constraints of that postulate. In addition, the Rawlsian framework makes it possible to see that all three arguments amount to contentions that government is a *necessary* tool for accomplishing certain ends, and that these ends are important enough that the third postulate does not rule government out. The tasks proposed for this chapter have been completed.

Chapter V

The Structure

of the Counter-Argument

The strongest possible argument against government would be any one of those deductively valid arguments, having true and absolutely uncontroversial premises, whose conclusions read: "Government can in no way be justified." Unfortunately, it is not at all clear that such arguments exist.

It is important, therefore, to emphasize again that it is not the intent of the present work to establish that it is *impossible* to justify government. Rather, the present work is intended as a critical analysis of a few justificatory attempts; the few attempts to be criticized here are singled out because they seem best to reflect the attitudes about government that most people share. It is assumed that if the present counter-argument succeeds in undermining these attitudes, then the thesis that governments should no longer be maintained will have received rather strong support.

The counter-argument will be formulated in accordance with the pattern set earlier in the essay, where the kinds of arguments in defense of government that are here to be considered were isolated (Chapters I-III). That is, attention will first be focused upon the argument for community and communal values in general, in the hope of providing a better feeling for what a non-governmental social structure might be like. Attention will then be directed to the three arguments in behalf of government, considered in the light of this non-governmental alternative.

The Rawlsian framework, adopted in Chapter IV, makes it possible to focus attention upon the arguments that it would be appropriate to raise in the three constitutional conventions, where the decisions for or against government are to be made. The framework also makes it possible to place the third postulate in perspective: saying that the

postulate is accepted as a basic assumption is construed as meaning that it is accepted, no matter
what else is, as a principle of justice in all
three initial situations. Thus it guides deliberation in all three constitutional conventions. This
means that, in their attempts to solve the problems
which are their responsibility, the party or parties to the constitutional conventions will be dis-
posed to avoid choosing coercive solutions wherever
this is possible. The third postulate thus places
the burden of argument upon the defenders of government. They must provide the "good reasons."

Each of the three defenses of government here
being considered regards government as a social
"tool" for achieving certain ends. The Rawlsian
framework provides a valuable perspective on controversies about how this tool is to be designed.
Among the three defenses, variations in the way in
which the framework is filled out lead to associated variations in the way in which the tensions
between the three factors of tool design are
resolved; that is, variations in the framework
lead to different designs for the tool.[1]

All three tools are governments, however. The
three defenses share a commitment to the thesis
that government is *necessary* if certain valued ends
(somewhat different in the three cases) are to be
achieved. In each argument in behalf of government, it is this commitment which leads to the
designed tool's being a government. If it were not
for this commitment--that is, if a non-coercive

---

[1] I am not sure, but it may be that this way of approaching
the problem is what Rex Martin has in mind when he argues
for "internalist" programs for justifying political authority. If so, then my later counter-arguments may involve the
sorts of changes in strategy that he thinks would be
required of the philosophical anarchist in responding to
these programs. I am not sure about all this, in part
because of Martin's vagueness on the general point, and in
part because it was not Martin's line of argument that led
me to adopt this strategy. See Rex Martin, "Two Models for
Justifying Political Authority" [80], and "Wolff's Defence
of Philosophical Anarchism" [81].

means were available for achieving the ends in
question--the use of government as a social tool
would violate the third postulate. It would be
rejected in the constitutional convention.[2]

The counter-argument, then, will be that government would be rejected in each of the three constitutional conventions, because of the availability of a non-coercive means of solving the various
problems being confronted there.

The counter-argument will proceed as follows:
in Chapter VI, the generalized "public goods" problem, left hanging in Chapter I, will be raised once
again; it will be recalled that, in that earlier
chapter, the possibility was raised that some coercion might be necessary if communal values are to
be achievable. The general discussion of the problem in Chapter VI will lead to a set of rather surprising constraints upon the provision of public
goods in a non-coercive social order. It will also
provide a good background for a general sketch of
the particular non-coercive social tool that is
here to be compared with government in the three
constitutional conventions. This favored tool will
be referred to as "the free market," or where that
gets too unwieldy, simply as "the market." The *general* discussion of public goods will give a fairly
clear idea of the sorts of gambits available to a
defender of the free market in confronting the
claim that government is necessary to achieve some
particular public good.

Chapters VII, VIII and IX can be regarded as
the "Proceedings" of the Hobbesian, Lockeian and
Marxian constitutional conventions, respectively.
The conclusions, it will be argued, would come out
somewhat differently from the way they were portrayed by Hobbes, Locke and Marx. That is, it will
be argued that government is *not* necessary for
peace, protection of rights, or valuable social
change, that its adoption therefore violates the

---

[2]For an intricate, and often interesting, discussion of "necessity" arguments in general, see Elizabeth Anscombe, "On
the Source of the Authority of the State" [1].

third postulate, and that it is thus morally unacceptable.

The argument will not be at all plausible, of course, unless care is taken to do justice to the kind of "necessity" that is attributed to government in each case. It is in this regard that the three principles of tool design are crucial. It will be argued that even though there are risks involved with the free market, government is yet riskier, and that therefore the uncertainty of the market cannot be held against it in the constitutional conventions, as part of the argument that government is necessary.

Rational parties, it will be contended, would reject government as a violation of a principle of justice. That will be the ethical argument against government.

One final point needs to be mentioned here, so that it may be ignored later. When the time comes to compare the various social tools from which the parties to the constitutional conventions are to choose as means to solving the problems met there, it will become apparent that a good deal of the controversy has to do with empirical claims about how various institutional arrangements function-- or would function--in society. It might be thought that philosophical works, like this one, ought to steer clear of such empirical debates.

Two comments are in order. First, it is probably futile to try to avoid empirical arguments. Differences about empirical matters seem, in one way or another, to contaminate *all* arguments that people are likely to have, and they seem to do so in such a way as to make non-empirical purity a fairly hopeless ideal. But second, even if this be denied, it must surely be admitted that once empirical claims are brought up in a philosophical discussion, they are fair game. One needs only to glance back at Chapters II and III to see how deeply the arguments here being discussed are influenced by empirical claims.

The three arguments for government rely on the

claim that government is necessary for achieving certain things. In criticizing these arguments, "empirical" questions--questions that are raised by the defenders of government--are addressed only in the course of utilizing the inocuous technique of argument by counter-example. A society that does not have a government is envisioned, and it is argued that there is no reason to think that this society need do without the certain things in question. It is concluded, therefore, that the arguments for the necessity of government fail.

So the fact that certain empirical claims get discussed from time to time in the course of the present argument will not be regarded as a shortcoming of the argument.

In response to Locke's concession that civil government is the proper remedy for the "inconveniences of the state of nature," Robert Nozick has noted that

> To understand precisely what civil government remedies, we must do more than repeat Locke's list of the inconveniences of the state of nature. We also must consider what arrangements might be made within a state of nature to deal with these inconveniences--to avoid them or to make them less likely to arise or to make them less serious on the occasions when they do arise. Only after the full resources of the state of nature are brought into play, namely all those voluntary arrangements and agreements persons might reach acting within their rights, and only after the effects of these are estimated, will we be in a position to see how serious are the inconveniences that yet remain to be remedied by the state, and to estimate whether the remedy is worse than the disease.
> (*Anarchy, State, and Utopia* [102], pp. 10-11)

It is this task which confronts the parties to the three constitutional conventions: they are to judge the state in the light of the free market alternative. There will be occasion, in what follows, not only to ask if the remedy is worse than the disease, but also to wonder whether civil government is really a remedy, or just a placebo.

Chapter VI

Public Goods and the Free Market

The ethical argument against government need not rely on the thesis that people do not need to cooperate with one another. Or at least, that was the claim in Chapter I. A typical argument supporting the value of *community* was there discussed--the Aristotelian argument--and nothing has been said since then that would in any way undermine that argument. The present work acknowledges that cooperation among people--"communal" cooperation in particular--is extremely valuable in human affairs.

Indeed, the stronger claim that *homo sapiens* is a social animal--that people *need* to cooperate if they are to survive--seems plausible enough that it, too, is accepted. One must, of course, make some qualifications to such a claim: that mere survival may be possible for many people without requiring the aid of others, that *some* people would probably be able to live in relative comfort in the absence of a community, and so on. But solitary life--the hermit's life--appears to be neither particularly attractive nor particularly practical for most people. At the very least, it must be acknowledged that people can flourish only given a background of some sort of communal cooperation.

The basic question of this essay, however, is whether people need government in order to achieve the appropriate kind of communal cooperation. Government is conceived of as an agency that may be characterized, in part at least, by its assumed right to coerce its own clients. As early as the first chapter, it was found to be necessary to consider the possibility that the kind of community life envisioned there would be possible only if the coercive agency--government--were in place. If government *were* necessary for achieving communal values, then, given the importance of those values, it would seem that government would be justified.

The question as to whether government is necessary was not resolved in the first chapter, how-

ever. There the point was made merely that it might
be. The Aristotelian argument in behalf of community was found to contain considerations both for
and against government in the present sense.

More or less undermining the idea of government was Aristotle's very definition of "the
state": he characterized the state as an association of persons who share a common view in matters
of good and evil, right and wrong, just and unjust,
and who therefore have the same general aim in their
lives. The state was no more and no less than that
institutional framework within which such an association pursued the aims held in common by its members. When Aristotle argued for the state, therefore, he defended something quite different from
the conception of the state set out in the introductory chapter of the present work. Aristotle's
argument supported the value and importance of a
community of like-minded people, working together
to achieve common goals in a common way. That
value is here conceded.

Moreover, there were elements in the argument
of the first chapter that suggested that government
in the present sense would not be acceptable. One
passage suggested that the choice as to whether to
enlist in particular cooperative ventures was to be
left to individuals. This is in keeping with the
idea that the community defended is one comprised
of "like-minded" persons. Another passage seemed
to imply that to rule people without their consent
would be tyranny, and tyranny, of course, would be
unacceptable. A third passage, finally, reinforced
the idea that involuntary rule is unjust, by comparing the notion of statesman-as-dominator to the
ways in which doctors and ships' captains practice
their respective crafts. The latter, it was noted,
are not justified in persuading or forcing patients
or passengers; the implicit question was: Why
should statesmen be considered justified in doing
so?

These several features of the argument discussed in the first chapter seem to work against
government. Governments, as they are understood
here, do not limit themselves to working in behalf

of those objectives shared by all of their clie
They are not merely associations of like-minded
people. Instead, they tend to be associations of
all those people who live within a specified geographical territory, whether they be like-minded or
not. Governments do not leave the choice to cooperate up to the individuals they rule. People often
have the choice of either cooperating or leaving
the community, of course, but granting this option
to people is not well described as "leaving the
choice to cooperate up to individuals." It's more
like an ultimatum. Governmental officials do not
offer their services to the community in the way
that doctors and ships' captains do, since such
officials *do* resort to force in maintaining their
clientele. Since governments and governmental
officials, in the present sense, do none of these
things that Aristotle says that states and statesmen, in his sense, should do, one might conclude
that his argument works against government.

The argument contains considerations in support of government, as well, however. As it happens, people differ as to what they value. Achieving *any* communal values requires that compromises
be made among people as to which aims get striven
for. Now, the *ideal* of the Aristotelian state
excludes coercion; but it may be that some public
goods require coercion if they are to be achieved,
and that among these, some are valuable enough that
compromise with this aspect of the ideal is justified. That is, it may be that government is justified by practical considerations.

This issue was left unresolved in the first
chapter. The second and third chapters were
devoted to exploring three representative arguments
that were favorable to government. It is now possible, given the methodological framework of Chapter IV, which provides a restricted context within
which the debate may be conducted, to set forth the
argument against government.

Certain practical restrictions upon the options
available to a non-coercive social order in its
efforts to secure public goods may be arrived at,
however, through further consideration of the gen-

eral problem of public goods. It will be valuable, therefore, to nail down these restrictions before a non-coercive model of social organization is sketched, and before that model is brought into competition with government in the three constitutional conventions. The tasks of the present chapter, then, are two: first, to further restrict the non-coercive options available to the party or parties in the constitutional conventions; and second, to characterize in a general way the particular non-coercive model that is there to be considered.

Surely one of the boldest strokes in recent work concerning the "public goods" problem is the one delivered by Mancur Olson in his influential work, *The Logic of Collective Action* [104].[1] Olson seems to have shown that large groups of rational persons will *not* organize for coordinated action merely because, as a group, they have a reason for doing so. That is, he has argued persuasively that one cannot reasonably expect public goods to be obtained in circumstances in which 1) the community is very large, 2) the members of the community behave rationally, and 3) the members of the community may choose to support the effort or not. Since it is obvious that such a result has important consequences for any effort to defend a non-coercive model of social organization, it is clear that the specifics of Olson's argument must be examined more closely.

A common, collective, or public good, for Olson, is " . . . any good such that, if any person x_i in a group $x_1, \ldots, x_i, \ldots, x_n$ consumes it, it cannot feasibly be withheld from the others in that group" (*The Logic of Collective Action* [104], p. 14). The important fact to note about public goods is that *if* the good is created or provided by some members of the group, there is no feasible way of excluding or preventing those members who have *not* contributed from sharing in the consumption of the

---

[1]For a somewhat different treatment of the problem of public goods, see Murray N. Rothbard, *Man, Economy, and State* [121], pp. 883–90.

good (pp. 14-15). It is not necessary, in the definition of public goods, that it be technically *impossible* to prevent non-contributors from partaking in what others have provided: it must only be infeasible or uneconomic (p. 14).

Public goods are thus defined with respect to specific groups of people. To avoid certain complications, it will help to limit attention to only those public goods which require that someone make some sort of investment--whether it be of labor, cash, or whatever--if they are to become available. Only things that people have to provide if they are to be consumed will be considered. For similar reasons, it is best to worry only about those situations in which the members of the group with respect to which some public good is defined are unanimous in their desire for that good. This restriction is justified by the fact that Olson will argue that *even* in cases where all of the members of a very large group are unanimous in desiring a public good, that good will not be provided, given that the members can choose whether or not they will help in providing the good, and that they make this choice rationally.

An example might help to clear up Olson's definition of public goods. Perhaps the clearest example is that of protection from nuclear attack. Consider, for example, the group made up of all the residents of metropolitan Boston. It is reasonable to assume that each member of this group would want the metropolitan area to be protected from nuclear attack. But such protection has certain costs. For the sake of the example, it may be assumed that there is some distribution of costs such that, for each individual, protection of Boston from nuclear attack is worth his share of the costs, under that distribution. That is, each person desires the protection enough that he would be willing to pay his share if he had to.

But consider, now, the case of Albert the Free Rider. Albert is a resident of the metropolitan Boston area. So he is a member of the group in question. He, like everybody else, wants Boston to be protected. But Albert is ready to gamble that

even if he does not bear his share of the costs,
protection will be provided anyway. That is, he
computes that there is another distribution of the
costs that would willingly be born by people in
protecting the area from attack, but that does not
require that he pay anything. He decides not to
pay, because he recognizes that nuclear protection
is a *public good*: that is, it is a good such that *if*
it is provided, there is no feasible way for those
who have paid the costs to withhold it from Albert.
Albert counts his money and grins.

If there are lots of people like Albert in the
group, then providing the public good may prove to
be much more difficult than one would otherwise
expect. It may be that the public good will not be
provided at all. A great deal will depend, of
course, on what the particular public good is, and
upon how much each person in the group values that
good. The problem of ascertaining whether certain
specific public goods would be provided voluntarily
within given groups will turn out to be the main
issue confronting the party or parties to the constitutional conventions, as they try to decide whether or not to establish government. Most of the
interesting features of that problem will therefore be discussed in subsequent chapters.

But Olson argues plausibly that provision or
non-provision of public goods also depends in an
important way upon certain fundamental characteristics of the group itself. To understand his argument, it is necessary to examine briefly his "taxonomy of groups," and his analysis of the varying
potentials that different kinds of groups have of
providing public goods in general.

In the first place, Olson distinguishes between
what he calls "exclusive" and "inclusive" groups.

An exclusive group is best characterized as
that sort of group, the members of which hope to
keep membership restricted as much as possible.
Within such groups, competition or rivalry is the
characteristic relationship holding between members. In general, the character of an exclusive
group is determined by the fact that the particular

public good sought is such that it is fixed in sup-
ply--that is, it is such that the more benefit one
member gets, the less others get (p. 37).

By far the most common examples of exclusive
groups are to be found among producers in a competitive economy. Given some particular commercial
product, all those individuals and firms who produce that same product make up an exclusive group.
The public good associated with such a group would
be an increase in the profit margin between cost
and selling price. If the selling price of the
product goes up, if demand is inelastic, and if
production throughout the industry remains the
same, with no increase in costs, then everyone in
the group will benefit. But if one producer sells
more products at the higher price, then the others
must sell less. The benefits of the public good
are fixed in supply. Thus competition is the rule,
and restricting membership in the group is the aim.
Monopoly is the ideal.

The analysis of exclusive groups is not, however, particularly important for the present discussion. It can safely be ignored, at least for
now. Of far greater significance is Olson's analysis of "inclusive" groups.

For a characteristic inclusive group, the larger the membership, the happier the individual members. In such groups, increasing the membership
hurts no one, and in fact typically leads to a
reduced cost burden on each member. For inclusive
groups, the benefit from a public good is *not* fixed
in supply: if one member gets more, others need
not get less.

A typical inclusive group is the contemporary
"lobbying" organization. Such organizations try to
get legislators to pass certain laws--laws that
would, if passed, benefit everyone in some given
group. But lobbying has its costs, and the more
people there are who help to bear these costs, the
less each contributor's burden becomes. An example
of an inclusive group that does not so obviously
have to do with governments and legislation is the
group mentioned earlier--the group made up of the

residents of the metropolitan Boston area, who hope
to provide themselves with protection against nuclear attack. That group clearly qualifies as one
of Olson's inclusive groups with respect to that
particular good.

Now, it is of course possible that the same
group of people could be characterized as an exclusive group with respect to one objective, and as an
inclusive group with respect to another. The firms
in some particular industry would be an exclusive
group with respect to efforts to raise prices by
restricting output, for example, but would qualify
as an inclusive group in lobbying the government
for lower taxes, tariffs, etc. (p. 39). But this
fact need not trouble the present discussion. It
must merely be remembered that it is the objective,
rather than the membership, of a group that determines whether it is to behave exclusively or inclu-
sively.

Olson's main contribution to the theory of
public goods is his well-argued contention that,
given a particular public good, the potential of an
inclusive group to provide that good changes dramatically with the size of that group. To understand
his argument, it will be necessary to explore a bit
further the Olsonian taxonomy of groups.

There are three kinds of inclusive groups:
"privileged" groups, "intermediate" groups, and
"latent" groups. With respect to the provision of
any one public good, the distinction between the
three kinds of groups is merely one of size.

Privileged groups are groups that are small
enough such that the cost of providing the public
good is so low that each member--or at least one of
them--would be willing to pay the whole cost if he
had to.

Intermediate groups are groups that are large
enough that the cost of providing the public good
is too large for any one member to be willing to
pay it, even if that were the only way to get the
good. But intermediate groups are still small
enough that failure of any one member to pay his

share will have a noticeable effect upon the burdens of the other members.

Latent groups, finally, are groups that are large enough that no one member would pay the whole cost of the public good, and are *so* large that failure of any one member to pay his share will have no significant effect upon the shares of other members (pp. 49-50).

Now, a privileged group defined with respect to one public good may be larger than a privileged group defined with respect to a different good. Much depends upon the cost of providing the good and the value that individuals place upon having it provided.[2] But the three kinds of groups are defined by Olson in such a way that interesting results may be obtained even when particular costs and particular values are ignored. Attention is focused, instead, upon the different courses of action that a rational person would take as a member of each of the three kinds of inclusive groups, and upon the differences this would make regarding provision of the public good.

It is clear that a definition of "rationality" is needed if such an inquiry is even to get off the ground. Olson's seems to be fairly uncontrover-

---

[2]Where the cost per unit decreases as the size of the group increases, it may very well be difficult to predict that increasing group size will invariably lead to a decreasing willingness (or capacity) to supply the public good. This will, I think, be the *general* tendency of increasing group size, but some increases may have opposite "local" effects on the curve. See William H. Riker and Peter C. Ordeshook, *An Introduction to Positive Political Theory* [118], pp. 73-74 (footnote 31). Similar complications may arise if the *value* that individuals place on the good changes as group size increases. But both of these issues seem to cause trouble only for a *dynamic* theory of the effects of increasing group size. If the various groups are defined as in the three paragraphs immediately preceding this one in the text, and if one deals with them without asking what happens *dynamically* as an intermediate group gets larger and larger (for example), the problems seem not to be raised.

sial. He does not assume that rational behavior
need be restricted to the pursuit of self-interest.
To say that people should be rational, for Olson,
is to say no more than that " . . . their objectives, whether selfish or unselfish, should be pursued by means that are efficient and effective for
achieving these objectives." Such a definition has
the advantage of neither implying self-interested
behavior nor being inconsistent with it (pp. 64-
65).

Olson's argument will rely upon the idea that
it is foolish-- irrational--to exert one's efforts
toward achieving goals that are not perceptibly
furthered by those efforts. His clearest example
is the following:

> A man who tried to hold back a flood with a pail
> would probably be considered more of a crank
> than a saint, even by those he was trying to
> help. It is no doubt possible infinitesimally
> to lower the level of a river in flood with a
> pail, . . . but . . . the effect is impercep-
> tible, and those who sacrifice themselves in the
> interest of imperceptible improvements may not
> even receive the praise normally due selfless
> behavior. (p. 64)

Such a man would be behaving irrationally.

Equipped with a definition of "rationality,"
it is now possible to try to determine what rational
individuals would do as members of first a privileged group, then an intermediate group, and
finally a latent group.

Privileged groups, by definition, contain at
least one member who would be willing to bear the
whole cost of the public good if he had to. Much
space can be saved by considering just this one
member. It may be that this member would simply
provide the good himself, out of generosity, perhaps; or maybe he would provide the good and then
ask for good-will reimbursements later. On the
other hand, he may, out of self-interest, try to
conceal from his fellow members the fact that he
would pay the whole cost, in the hope of either

getting someone else to pay the cost, or, at least, of bearing a smaller burden himself. In any case, however, the presumption is that, in a privileged group, the public good will be provided. For if all else fails, there is at least one member who will pay the whole cost.

The situation is more complex in intermediate groups. There, each person will know that someone else must bear at least *part* of the cost of the public good, since he knows that he, anyway, would not be willing to bear the whole cost. Perhaps each person will bank on the possibility that the group he is in is really a privileged group, and wait for that one person to pick up the tab. Or perhaps he will be more fair to the others, and contribute his fair share. Presumably people will know that their group is not a privileged one after they have waited awhile for some one member to pay the whole cost, and no one has done so. So even in the case of radical self-interest, it should dawn on everyone eventually that some cooperation is necessary.

It is necessary, in an intermediate group, to arrange some distribution of costs. Where the members are not acting in a radically self-interested way, there is some presumption that a distribution will be arranged, and that the public good will be provided. But in the case of selfish behavior, certain interesting complications arise. Intermediate groups, by definition, are ones in which the failure of any one member to pay his share will have noticeable effects upon the burdens of the other members. The self-interested intermediate group member will know that he might be able to get away with a smaller share in the distribution if he strikes an appropriate bargaining position. Each of the other members will realize that if the position he is taking is an accurate measure of the real extent to which he values the public good, then they had better alot to him no more than the share which his bargaining position demands. For if they ask him to pay more, he will simply refuse, and his failure to pay any of the costs would have a noticeable effect upon them: they will have to pay more.

But if the self-interested member's bargaining

position does *not* accurately reflect the amount he
would be willing to pay, then the other members
will want to find this out, too. For if he would
pay more, giving him the distributive share demanded
by his position would also mean that the other members are bearing more of the burden than they have
to.

Where several members of the group strike such
positions, or at least *seem* to from the perspective
of the rest of the membership, the bargaining may
become extremely complicated. It may be that some
distribution will be agreed to that all members
will be content with. Or it may be that the bargaining situation will break down under the stress
of suspicions that some members are simply holding
out for a better deal. Perhaps no distribution
will be agreed to. In the first case, the presumption is that the public good would be provided; in
the second, one assumes that it would not. In general, it would be necessary to know a great deal
more about particular intermediate groups and the
particular public goods in question in order to
determine whether the goods would be provided or
not. The intermediate group case is indeterminate.

In latent groups, finally, the failure of any
one member to pay his share of the costs of the
public good will have no perceptible effect upon
the burdens of the other members. This situation
is much better for that member who acts rationally
in his own self-interest, for it does not seem to
be necessary to pay any of the costs. Like Albert
the Free Rider, the rational egoist will note that
the public good will probably be provided even
without his help, so he will save his money. After
all, he would think: his abstention will not
really hurt anyone else, and so no one will have a
motive to react in any way to his refusing to pay.
He doesn't even have to bargain.

But, Olson argues, it would not be just those
members who think primarily in terms of their own
self-interest who would abstain from supporting the
group effort:

Even if the member of a [latent] group were to

neglect his own interests entirely, he still
would not rationally contribute toward the provision of any collective or public good, since
his own contribution would not be perceptible.
A farmer who placed the interests of other farm-
ers above his own would not necessarily restrict
his production to raise farm prices, since he
would know that his sacrifice would not bring a
noticeable benefit to anyone. Such a rational
farmer, however unselfish, would not make such a
futile and pointless sacrifice, but he would
allocate his philanthropy in order to have a
perceptible effect on someone. (p. 64)

A rational member of a latent group, whether selfish or altruistic, would abstain from contributing
toward the public good.[3] To the extent that the
members of a latent group are rational in Olson's
sense, therefore, the presumption is that the public good would not be provided.

The impact that this conclusion has upon the
present discussion seems to be rather dramatic.
The implication is that public goods are not likely
to be provided in any community that meets the following three conditions: 1) the community is a
latent group; 2) the members of the community have
the option to abstain from supporting the effort to
secure the public good; and 3) the members behave
rationally.[4]

---

[3]Analyses of human behavior are obviously inadequate wherever
they assume either absolutely self-interested behavior on
the part of everyone, or absolutely altruistic behavior. An
interesting defense of charitable institutions as social
devices for providing public goods--a defense that seems to
fall into neither trap--is provided by Richard C. Cornuelle,
Reclaiming the American Dream [22]. When it comes time to
propose a model for an ungoverned society in what follows,
it will be crucial to avoid inadequacies of both the "rugged
individualist" and "perfect communitarian" kinds. The "free
market" model of social organization, introduced later in
the present chapter, is to be understood as neither presup-
posing rugged individualism--or predominantly self-interested
behavior--nor as ruling it out.

[4]For recent efforts at applying public good theory to ethics

Whatever the merits of Olson's argument, it seems reasonable to imagine that it would at least be presented to the parties in the constitutional conventions. Phrased as it is, it would appear to support the conclusion that public goods can be provided to latent groups--i.e., to communities that meet the first of the three conditions--only if either the community members behave irrationally, or if they are not given the choice to opt out of the communal effort. Since it is not terribly reasonable to try to provide a social order in which people must behave irrationally, it would seem that the only way to provide public goods to large communities is to take away the option of abstaining. That is, it may be concluded that coercion is necessary to provide public goods to large groups. That would be a dramatic conclusion indeed.

There are, however, at least five plausible ways of defending the non-coercive social order in the constitutional conventions, once Olson's argument has been presented. That is, it is not reasonable to imagine that the parties to the constitutional conventions would accept government, simply on the basis of the Olsonian argument, without first carefully scrutinizing that argument. Such an examination would show that there are at least five potential weak spots in the argument, which, if attacked, might tend to break the apparent link between the argument and the conclusion that coercion is necessary. Thus the five weak spots represent five options available to defenders of a non-coercive social order in the constitutional conventions. They are as follows.

1. It might be argued that Olson is wrong in thinking that helping to provide a public good in a latent group is irrational. One might think that the careful reasoning of Olson's argument would be taken into consideration by a rational person in a latent group. In considering whether to help pay for the good, a rational person might think: "But

---

in general, see James M. Buchanan, "Ethical Rules, Expected Values, and Large Numbers" [19], and Richard B. McKenzie, "The Economic Dimensions of Ethical Behavior" [77].

if everybody avoids paying, the good won't get provided." It is difficult to feel comfortable with
calling a decision to pay on the grounds of this
kind of consideration irrational. Olsonian rationality, applied to decisions in latent groups, seems
to violate what might as well be acknowledged as
Kant's *categorical imperative*; and it seems a bit
strong to call that principle irrational in such
situations, especially since it seems to be supported by Olson's conclusion that, if people were
to act as he thinks rationality dictates, then they
would fail to get what they wanted.

Such an argument may not be too helpful, however, even if it could be made to work. Olson's
line of reasoning may be reformulated in such a way
that instead of dealing with what it is *rational* for
people to do as members of latent groups, it deals
with what people *in fact* do, or with what the parties
to the constitutional convention may reasonably
expect people to do, as members of such groups.
Olson lists several historical examples of latent
groups and their behavior in his book. These examples seem to support, with certain important qualifications (see below, option (4)), the thesis that
latent groups don't manage to provide themselves
with public goods. So the first option is less
attractive than it may at first seem. In order to
make effective use of it in the constitutional conventions, one would have to be able to argue plausibly that the particular goods being considered
there are such that people could be expected to
help in providing them, even as members of latent
groups.[5]

---

[5]Olson does qualify the potential value of his theory by not-
ing that it may not be of much (or any) use as regards
"non-rational" or "irrational" groups (pp. 159-65). Among
such groups, it seems, he would include those characterized
by "ideologically oriented behavior" (p. 162). Karen Johnson, in "A Note on the Inapplicability of Olson's Logic of
Collective Action to the State" [60], has argued, along the
lines of this first option of ours, to the conclusion that
the *state* is just the sort of group *not* covered successfully
by Olson's analysis. Her notion of the state is considerably
broader than the one being considered here, however, and it

2. It might be argued that there is a non-coercive means of insuring that the particular goods that are being considered in the constitutional conventions would be demanded only by privileged groups. Since there is a presumption that public goods would be provided in privileged groups, this option would be a very attractive one, if it could be utilized plausibly.

3. It might be argued that there is a non-coercive means of insuring that the particular goods that are being considered would be demanded only by (at the largest) intermediate groups. This option is obviously much less attractive than the last, since whether intermediate groups will be able to provide themselves with public goods is, in general, indeterminate. But it might be that knowing which goods were in question would allow one to have a better idea about the likelihoods involved. If this option were to be effective, it would have to make it plausible that these particular goods would be provided even by intermediate groups.

4. It might be argued that public goods could be provided to latent groups by a provision of non-public goods to those who pay, or by some sort of non-coercive disincentives to those who fail to pay. This option is suggested by Olson himself, and he lists several examples of latent groups which *do* seem to manage to provide themselves with public goods in this way. But as he notes--and as will become clear in a later chapter--there is a hidden trap to this option. It has been used--unsuccessfully, it would appear--in at least one relatively recent defense of the particular non-coercive model that will here be examined. If this option were the only one available, then it seems likely that the model would fail. This option might be useful in conjunction with one or more of the others, however.

---

is not clear how she would respond to the claim made in the Introduction about necessary conditions of statehood. Her argument seems, at least, to parallel some remarks made below, especially in Chapter VII, regarding voluntary provision of "public" goods.

5. It might be argued that the goods being
considered in the constitutional convention were
private goods, rather than public goods. That is,
it might be argued that there *is* a feasible way of
withholding the goods in question from those who
fail to help in providing it. This option would be
very powerful if, in addition, it could be argued
that one could *expect* the goods to be provided pri-
vately in a non-coercive society.

These, then, are the five options available to
the defender of a non-coercive social order in the
constitutional conventions. If all of these options
fail, and if no other options seem to be available,
then the parties to the convention will opt for
coercion. They will adopt government.

The discussion of Olson's argument has had a
decidedly valuable effect, therefore. It has
placed certain restrictions upon the kinds of arguments to be used in opposition to government in the
three constitutional conventions. It has thus provided guidelines for what will be acceptable as an
alternative to government. Any acceptable non-
coercive model of social organization will have to
avail itself of one or more of the five options if
it is to be chosen over government. With this in
mind, it is now possible to give a preliminary
sketch of the model to be examined in the present
work.

In the present context, it may be most fruitful to begin the sketch of the model by recalling
once again an extremely interesting remark of Aristotle's that was cited earlier in the present chapter, as well as in the first chapter. In discussing the view of "most people" that domination and
government are "one and the same thing," Aristotle
noted that "One does not find this insistence on
power in any of the other professions; it is not
the job of a doctor or ship's captain to persuade
or to force patients or passengers" (*Politics*, p. 260).
The question implicit in this remark is the following: If doctors and ships' captains are not considered to be justified in maintaining their clien-
telle by force, why is it that people feel that
statesmen are justified in doing so?

- 113 -

The statesman, for Aristotle, is someone who, like the doctor or the ship's captain, provides certain services to the community. These services seem to be valuable ones. As such, it is not immediately clear why they could not be provided on the market, like the services of other professionals. On the market, those who desire more of the statesman's services could purchase more, and thus bear a larger share of the burden of supporting the provision of these services to the community. Furthermore, those who did not care for the way a particular statesman did business could turn to another statesman, or they could make arrangements for providing the services themselves, or they could decide to try to make do without the services.

Answers to the question implicit in the Aristotelian remark have, of course, been ventured. The most important of these answers are the ones that have been sketched, in a general way, in preceding pages. They all share a common element: they share a commitment to the thesis that the market would *not* provide the services in question, at least not in an acceptable way. Coercion is necessary if certain public goods are to be provided. That is why the statesman is justified in maintaining his clientele by force.

These answers ought not to be accepted on face value, however. There is no reason to expect that the parties to the constitutional conventions would accept them without listening to counter-arguments in behalf of market provision of the goods that it is hoped governments would provide. The parties share, after all, a commitment to the third postulate, which was adopted as a principle of justice. They share, therefore, a certain bias against coercion. It is assumed, of course, that the parties will realize that simply *asserting* that people are not to be coerced in the absence of good reasons to the contrary will not insure that there will be no coercion in the community once all veils are lifted. They need a means of safe-guarding peace, rights, and valuable social change in the real world. But their acceptance of the third postulate dictates that they would prefer non-coercive means to this end over coercive means, if they were

- 114 -

available, and if they could plausibly be defended
as effective. They would consider, therefore, the
possibility that the services in question could be
provided on the market. That, in fact, is the main
issue before the constitutional conventions.

The non-coercive model of social organization
that will be presented to the parties in the present
work is what will here be referred to as the "free
market" model. There is a sense in which this
model is not well characterized merely as that situation which would result if government were
rejected in the constitutional conventions, for it
borrows heavily from a background which presumes
acquaintance with the "free market capitalist" mode
of production and consumption of goods. Real people making decisions about government in the
absence of such a background might be expected to
opt for government, being unaware of the complex
machinery available within the free market. For if
they rejected government, not only would their
decision be irrational, since they would have no
reason to expect that public goods would be provided to them, but the goods may actually not get
provided. Where no one knows about the market,
there may be no one who would think to try to gain
personal benefits by providing social goods. The
advent of the capitalist mode of production is,
after all, a relatively recent historical phenomenon; furthermore, it never did win complete freedom from older modes of social organization--i.e.,
governmental modes--and it has in the last century
been steadily adulterated with increasing governmental interference. It is to be expected that
real people might not imagine the free market model
to be the result of rejecting government, simply
because they do not know about the model.

The parties to the constitutional conventions,
however, *do* know about the model. Since they will
also know that real people may be ignorant of it,
in certain times and in certain places, they will,
if they choose the free market, also adopt measures
to educate people. But if the free market is
deemed the best form of social organization in the
constitutional convention, it will not be rejected
because real people are ignorant of it. It will be

accepted.

The free market model, then, is hardly being
presented for the first time in these pages.
Because of its links with capitalistic modes of
production and consumption, it has been called
"anarcho-capitalism," or sometimes "radical capitalism," by some of its exponents. That precedent
will not be followed here, however, because of the
confusion that such designations seem to provoke
among people who think of capitalism as the sort of
system exemplified, for example, by the United
States, where producers typically receive considerable support from government. Furthermore, to refer
to the model as a version of capitalism would seem
to suggest that non-capitalistic modes of organization would not appear in a society organized within
its guidelines. It is not clear that this would be
the case on the free market. For these reasons, it
seems best to keep "capitalism" out of the name of
the model.

The model has also been called "radical libertarianism." This seems to be a more appropriate
designation, but it, too, has problems. Many would
argue that the term "libertarian" applies most
appropriately to those socialist anarchists of the
nineteenth and twentieth century who applied that
name to themselves. Since these thinkers were
often at least as much opposed to the capitalist
mode of production as they were to governments, it
might be confusing to apply that name to the free
market. The market does not insist upon capitalistic organization, but it does allow it. It allows
any form of explicit, voluntary cooperation among
persons.

A society that conducted its business by voluntary contract, rather than by government, would
be extraordinarily complex. It is extremely
unlikely that any one contract or agreement would
provide people with all of the diverse services
presently associated with governments. The free
market society is simply, as its name suggests, an
unfettered market place, where all commodities and
services could, it is hoped, be made available,
limited only by the market principles of supply and

demand.

This is not to say that everything on the market must be bought and paid for in cash. Rather, the market relies upon the principle of *value exchange*; value may be computed in terms of money, but this need not be the case. In fact, there are many valuable commodities and services that are most conveniently exchanged directly, without monetary intermediary. The market is no more and no less than the locus of *all* voluntary exchange.

It seems best to stick to "the free market" as the name of the particular non-coercive model of social organization that is here to be discussed. Rooted most evidently in the thought of nineteenth century American anarchists, Lysander Spooner being perhaps the most influential among them in terms of theoretical foundations, the model has recently been expounded in considerable detail by such thinkers as Murray Rothbard, by Morris and Linda Tannehill, by Jerome Tuccille, and by David Friedman. In addition, the model owes a considerable debt to the work of Ayn Rand.[6] The arguments and suggestions contained in the works of these writers will prove to be a valuable resource in the constitutional conventions.

Very general considerations, then, suggest that the free market ought to be considered as an alternative to government. It is not immediately obvious that the market would not work, and the third postulate seems to be biased somewhat in its favor. The question now is whether the free market can meet the rigors of the constitutional conventions.

---

[6]For specific works by these authors, see Works Cited.

Chapter VII

Peace on the Market

Is government necessary for the preservation of peace? This is the question before the Hobbesian constitutional convention.[1]

For Hobbes, human nature is such that, in the absence of government, people would have reason to fear that others would behave aggressively toward them. This being the case, people would take steps to defend themselves through pre-emptive attacks. Universal war--a result of the behavior of both aggressors and pre-emptive defenders--would be the natural state of affairs.

Government, for Hobbes, is the remedy for this unpleasant situation. This is because of the fact that, even though people in the state of nature would recognize the value of obeying the "Law of Nature," which dictates that people place limitations upon the ways in which they behave toward one another, it would be foolish to refrain from attacking others unless there existed some "common power,' which could guarantee that others would do so too. The only way to erect such a common power is to establish government.

Now, it is crucial that a potential source of confusion be cleared up immediately.

The first postulate, set out in the Introduction to this essay, suggests that government is a fundamentally coercive agency. The third postulate suggests that unless there are good reasons to the contrary, people should not be coerced. The aim of the present project is to make plausible the thesis that there are not good reasons for governmental coercion, since arguments to the contrary rely on

---

[1]For a critique of Hobbes that takes an approach somewhat different from the one offered here, but which comes to the same general conclusion, see David B. Suits, "On Hobbes's Argument for Government" [137].

the claim that government is necessary to achieve
certain valued ends, and since consideration of the
free market alternative will show that this claim
is false.

But there are at least two senses in which
government may be said to be a "fundamentally coercive agency," and ambiguity between these two
senses may cause confusion with respect to the
Hobbesian line of argument.

On the one hand, government is coercive in
that one of its assigned tasks is to *defend its clients*, if necessary, by force or threat of force. It
is designed to supplement the resources of individual clients for their self-defense, and thereby to
make successful aggression less likely.

On the other hand, government is coercive in
that it *maintains its clientele* by force. Not only
must an individual citizen accept the services provided by his government, whether he wants the services or not, and whether he thinks the government
is providing the services well or poorly, but he is
typically forced to pay for them, whether he wants
them or not, as well.

Now, when it is here contended that the free
market model refutes the claim that governmental
coercion is necessary, it is not implied that *defensive* force may not be necessary and justified.
Rather, the free market is conceived of as a means
of *providing* defensive services, for example, without
coercing those to whom these services are provided.
It is the claim that the *second* kind of governmental
coercion is necessary, which the free market alternative shows to be false. It is because *this* claim
is false that government proves to be unnecessary,
and it is this claim that must be true if government were to be justified within the guidelines of
the third postulate.

It is to avoid the confusions surrounding the
notion of government as a "coercive agency" that
the first postulate is worded as it is: "An essential character of government is its assumed right
to coerce its own 'clients'."

The question before the Hobbesian constitutional convention, therefore, is this: can it reasonably be expected that peace would be provided on the market, at least as well as it would be provided by governments? If so, then government would be rejected, given the third postulate.

The free market, it will here be argued, provides at least as efficient a remedy to the ills of the state of nature as does government. In presenting the argument, it will be fruitful to consider separately those defensive services which seem most clearly to be "private goods," on the one hand, and those that seem to be "public goods," on the other. This will be helpful because of the fact, discussed in the last chapter, that there are special problems involved with supplying public goods on a voluntary basis. That some defensive services--indeed, that most "domestic" defensive services--are private goods, rather than public goods, will become clear in the course of the discussion.

First, then, to domestic defensive goods.

The individual in the state of nature is obliged to defend himself. This means, first and foremost, that he is himself responsible for preventing other individuals from doing him physical harm, and from snatching away the things he has provided himself with for the satisfaction of his "desires." More briefly, he must protect himself and his property[2] from the depredations of others.

Not only is the individual in the state of nature obliged to defend himself, he must *constantly* be on the defensive. This is, to say the least, a rather unpleasant way to live one's life. But each time a person adds to his ability to enjoy life, whether it be through acquisition of one more desired item, or through the acquisition of a bit more power to get desired items, he increases his

---

[2]No particular definition of "property" need here be implied, although it should be noted that only those things that are at least somewhat difficult to come by need to be protected.

vulnerability to attack. Finally, the situation is
such that there is a rather low probability that
anyone will live long enough to enjoy much of anything. No matter how powerful an individual is,
his power can always be offset by a coalition of
aggressors. An individual in the state of nature
would obviously be willing to sacrifice a great
deal for a tool that would make his life more
secure; for without such a tool, he is likely to
have to sacrifice everything.

The parties to the Hobbesian constitutional
convention consider the possibility that government
might be just the tool needed to avoid the evils of
the state of nature. But in deciding whether to
adopt government or not, they will examine its efficiency with respect to the three principles of tool
design mentioned in Chapter IV, comparing it with
other possible tools. They will consider, that is,
1) the reliability of government in achieving its
end, namely, domestic peace; 2) the extent to
which government fits the known characteristics of
those who may be expected to "use" it; and 3) the
extent to which the use of the governmental tool
will be dangerous--that is, the extent to which
nasty consequences may be expected through using
the tool.

Examining government in the light of the tool
principles reveals an obvious, but important, fact:
government is hardly a perfect tool for the job it
is meant to accomplish.

For one thing, the parties to the constitutional convention will not anticipate that the
adoption of government will guarantee that domestic
peace will be preserved. Compared to the "state of
nature" envisioned in the Hobbesian argument, it is
likely that people will be less subject to being
attacked by their neighbors under government. But
the parties will not expect that all interpersonal
aggression will be eliminated. Government is, at
best, a device that can be expected to *minimize* the
risk of attack upon person and property.

In addition, the principles of tool design,
when used to test government as a social tool, will

direct attention to the fact that government is
less than perfectly suited to the known characteristics of the tool user. Stated in this way, the
point is much too vague; but it is an important
point, and it will pay to devote a few lines to
clearing it up.

In thinking of government as a tool, there are
at least two classes of people who could plausibly
be thought of as the tool "users."

On the one hand, it might be thought that it
is the class of those who are governed that use the
tool. To the extent that government is a tool to
be used by the governed, the point about suitedness
suggests that government requires, if it is to be
used most efficiently, characteristics on the part
of those who use it that the governed, as a class,
cannot reasonably be expected to have. Democratic
societies, for example, seem to suppose that government is to be used by the people. But democracies have always been troubled by the fact that
people do not seem to be able to make efficient use
of their governments. Either people tend to make
little or no effort to use government at all--per-
haps as a result of the kinds of "rational" considerations discussed by Mancur Olson--or, where they
do make use of it, they do not seem to be able (or
willing) to take a broad, society-wide perspective
on what the government should do--a perspective
that, it seems, is required if the governmental
tool is to be used in some consistent, productive
fashion. Where the governed are perceived as the
tool users, there is a sense in which government
appears to be somewhat too utopian: it does not
fit the known characteristics of people as members
of the governed class. Stated somewhat differently,
this is, in fact, one of the best known arguments
against democracy.

On the other hand, however, it might be thought
that the "users" of the governmental tool are the
members of the class of governors. It may be that
in this case the *end* of government continues to be
the good of "the people"; the difference is to be
found, however, in the fact that in the first case,
the governed were thought to use government

- 123 -

directly, whereas in this case, it is the governors
who use government, albeit in behalf of the governed. Benevolent dictatorships, representative
republics, and, in general, "political steward-
ships,"[3] seem to make this assumption regarding the
question as to which class of people is to be identified as the "user" of government as a tool. But
such political systems, as benevolent as their
intentions may be, always seem to run into trouble
from the fact that the governors do not know enough
about the individual needs of the citizens--and
about efficient means for meeting those gross needs
they *do* know about--to make efficient use of the
governmental machinery they are supposed to wield.
Where the governors are perceived as the tool users,
government again appears to be somewhat too utopian
a tool: government requires that the governors
know a great deal more than may reasonably be
expected of them. It seems almost to demand omni-
science. This, in fact, is one of the main arguments against political stewardship.

In both cases, then, the parties to the constitutional convention will recognize that government is less than perfectly suited to the known
characteristics of people.

Finally, examining government in the light of
the three principles of tool design will lead the
parties to recognize that there are certain definite dangers involved with choosing government as a
social tool.

In the first place, to establish a government
is, on the present definition, to establish an
institution that claims the right to coerce its own
clients, at least as regards maintaining their support. It is also empowered with the *means* of coercing its citizens. The parties to the constitutional convention will realize that it will be
rather difficult to make adjustments in an institution that claims this right and has this power, in
the event that it becomes inefficient. Even the

---

[3]This felicitous expression seems to have been coined by
Robert Paul Wolff, *In Defense of Anarchism* [158], p. 31.

best motivated government could, through ineffi-
ciency or misguided policy, lead society down a
path that might be worse than the state of nature.

But in the second place, the parties will recognize that there are no guarantees that the government *itself* might not initiate attacks upon its
citizens. Government is established as a means for
preserving domestic peace, among other things, but
it might very well violate the peace itself. The
kinds of such violation that are possible are unlim-
ited, ranging from invasions of privacy to murder.
This is no wild-eyed fantasy. Governments do these
things all too frequently. The parties will recognize that establishing a government will make it
extremely difficult for people adequately to defend
themselves if their "protectors" turn to attacking
them. They will take into account the dangers of
government as a social tool.

The examination of government in the light of
the principles of tool design need not, of course,
lead to immediate rejection of government. It may
be that government is the only means for achieving
relative domestic peace, and if so, it might be
that some *particular* design for government would render its imperfections less severe. If government
were adopted in the constitutional convention, then
the parties would keep the tool principles in mind
as they designed a particular government.

It is crucial to note, however, that the examination of government has an important effect upon
any attempt to outline a non-coercive alternative.
For it shows that such an alternative need not be a
perfect tool, if it is to be chosen over government
in the constitutional convention. It need only be
the case that the parties could rationally expect
that the alternative would do at least as good a
job of providing domestic peace (for example) as
government can be expected to do. In particular,
the free market model need not be able to *guarantee*
that peace will be preserved; it need only be as
promising as government. Neither does the free
market have to be *perfectly* suited to human characteristics, or absolutely free of risk.

In defending the free market, it is only necessary that a plausible case be made that the market could be expected to do at least as good a job in providing peace, to be at least as well suited to human characteristics, and to be at least as safe, as government. It is true that people are not angels, but this fact does not rule out the free market any more than it rules out government. If the market is at least as good a tool as government, given the three principles of tool design, then government is not "necessary"; it would be rejected.

How well, then, can the free market be expected to do in providing domestic peace? As a rough approximation, this question can be rephrased as follows: how well could the market be expected to provide those services that police departments are supposed to provide in governed societies? The approach to this question taken by David Friedman, in his *Machinery of Freedom* [31], seems to provide a mercifully short route to the interesting issues, and it is this approach that will be taken here.

Friedman observes that even in governed societies, protection from coercion is available, at least to some extent, on the market (p. 156). In twentieth century America, for example, such protection is sold in a variety of forms, such as "Brinks guards, locks, burglar alarms," etc. It is true, of course, that the particular services and devices presently available seem more like attractive supplements to the services provided by the police, rather than reasonable replacements for those services, but Friedman notes that "As the effectiveness of government police declines, these market substitutes for the police . . . become more popular" (p. 156).[4] It is reasonable to suppose that

---

[4]Examples are plentiful. The city of Lexington, Kentucky, has hired private companies to patrol certain high-crime areas, such as housing projects, twenty-four hours a day. In one case, the crime rate dropped to zero after a company took over the policing. St. Petersburg, Florida, has had a private firm patrolling its parks. In New York City, the

the variety and amount of protective goods available would vary with demand, as is the case with any other market commodity.

Friedman suggests that the free market society--wherein all protective goods and services are available on the market, and none are provided by a governmental agency--can be envisioned by projecting a hypothetical trend of decreasing governmental effectiveness and increasing market popularity to the end-state that would be produced by that trend, were it to continue unchecked. Instead of by a single governmental police agency, one can imagine that protective services would be provided to a given area by a variety of "private protection agencies": variations on present day security companies, perhaps, that have grown and broadened their services to meet demand. These agencies "sell the service of protecting their clients against crime" (p. 156).

Some of the most striking differences between the free market defense system and the government defense system may be summarized rather briefly. Imagine two neighbors, Friedman and Joe. Under the governmental arrangement, they must each purchase (through taxation) protective services. This is not the case on the market: Friedman may choose to buy protection, but Joe need not. Under government, both neighbors will have to be content with the same amount of protection, or at least with the

---

number of private guards exceeds the number of city police. Munich, Germany, has hired private guards to patrol its subway stations (see [147]). In general, the free market model may be thought of in terms of what Richard Wagner has called "political entrepreneurship." See Richard E. Wagner, "Pressure Groups and Political Entrepreneurs: A Review Article" [154]. See also William H. Riker and Peter C. Ordeshook, *An Introduction to Positive Political Theory* [118], especially pp. 69-77. It provides incentives for more traditional "entrepreneurs" to enter the market, and it eliminates many of the incentives that motivate contemporary *political* entrepreneurs. Nevertheless, *some* of the factors that motivate political entrepreneurship in the state will surely still be present on the free market.

same *minimum* of protection. This is not necessarily
the case on the free market: Friedman might decide
to purchase the Pinkerton "Paranoid Plan," while
Joe might make do with a couple of locks and a little wire that turns on an "aa-oo-ga" horn when
tripped. Governed, both Friedman and Joe will have
no choice as to what agency they do business
with--there would be only one. On the free market,
one might decide that Tannahelp, Inc. was by far
the most reliable name in the industry, while the
other might prefer Dawn Defense. Finally, consider
Maxine. She lives across the street from Friedman
and next door to Joe. She would like the Paranoid
Plan, but is able to afford only one small Yale
lock. She is presently saving her money toward the
day when she can afford an aa-oo-ga horn like Joe's.
Under the governmental system, Maxine would be
assured of getting the rough equivalent of one more
lock *and* the horn, for the government would see to
it that Friedman and Joe paid for it for her. This
is not the case on the free market. Maxine must
continue to scrimp and save, perhaps having to go
without sufficiently nutritious meals, until she
has managed to purchase the horn.

This, of course, is a rather superficial
sketch. As Friedman notes in his book, the question regarding how protective agencies would provide services on the market is as much an economic
question as anything else. It would depend on the
costs and effectiveness of different alternatives:

> On the one extreme, they might limit themselves
> to passive defenses, installing elaborate locks
> and alarms. Or they might take no preventive
> action at all, but make great efforts to hunt
> down criminals guilty of crimes against their
> clients. They might maintain foot patrols or
> squad cars, like our present governmental police,
> or they might rely on electronic substitutes.
> In any case, they would be selling a service to
> their customers and would have a strong incen-
> tive to provide as high a quality of service as
> possible, at the lowest possible cost. It is
> reasonable to suppose that the quality of ser-
> vice would be higher and the cost lower than
> with the present governmental protective system.
> (pp. 156-57)

It is reasonable to suppose this because of the
fact that protective services would no longer be
monopolized by a single coercive agency: competitive pressures would tend to keep quality up and
cost down.

This, then, is more or less how an advocate of
the free market would portray the system to the
parties to the constitutional convention. It is
reasonable to expect, however, that the parties
would tend to remain somewhat skeptical of such a
glowing story, just as they would be suspicious
about grand pronouncements concerning the glories
of the state. In particular, there are three areas
that need more discussion. First, the parties will
want to have a better idea as to what might be
expected to happen in the event of a conflict
between Friedman and Joe, and thus between their
respective agencies. Second, the parties will wonder whether the free market might not itself lead
to a monopoly in protective services, and if so,
whether this might not cancel out the apparent differences between market and state. Third, the parties will be concerned about Maxine. If she is not
able to get adequate protection under the free market system because of her poverty, that might be
grounds for thinking that the market does *not* provide protective services as well as does government.

First, then, to the problem raised by the possibility of conflict between two members of a free
market society, and the apparent danger of a result-
ing conflict between protective agencies. In
Machinery of Freedom , Friedman outlines this case, in
which he and Joe get into a conflict, in such a
compelling way that his story will be repeated here
at some length.

> Inevitably, conflicts would arise between one
> protective agency and another. How might they
> be resolved? (p. 157)

> I come home one night and find my televi-
> sion set missing. I immediately call my protec-
> tion agency, Tannahelp Inc., to report the
> theft. They send an agent. He checks the auto-

matic camera which Tannahelp, as part of their service, installed in my living room and discovers a picture of one Joe Bock lugging the television set out the door. The Tannahelp agent contacts Joe, informs him that Tannahelp has reason to believe he is in possession of my television set, and suggests he return it, along with an extra ten dollars to pay for Tannahelp's time and trouble in locating Joe. Joe replies that he has never seen my television set in his life and tells the Tannahelp agent to go to hell.

The agent points out that until Tannahelp is convinced there has been a mistake, he must proceed on the assumption that the television set is my property. Six Tannahelp employees, all large and energetic, will be at Joe's door next morning to collect the set. Joe, in response, informs the agent that he also has a protection agency, Dawn Defense, and that his contract with them undoubtedly requires them to protect him if six goons try to break into his house and steal his television set.

The stage seems set for a nice little war between Tannahelp and Dawn Defense . . .

But wars are very expensive, and Tannahelp and Dawn Defense are both profit-making corporations, more interested in saving money than face . . .

The Tannahelp agent calls up his opposition number at Dawn Defense. 'We've got a problem . . . After explaining the situation, he points out that if Tannahelp sends six men, and Dawn eight, there will be a fight. Someone might even get hurt. Whoever wins, by the time the conflict is over it will be expensive for both sides. They might even have to start paying their employees higher wages to make up for the risk. Then both firms will be forced to raise their rates. If they do, Murbard Ltd., an aggressive new firm which has been trying to get established in the area, will undercut their prices and steal their customers. There must be a better solution.

The man from Tannahelp suggests that the
better solution is arbitration. They will take
the dispute over my television set to a reput-
able local arbitration firm. If the arbitrator
decides that Joe is innocent, Tannahelp agrees
to pay Joe and Dawn Defense an indemnity to make
up for their time and trouble. If he is found
guilty, Dawn Defense will accept the verdict;
since the television set is not Joe's, they have
no obligation to protect him when the men from
Tannahelp come to seize it.

What I have described is a very makeshift
arrangement. In practice, once [free market]
institutions were well established, protection
agencies would anticipate such difficulties and
arrange contracts in advance, before specific
conflicts occurred, specifying the arbitrator
who would settle them. (pp. 157-58)

The idea of third party arbitration in conflicts between firms is not, of course, original
with Friedman. Even in governed society, use of
the state's legal machinery often seems much too
expensive or much too time-consuming for firms to
rely exclusively upon them. Private, third party
arbitration has evolved as a necessity from within
the governed system.

Furthermore, it does not appear to be the case
that the effectiveness of private arbitration within
the governed system has been dependent upon the
existence of governmental courts as an ultimate
recourse in the event of failure to agree. This
issue will be treated at greater length in Chapter
VIII, but it will be helpful in the present context
to steal some of that chapter's thunder (or patter,
for those who are not convinced) in order to provide support for the contention that private arbitration does not rely upon a governmental background. That private arbitration is currently
strong, that it has a noble history, and that it
does not require governmental support, has been
well documented by Murray Rothbard:

Currently, the American Arbitration Association, whose motto is 'The Handclasp is Mightier
than the Fist,' has 25 regional offices through-

out the country, with 23,000 arbitrators. In
1969, the Association conducted over 22,000 arbitrations. In addition, the insurance companies
adjust over 50,000 claims a year through voluntary arbitration. There is also a growing and
successful use of private arbitrators in automo-
bile accident claim cases.

It might be protested that, while perform-
ing an ever greater proportion of judicial functions, the private arbitrators' decisions are
still enforced by the courts, so that once the
disputing parties agree on an arbitrator, his
decision becomes legally binding. This is true,
but it was *not* the case before 1920, and the
arbitration profession grew at as rapid a rate
from 1900 to 1920 as it has since. In fact, the
modern arbitration movement began in full force
in England during the time of the American Civil
War, with merchants increasingly using the 'private courts' provided by voluntary arbitrators,
even though the decisions were not legally binding. By 1900, voluntary arbitration began to
take hold in the United States. In fact, in
medieval England, the entire structure of mer-
chant law, which was handled clumsily and inef-
ficiently by the government's courts, grew up in
private merchants' courts. The merchants'
courts were purely voluntary arbitrators, and
the decisions were not legally binding. (*For a
New Liberty* [120], pp. 229-30)

For the most part, the parties to the constitutional convention would expect that protection
firms on the free market would agree to peaceful
arbitration whenever it was profitable to do so.
It is not likely that they would go to war over a
dispute between their clients. The parties would
reasonably anticipate that the free market would
provide defensive services, and that there is no
more reason to expect that disputes between clients
would erupt in interagency battle than there is to
expect war between different police departments
within a given state.

The second concern of the parties to the constitutional convention was that the free market

might itself lead to a monopoly in protective services, and that this might render meaningless the
apparent differences between the market and the
state. There seem to be two possible ways in which
it might be thought that the free market might deteriorate to monopoly: either by economic means or by
coercive means.

The case for monopolization of the defense
industry by purely economic means is either not
particularly compelling, or not particularly alarming, depending upon how the projected monopolistic
end-state is viewed. If one envisions a situation
in which a single protective agency has all the
business in some particular area, and is able to
maintain low quality and a high price, then there
would indeed be little practical difference between
this situation and the governed situation. But
there are good reasons for thinking that no such
situation could be brought about on the free market
through purely economic means. If one envisions a
situation in which just one agency has all the business, but in which the agency has to keep quality
up and costs down in order to *keep* the business,
then there are reasons to expect that this situation could arise, in some circumstances, on the
free market. But such a situation seems to preserve all of the interesting differences between
the market and the state, and there seems to be no
reason to be alarmed over the possibility that it
might arise. It will pay to explore these two situations in some detail.

It might be thought that competition on the
market would be only a temporary phenomenon, until
one firm, or a relatively small group of firms
acting in concert, managed to gain a monopoly or
virtual monopoly in the defense industry. Once
such a monopoly has been gained, it might be argued,
the monopolist would be free to charge almost any
price for defensive services, since the demand for
such services is relatively inelastic. Neither
would it be necessary for the monopolist to maintain the quality of the services he provides, since
his customers would have no alternative to accepting what he made available. The quality of defensive services could be expected to deteriorate, as

the monopolist invests less on providing the goods, and the price would go up, as the monopolist seeks to maximize profits.

This argument would not be accepted by the parties to the constitutional convention, since it ignores the most crucial features of free market competition.

In the first place, it is extremely difficult even to *establish* a monopoly by economic means; for there seem to be just two possible ways of gaining a corner on a previously competitive market: either one provides goods of a better quality or at a lower price, in a consistent fashion, thus attracting business away from competitors, or one tries to coordinate the pricing policies throughout the industry, thus forming a cartel or oligopoly.[5] Since the first alternative conjures up images of defense agencies competing with one another to provide better services at lower costs, and since such a state of affairs can hardly be construed as a *disadvantage* of the market, the first alternative does not need to be considered here. It is the attempt to create monopoly power through voluntary price coordination which, if it could be expected to be successful, would work as part of an argument against the free market. There are two variations on this theme.

First, one might expect that competitors in an industry would see that a cartel would be in their common interest. They would get together, agree to fix prices, and the monopoly would be formed. But there are good reasons to expect that it would not be this easy. The point is a familiar one among students of economics, and is lucidly articulated by Friedman:

A cartel is strongest in an industry where

---

[5]Local price-cutting will be discussed below. It is not listed here as a "possible way of gaining a corner on a previously competitive market," because it does not seem to be one. It must be discussed, however, because of its popularity as a critique of market operations.

there is almost a natural monopoly [i.e., where
the optimum size for a firm, in terms of profit-
ability, is so large that there is room for only
one such firm on the market]. Suppose, for instance, that the optimum size of a firm is such
that there is room for only four firms large
enough to be efficient. They agree to raise
prices for their mutual benefit. At the higher
price the firms, which are now making a large
profit on every item sold, would each like to
produce and sell more. But . . . They must in
some way divide up the total amount of business.

A firm that sells more than its quota can
greatly increase its profit. Each firm is
tempted to 'chisel' on the agreement, to go to
special customers and offer to sell them more at
a slightly lower price 'under the counter,'
without letting the other members of the cartel
know about it. As such chiseling becomes wide-
spread, the cartel agreement effectively breaks
down . . . 'Chiseling,' of course, is what the
other cartel members call it; from the stand-
point of the rest of us it is a highly desirable
form of behavior.

If a cartel manages to prevent chiseling
among its members, it . . . still has the problem of keeping new firms from being attracted
into the industry by the high prices and consequent high profits. Even where there is almost
a natural monopoly, such that any new competitor
must be very large, this is difficult.

The obvious strategy of the cartel members
is to tell any potential competitor that, as
soon as he has sunk his capital into constructing a new firm, they will break up the cartel
and return to competition. The new firm will
then find himself the fifth firm in an area with
room for only four. Either one of the firms
will go broke or all will do badly. Either way,
it does not look like a very attractive specula-
tion.

That strategy will work as long as the cartel does not raise prices much above their mar-

ket level. When it does, a profitable counter-
strategy becomes available. The potential competitor, before investing his capital in building a new firm, goes to the major customers of
the cartel. He points out that if he does not
start a new firm, the cartel will continue to
charge them high prices, but that he cannot risk
investing money until he has a guaranteed market.
He therefore offers to start the new firm on
condition that the customer agrees to buy from
him, at a price high enough to give him a good
profit but well below the cartel's price, for
some prearranged period of time. Obviously, it
is in the interest of the customers to agree.
Once he has signed up a quarter of the total
business, he builds his factories. Either the
cartel restricts output still further, keeps its
prices up, and accepts the loss of a quarter of
the market, in which case the newcomer may eventually expand, or it competes for the customers
the newcomer has not already tied up. Since
there is only enough business to support three
firms, one of the four goes broke.

    Although an artificial monopoly or cartel
may be able to influence prices slightly, and
although it may succeed for a while in gaining
additional profits at the cost of attracting new
competitors, thus reducing its share of the market, any attempt to drive prices very far above
their natural market level must lead to the monopoly's own destruction. (pp. 46-48)

    That it is extremely difficult to establish
monopoly by cartel seems to be born out by available
historical evidence. It is often thought that history refutes the "theoretical" argument that cartels
are unstable. It is often thought that the most
conclusive refutation is provided by the example of
the rail industry during the late nineteenth century. It is frequently held that the cartel formed
by the "Robber Barons" of the rail was *so* successful that it took direct intervention on the part of
the United States government to keep it in line.
The facts, however, suggest otherwise.

    Railroads and Regulation [63], by socialist his-

torian Gabriel Kolko, is representative of the
growing "revisionist" trend in American historical
study. In his book, Kolko builds a powerful case
for the thesis that the common view of the relationship between the rail industry and government
in the nineteenth century is simply backwards.
Kolko argues that, far from being formed to restrain
a powerful rail cartel, the federal regulatory com-
missions were formed, primarily at the instigation
of *unsuccessful* monopolists, to prevent the competition which had ruined previous attempts at forming
a cartel. Not only does the example of nineteenth
century railroad monopoly fail as a refutation of
the instability thesis, it supports it.

> The conventional interpretation of federal
> railroad regulation warrants a radical reap-
> praisal, for the motives and consequences of
> regulation have been misunderstood. Historians
> have overlooked all-too-many crucial factors.
> The railroad industry continued to remain opera-
> tionally competitive despite the merger and con-
> solidation movement of the 1890's led by J.P.
> Morgan. Rates were not affected by mergers,
> because at the very time that vast railroad sys-
> tems were being tied together there were many
> smaller, successfully run companies remaining,
> and new entries meant that the absolute number
> of operating railroads was actually to increase
> until 1907. Despite the vast capital resources
> available to him, Morgan was never able to ful-
> fill his ambition of consolidating regional
> railroad systems to the extent necessary to con-
> trol the rates of the area, in large part
> because the managerial abilities of Morgan's
> assistants proved to be inadequate and often
> incompetent. Pooling efforts, although technic-
> ally illegal, failed not because of the law but
> because of the inability of dozens of important
> railroads in the major regions to act in a con-
> certed, cooperative manner for sustained periods.

> The railroads realized that they needed the
> protection of the federal government, and they
> became the leading advocates of federal regula-
> tion on their own terms. The principle of fed-
> eral railroad regulation per se was accepted by

an important segment of the railroad community
by 1880, and the relative importance of this
group increased gradually over the period until,
by 1916, it included the vast majority of railroad men interested enough to leave some record
of their views . . .

The federal regulation of railroads from
1887 until 1916 did not disappoint the American
railroad industry. If railroad leaders often
disagreed on the details--disagreements that
extended into their own ranks on any specific
issue--the railroads nevertheless supported the
basic principle and institution of federal regulation. And . . . they enthusiastically worked
for its extension and for the supremacy of federal regulation over the states . . . Under the
benevolent supervision of the Interstate Com-
merce Commission, the conditions of the industry
improved sharply, as internecine competition was
replaced by rate maintenance and the elimination
of rebates, and as the railroad system received
protection from the attacks of both the states
and powerful shippers. The percentage of railroad stock paying dividends increased from 39
per cent in 1888 to 67 per cent in 1910, and the
average rate of dividends on all stock rose from
2.1 per cent to 5 per cent over the same period.
If the federal regulation of railroads was only
partially responsible for this improved performance, the Five Percent decision of 1914 formal-
ized the federal government's responsibility to
maintain private profit, and the Transportation
Act of 1920 determined a level of profit which
had been the cherished and usually unattained
goal of the railroads since the 1870's. (*Railroads and Regulation*, pp. 231-33)

The "Robber Barons" were *not* able to get together
voluntarily to control rates by cartel. Only when
they enlisted the coercive support of the federal
government were they successful. The phenomenon of
federal control of the railroads " . . . was not an
effort to democratize the economy via political
means, but a movement to establish stability and
control within the railroad industry so that railroads could prosper without the fearful consequences

- 138 -

of cutthroat competition" (p. 238). The railroads used the power of the federal government " . . . to solve internal economic problems which could not otherwise be solved by voluntary or non-political means" (p. 239). What is often taken as the most dramatic illustration of the danger of the market turns out to be simply an historical mistake. It is exceedingly difficult--if not impossible--to establish monopolistic control over an industry by voluntary cooperation among firms.[6]

There is a second variation, however, to the theme presently under scrutiny. If monopolistic cooperation within a particular industry cannot reasonably be expected through voluntary collusion of the constituent firms, it may still be possible for one firm to achieve the same effect through merger and acquisition. As John S. McGee has put the matter, in an extremely valuable study of the Standard Oil Company, perhaps the most brilliant practitioner of the acquisition technique,

> Unless there are legal restraints, anyone can monopolize an industry through mergers and acquisitions, paying for the acquisitions by permitting participation of the former owners in the expected monopoly gains. Since profits are thus expanded, all of the participants can be better off even after paying an innovator's share to the enterpriser who got the idea in the first place.

> Under either competition or monopoly, the value of a firm is the present worth of its future income stream. Competitive firms can be purchased for competitive asset values or, at worst, for only a little more. Even in the case of important recalcitrants, anything up to the present value of the future monopoly profits from the property will be a worthwhile exchange to the buyer, and a bountiful windfall to the

---

[6]That the railroad case is not an exceptional one is documented in Kolko's more general work, *The Triumph of Conservatism* [64].

seller.[7]

Unfortunately for the would-be monopolist, however, there is a rather nasty shortcoming to this technique: it encourages people to invest in what the monopolist is trying to acquire a monopoly over, in the hope that he will be willing to grant them a share in the expected bounties (Friedman [31], p. 45). In the case of Standard Oil, for example, the company's attempts to buy up competing refineries amounted to making a "demand" on refineries for which others were quick to provide the supply. The case of David P. Reighard is perhaps the most gratifying example of this phenomenon:

> In 1875 or 1876, Mr. David P. Reighard started the Empire Oil works in Pittsburgh. When Holdship & Irwin [a Pennsylvania oil refining business which shared a pipeline system with Empire] sold in 1886, Reighard also sold out to Standard. Reighard stayed out of the oil business till 1887, when he built the Globe Refining Company at Pittsburgh. He ran the Globe for 18 to 20 months, then sold out to Standard again. At the same time, Mr. Reighard sold a large Philadelphia refinery, which he was in the process of building. The sale was no occasion for sadness, for as Mr. Reighard put it: 'Well, the reason I sold out was I found that the bonus that I asked those people (the Standard Oil) was as much as I could actually make on the profits for 15 or 20 years to come.'

> Reighard sold for $1,224,800 in trust certificates and $50,000 cash. Each of the last two refineries that Reighard sold to Standard had cost between $200,000 and $250,000. Thus it was that Mr. Reighard managed to build and sell three refineries to Standard, all on excellent terms. (McGee [76], pp. 147-48)

The acquisition technique did prove profitable to Standard Oil, but not because it allowed them

---

[7]"Predatory Price Cutting: The Standard Oil (N.J.) Case" [76], p. 139.

ultimately to charge exhorbitant prices on a cornered market. The company grew by leaps and bounds,
and profits were earned through the increased volume of oil sold. But Standard never did manage to
gain exclusive control of the market, partially
because its own activities made it profitable for
others to enter the industry:

> From the beginning of Standard's power, and
> throughout the period of its greatest strength,
> new firms sprang up and prospered; old firms
> survived and grew. (p. 157)

Standard Oil, of course, is often thought of
as the "arche-type of predatory monopoly" (p. 137).
In the famous case of *Standard Oil Co. of New Jersey v.
United States*, in 1911, even ex-employees of the company testified to the vicious tactics that had been
used by their old employer to dominate the market.
As McGee has shown, however, it seems that there
was nothing at all vicious about Standard's technique: they tried to buy out their competition, at
terms extremely profitable to the seller. As Prof.
McGee notes,

> It is interesting that most of the ex-Standard
> employees who testified about Standard's deadly
> predatory tactics entered the oil business when
> they left the Standard. They also prospered.
> (p. 167)

The case of Standard Oil is representative of
situations in which a company tries to gain monopolistic power by merger and acquisition. But this
technique seems no better suited to gaining a corner
on the market than does voluntary cooperation among
separate firms. The parties to the constitutional
convention would agree that neither method is a
plausible means of gaining sufficient power to
raise prices--or lower quality--at will. It would
appear that the only method likely to lead to a
corner on the market is the method of consistently
providing goods that are of higher quality or lower
price than those provided by competitors.

The adverb "consistently" is important in this
formulation; for although it is often thought that

monopoly can be gained through temporary localized
price cutting, this seems to be highly unlikely.
Standard Oil, again, is often thought to have mas-
tered this technique, and to have used it as its
primary method of winning the market. McGee's study
not only shows that this thesis is false--Standard
used the acquisition technique, and not predatory
price cutting--but also gives a compelling theoretical account of why it is likely never to be used
in a free market:

> Assume that Standard had an absolute mono-
> poly in some important markets, and was earning
> substantial profits there. Assume that in ano-
> ther market there are several competitors, all
> of whom Standard wants to get out of the way.
> Standard cuts the price below cost. Everyone
> suffers losses. Standard would, of course, suf-
> fer losses even though it has other profitable
> markets: it could have been earning at least
> competitive returns and is not. The war could
> go on until average variable costs are not cov-
> ered and are not expected to be covered; and
> the competitors drop out. In the meanwhile, the
> predator would have been pouring money in to
> crush them. If, instead of fighting, the
> would-be monopolist bought out his competitors
> directly, he could afford to pay them up to the
> discounted value of the expected monopoly prof-
> its to be gotten as a result of their extinction.
> Anything above the competitive value of their
> firms should be enough to buy them. In the pur-
> chase case, monopoly profits could begin at
> once; in the predatory case, large losses would
> first have to be incurred. Losses would have to
> be set off against the prospective monopoly prof-
> its, discounted appropriately. Even supposing
> that the competitors would not sell for competi-
> tive value, it is difficult to see why the pred-
> ator would be unwilling to take the amount that
> he would otherwise spend in price wars and pay
> it as a bonus.

> Since the revenues to be gotten during the
> predatory price war will always be less than
> those that could be gotten immediately through
> purchase, and will not be higher after the war

is concluded, present worth will be higher in
the purchase case. For a predatory campaign to
make sense the direct costs of the price war
must be less than for purchase. It is necessary
to determine whether that is possible.

Assume that the monopolizer's costs are
equal to those of his competitors. The market
has enough independent sellers to be competitive.
Otherwise the problem of monopolizing it ceases
to concern us. This implies that the monopolist
does not now sell enough in the market to control
it. If he seeks to depress the price below the
competitive level he must be prepared to sell
increasing quantities, since the mechanism of
forcing a lower price compels him to lure customers away from his rivals, making them meet
his price or go without customers. To lure customers away from somebody, he must be prepared
to serve them himself. The monopolizer thus
finds himself in the position of selling more--
and therefore losing more--than his competitors.
Standard's market share was often 75 per cent or
more. In the 75 per cent case the monopolizer
would sell three times as much as all competitors taken together, and, on the assumption of
equal unit costs, would lose roughly three times
as much as all of them taken together.

Losses incurred in this way are losses
judged even by the standard of competitive
returns. Since the alternative of outright purchase of rivals would have produced immediate
monopoly returns, the loss in view of the alternatives can be very great indeed. Furthermore,
at some stage of the game the competitors may
simply shut down operations temporarily, letting
the monopolist take all the business (and all
the losses), then simply resume operations when
he raises prices again. At prices above average
variable costs, but below total unit costs, the
'war' might go on for years.

Purchase has an additional marked advantage
over the predatory technique. It is rare for an
industrial plant to wear out all at once. If
price does not cover average variable costs, the

operation is suspended. This will often leave
the plant wholly intact. In the longer run, it
may simply be the failure of some key unit, the
replacement of which is uneconomic at the present price level, that precipitates shut-down.
In either case, physical capacity remains, and
will be brought back into play by some opportun-
ist once the monopolizer raises prices to enjoy
the fruits of the battle he has spent so much in
winning.

    All in all, then, purchase would not be
more expensive than war without quarter, and
should be both cheaper and more permanent. It
may at first be thought that predatory pricing
more than makes up for its expense by depressing
the purchase price of the properties to be
absorbed. In effect, this requires that large
losses reduce asset values less than smaller
losses. This is not at all likely. Furthermore,
assuming that the properties in question are
economic, it is unlikely that their long-run
market value will be much reduced by an artifi-
cially low price that clearly will not be permanent. The owners can shut down temporarily,
allowing the monopolist to carry all of the very
unprofitable business, or simply wait for him to
see the error of his ways and purchase. Even if
there is widespread bankruptcy, wise men will
see the value to the monopolist of bringing the
facilities under his control, and find it profitable to purchase them at some price below what
the monopolist can be expected to pay if he
must. Since the monopolist is presumably interested in profits, and has a notion of the effect
of discount factors upon future income, he cannot afford to wait forever. Properties that a
would-be monopolist needs to control can be an
attractive investment. (pp. 139-41)

    Price cutting, then, is a good way for a
would-be monopolist to lose his shirt.[8] Far more

---

[8]Lester G. Telser ("Abusive Trade Practices; An Economic
Analysis" [141], and "Cutthroat Competition and the Long
Purse" [142]) has expanded on the possibility that the

promising is the acquisition technique actually used by Standard. But as should by now be clear, even that technique is unlikely to lead to control of the market, although it may be profitable for other reasons.

There seems to be only one effective economic means of gaining monopolistic control of the market, therefore: the *consistent* production of goods at a higher quality or lower price (or, preferably, both) than is possible for the competitors. It is obvious that this method of *acquiring* a monopoly is highly beneficial to consumers. It is necessary now to consider the possible evil consequences of a monopoly acquired in this way.

The parties to the constitutional convention would recognize that it is extremely difficult even to establish a monopoly by economic means; the

---

threat of predatory price-cutting may play an important role in setting the terms of acquisition or merger. Kenneth G. Elzinga ("Predatory Pricing: The Case of the Gunpowder Trust" [29]) provides some support for McGee's thesis in his study of the "Powder Trust" case of 1907. Yet he mentions the possibility that there may be some value for a large firm or cartel in having a *reputation* as a predatory pricer, mostly for the purpose of discouraging entry (p. 240). B.S. Yamey ("Predatory Price Cutting: Notes and Comments" [160]) explores several circumstances in which predatory pricing might be rational, including the ones discussed by Telser and Elzinga, and concludes that such practices deserve more attention than is implied by McGee's article. Nevertheless, Yamey observes, in an important footnote (p. 131), that such tactics may be available to--and rational for--*both* sides of a market "war." Elzinga's study seems to document the initiation of price-cutting by independents, and Yamey's work does a good job of showing why they might be inclined to try such a maneuver. The argument that a reputation as a price-cutting trust can deter some entrants seems to be acceptable, but the earlier studies suggest that other entrants often make large profits by calling the bluff of such trusts.

Yamey argues against defining "predatory pricing" as setting price below cost, on the grounds that "Any deliberate price cut to achieve some ulterior aim involves a sacri-

only effective way of doing so is through a process that is socially beneficial. But once a monopoly is formed, isn't it possible for the monopolist then to begin preying upon the consumer, lowering the quality of the goods and raising the price? In fact, this does *not* seem to be possible without resorting to force; the reasons for this should by now be apparent.

Monopolies that evolve in the fashion now under discussion are often referred to as "natural monopolies." Such monopolies come to be because they are able to make a profit on their goods at a price at which other companies lose money. It is typically because of the size of the monopoly that it can do this: smaller competitors are not able to

---

fice of profits of this kind" (p. 133). This, of course, raises new problems. Should we consider, as predatory pricing, *any* attempt to gain a larger market by manipulating price, whether on the part of a "small" firm or a "big" firm? If so, the "predatory" nature of such practices seems to have gotten lost somewhere in the course of the analysis. Yamey is aware of this problem, and one of his more important contributions is his calling attention to the fact that whether price-cutting is "predatory" or not depends mostly upon intent. This is notoriously hard to measure. Furthermore, although it is not mentioned anywhere in these articles, it may be that the meaning of "predatory" excludes the possibility of independents' engaging in predatory pricing. Can the attack of a mouse upon a lion--no matter how viciously prosecuted--be properly called "predatory"? The concept may presuppose superior size or strength. Such factors seem to confound the analysis.

At most, it seems that one might agree that predatory price-cutting may be successful with respect to some *aspects* of an attempt to monopolize a market, but not as the major tactic. Such practices can discourage some entrants and can make an impact on the terms of merger or acquisition, but McGee's main point seems still to be unrefuted: attempts to monopolize a market by adopting a price-cutting policy are far more costly than attempts to do so through merger and acquisition, and don't seem to have been adopted by those firms and cartels that have been most often accused of it.

I am indebted to David Henderson for calling my attention to the pieces discussed in this note.

produce as efficiently. This means that natural
monopolies can arise only in those areas of production in which efficiency increases with size, at
least up to that point where the size of the firm
is such that total demand is being met. Areas of
production that meet this requirement seem to be
relatively rare, but such areas do exist.

The reason for the existence of natural monopolies is also, however, the reason that such monopolies are not at liberty to raise prices at will
once the market has been cornered; for it retains
dominance of the industry only so long as other
firms cannot make a profit in it. Raising prices
arbitrarily allows reentry to those firms driven
out earlier. The monopolist is forced to continue
delivering the goods at the high quality and low
price that have given him his monopoly.

Alcoa Aluminum is a case in point. Alcoa dominated supply of primary aluminum for years, but
was never able to control prices at its will. The
method by which the company maintained its dominance was by producing the highest quality metal at
a price well below what its competitors could
afford to charge. This policy of giving better
service to its customers, and thus driving out competition and preventing entry, was much resented,
of course, by those who wished to make money in the
aluminum business. Indeed, it was this lack of
consideration for its competitors that led Judge
Learned Hand to rule against Alcoa in *United States
v. Aluminum Company of America*:

> It was not inevitable that it [Alcoa] should
> always anticipate increases in the demand for
> ingot and be prepared to supply them. Nothing
> compelled it to keep doubling and redoubling its
> capacity before others entered the field. It
> insists that it never excluded competitors; but
> we can think of no more effective exclusion than
> progressively to embrace each new opportunity as
> it opened, and to face every newcomer with new
> capacity already geared into a great organiza-
> tion, having the advantage of experience, trade

connections and the elite of personnel.[9]

The parties to the constitutional convention, concerned with efficient provision of quality goods at
a low price, rather than with maintaining the standard of living of inefficient producers, would not
share Judge Hand's disgust over the vicious lack of
consideration shown by companies like Alcoa Aluminum.

The argument of the last several pages should
provide sufficient support for the claim made earlier, that the case for monopolization of the
defense industry by purely economic means is either
not particularly compelling, or not particularly
alarming, depending upon how the projected monopolistic end-state is viewed. If the end-state is
viewed as a situation in which one defense agency
is able to lower quality and raise prices at will,
then there is no reason to expect that the free
market will lead to this end-state. If the
end-state is viewed as a situation in which one
agency has all the business, but is forced to keep
quality high and prices low in order to *keep* the
business, then it is possible, if the defense
industry is one of those which can support a natural monopoly (i.e., if efficiency in providing
defensive services increases with agency size at
least up to that size capable of meeting the entire
demand for such services), that the free market
might lead to this end-state. But there is nothing
alarming about this possibility, and the parties to
the constitutional convention would not think of
this possibility as a consideration *against* the free
market.

There is still the possibility, however, that
agencies competing on the free market might establish monopolistic control over the industry by
non-economic means. That is, the agencies might
resort to coercion in their attempts to secure
higher profits. That, in fact, is what the monopolistic interests of turn-of-the-century America
did, if Kolko's analysis is accurate: they turned

---

[9]Quoted in Ayn Rand, *Capitalism* [111], p. 57.

to the federal government for coercive support in
their efforts to keep prices up and to restrict new
entry. The state is not available to defensive
agencies acting on the free market, but wouldn't it
be possible for them to establish a monopoly and
prevent competition through the use of force?

They are, after all, defense agencies. As
such, it is to be expected that a great deal of
coercive power will be available to them. It was
argued earlier that it is unlikely that agencies
will do battle as a result of a conflict between
clients, since this would appear to be an extremely
unprofitable way to do business. But it is at
least conceivable that profits could be expected
through coercive domination of the market, and this
possibility must be examined.

Either there will be many private protection
agencies in a free market society, or there will be
few. There are some reasons to expect that there
will be many agencies, if the population to be
served is comparable to that of present nation-stat
since the number of agencies will depend upon economies of size. That is, the number of agencies
depends upon what size agency does the most efficient (and thus the most profitable) job of protecting its clients. If the number of security
agencies presently doing business in the United
States is any indication, the number of private
protection agencies can be expected to be fairly
huge. Another possible source of data is the efficiency of existing governmental police departments:
as Friedman has observed,

> If the performance of present-day police forces
> is any indication, a protection agency protect-
> ing as many as one million people is far above
> optimum size. (p. 170)

Such data are obviously far from conclusive,
however. Although there may be some reasons to
expect a large number of protection agencies in a
free market society, it is necessary to consider
the risks of coercive monopolization in both the
case where the number is large, and the case where
the number is small.

If there are a large number of protection agencies, then the risk of coercive monopoly, and the risk of one or more agencies' trying to win such a monopoly by coercive means, is relatively slight. This case is covered well by Friedman:

> An agency which settles its disputes on the battlefield has already lost, however many battles it wins. Battles are expensive--also dangerous for clients whose front yards get turned into free-fire zones. The clients will find a less flamboyant protector. No clients means no money to pay the troops.
>
> Perhaps the best way to see why [the free market] would be so much more peaceful than our present system is by analogy. Consider our world as it would be if the cost of moving from one country to another were zero. Everyone lives in a housetrailer and speaks the same language. One day, the president of France announces that because of troubles with neighboring countries, new military taxes are being levied and conscription will begin shortly. The next morning the president of France finds himself ruling a peaceful but empty landscape, the population having been reduced to himself, three generals, and twenty-seven war correspondents.
>
> We cannot all live in housetrailers. But, if we buy our protection from a private firm instead of a government, we can buy it from a different firm as soon as we think we can get a better deal. We can change protectors without changing countries. (pp. 167-68)

Where there is a large number of alternative agencies, attempts by one of them or a small group of them to wage war on the others will send clients scurrying to less imperialistic, and consequently less expensive and more secure, alternatives. Waging war not only costs more than maintaining the peace, it also imposes the risk of retaliation. There is no real risk of coercive monopolization, so long as the number of agencies is large.

Although it is somewhat less likely, it is

nevertheless possible that economies of size will
yield a free market society in which there is only
a small number of protective agencies serving society. In that case, the danger that they might form
a coercive cartel, and thus form a government,
becomes significant. The economic arguments against
monopolization, discussed previously, do not rule
out this new possibility, since the cartel may be
maintained, and entry into the defense industry
restricted, by force. No matter how profitable it
may be for one member of the cartel to welsh on the
agreement, or for a new firm to enter the industry,
such actions may not occur, because of the threat
of coercive reaction. Government-backed cartels
and state monopolies are effective for precisely
this reason.

This raises an important point, however. The
free market is advanced as an alternative to government, and risks of the market must be compared to
risks of government. No claim is made that the
free market is perfect. It is only alleged that
the free market is better than government. With
respect to the issue of monopolization by coercive
collusion among society's protectors, it is useful
to pursue the comparison between the two alternatives:

> . . . our present police departments, national
> guard, and armed forces already possess most of
> the armed might. Why have they not combined to
> run the country for their own benefit? Neither
> soldiers nor policemen are especially well paid;
> surely they could impose a better settlement at
> gunpoint.
>
> The complete answer to that question com-
> prises nearly the whole of political science. A
> brief answer is that people act according to
> what they perceive as right, proper, and practi-
> cal. The restraints which prevent a military
> coup are essentially restraints interior to the
> men with guns.
>
> We must ask, not whether [a free market]
> society would be safe from a power grab by the
> men with the guns (safety is not an available

option), but whether it would be safer than our
society is from a comparable seizure of power by
the men with the guns. I think the answer is
yes. In our society, the men who must engineer
such a coup are politicians, military officers,
and policemen, men selected precisely for the
characteristic of desiring power and being good
at using it. They are men who already believe
that they have a right to push other men
around--that is their job. They are particularly
well qualified for the job of seizing power.
Under [the free market] the men in control of
protection agencies are 'selected' for their
ability to run an efficient business and please
their customers. It is always possible that
some will turn out to be secret power freaks as
well, but it is surely less likely than under
our system where the corresponding jobs are
labeled 'non-power freaks need not apply.' (pp.
168-69)

Since it is possible that economies of size
might yield a free market society in which the number of protection agencies is small, the parties to
the contitutional convention must consider the possible dangers arising from this situation. They
will compare these dangers to the dangers of insti-
tuting government.

The significant danger is not merely that the
free market might lead to monopolization of the
defense industry, for the free market, which also
might *not* lead to such monopolization, is clearly
superior to government in this respect, since government closes out the possibility of competition
at the outset.

The significant danger is that the state formed
through free market collusion (for a state is what
it would be) might be worse than a state chosen in
the constitutional convention. But even here, the
parties will recognize that the danger of an especially evil state exists for both alternatives.
What they will consider is the issue as to which
choice makes it less likely that the danger will be
realized. They will consider that this result--call
it "tyranny"--is possible on the free market only

- 152 -

if economies of size yield a small number of agencies capable of forming a cartel, whereas the size requirement will be met by any governmental solution. They will consider that the "checks and balances" on the free market--the competitive economic atmosphere prevailing up to the time when a cartel is actually formed--are likely to be reinforced by the fact that the agencies have a relatively comfortable way of life, and can expect to improve it even without forming the cartel, whereas the checks and balances of governmental systems rely most commonly upon more shaky motivators: such things as honor and responsibility to one's fellows. Finally, they will consider Friedman's point: the governmental system seems to attract and reward precisely those people who are "best qualified" for the job of seizing power, whereas this is not true (at least to the same degree) of the free market system.

The parties to the constitutional convention would, it seems, opt for the free market. Stated briefly, the reason is this: the question as to whether government is more or less likely to lead to tyranny than the free market is fairly indeterminate. In addition to the considerations outlined in the last paragraph, however, the parties will note that, historically, governments have always deteriorated, no matter how noble the intent of their founders. Tyrannies have been painfully common in the world, and "benevolent" governments have been extremely short-lived. Adding these historical considerations to the points about stable checks and balances and about relative dispositions to seize power, the parties will, at least, have no reason to expect that the dangers of government are less than those of the free market. In fact, they will have some reason to expect the opposite. Even if they were to try to be as generous as they could be to the defenders of government, therefore, the parties could only agree to disregard the question as to whether government is more or less likely to lead to tyranny than the free market, because of its relative indeterminacy. For if they considered this question, they would have to lean toward the market.

Disregarding the tyranny question, however, leaves only the danger that the free market might itself lead to some not-necessarily-tyrannical form of the state. That is, if the parties decide not to consider the question as to the relative probabilities of tyranny evolving out of the market and out of the state, they still must consider the possibility that the market might lead to a state. They will note, however, that on the market there is at least the possibility of avoiding the state, and in this respect the market is vastly superior to government. Their decision will be that the free market is a better option, and this decision will be reinforced by the likelihood that economies of size will make monopolization--and the state-- impossible anyway. The monopoly issue will not lead to the rejection of the free market.[10]

The parties to the Hobbesian constitutional convention will be satisfied, therefore, that the first two of their three concerns over the provision of domestic protection services can be met on the free market. They will agree that they need not fear that conflicts between individuals would flare up into inter-agency warfare, and they will agree that they need not fear the kind of monopolization of the defense industry that would cancel out the apparent differences between market and state. It remains to be seen, however, whether their third concern about the market can be answered.

The parties were concerned about the case of Maxine. It will be recalled that Maxine was too poor to purchase the kind of protective services

_____

[10]Once the problem of providing justice on the market has been discussed, in Chapter VIII, and once the resources of the market have been developed with respect to the issues raised in all three constitutional conventions, it will be necessary to return to the monopoly question, at least briefly, in Chapter X. The possibility that a "*de facto*" monopoly in defensive services might arise on the free market without violating anyone's rights--a possibility recently raised by Robert Nozick [102]--will there be discussed.

that she took to be necessary. The parties were
concerned that there might be grounds for thinking
that the market does *not* provide protective services
as well as does government, if Maxine is unable to
get adequate protection on the market simply because
of her poverty.

The parties will recognize, however, that the
problem of Maxine is not unique to the free market
arrangement. They will realize that any plausible
governmental solution is likely to have its Maxines
too. There have always been groups of people in
human society who have been inadequately protected
by their governments. Sometimes it has been ethnic
groups, sometimes religious groups, sometimes just
"non-conformists"; police services have, from time
to time, been inadequately provided to people
because of their sex, because of their social
beliefs, because of their personal life-styles,
because they are black, because they are white,
because they are yellow, because they are red,
because they are rich, because they are poor,
because they believe in Jesus, and because they
don't believe in Jesus. There have always been
Maxines in governed societies, and it is unreasonable to expect that the parties to the constitutional convention would reject the free market
because there might be people who would lack adequate protection. To do so would be to ignore the
fact that governments not only share this disadvantage, but are also ideally suited to making life
yet more miserable for those they fail to protect.
It would be very much like arguing that one should
buy a Cadillac rather than a Volkswagen, because
Volkswagens use up precious petroleum products.

Maxine does, after all, have a recourse on the
free market. She can get together with others in a
similar situation to cooperatively provide the most
important of defensive services, in a protective
association.[11] Such communal solutions to defense

---

[11]It is also possible, of course, that defensive services may
be sold on some sort of credit plan. It is necessary, however, to consider the case of people, like Maxine, who
could not even afford defensive services on that basis.

problems are as readily available to people living
in a market society as are the profit-seeking
defense agencies, since the free market is the
locus of *all* voluntary exchange, and not just the
locus of monetary exchange for goods and services.
There are advantages of agencies over associations
for those who can afford them, of course, but these
advantages do not necessarily include being adequately protected. Lacking the cash to pay an
agency, Maxine may find herself devoting part of
her time to participating in night patrols of the
homes of association members.   Indeed, she might
find this method of defending herself philosophi-
cally more palatable than giving money to some
greedy capitalist.   In any case, she need not do
without adequate protection.

It might be objected that such a scheme would
have little chance of getting off the ground, given
the vested interest that the agencies would have in
keeping competitive associations off the market.
But here, as before, the economics of the matter
seem to suggest otherwise. An agency that embarked
on "adventures" against an association would lose
customers, because of the necessary added expense
of aggression, which would have to be passed on to
clients, and because of the dangers to clients of
retaliation by the association.   It is true that
governments have been reasonably successful in
squelching cooperative protection schemes among
those people they oppress, such as the group of
citizens who patrolled the ghetto streets in Detroit
during the riots of 1967.   But it is not likely
that the same could be expected from private protection agencies.   Governments risk little in sub-
duing citizens who seek alternative protection
schemes.   The cost of such efforts can simply be
covered by increased taxes, which "clients" must
(for the most part) pay, since they have no alternative before the next election.   It is not the
least of the advantages of the free market that it
provides the alternatives which can be expected to
keep society's "protectors" honest.

In governed society, one must ask what recourse
people have if their protectors fail to protect, or
if they turn against the people.   The question is

very difficult to answer satisfactorily: it seems
that there is *no* adequate recourse. On the market,
the situation is different. If one agency proves
inefficient or aggressive, there are other agencies
and associations to turn to. The social order will
not be perfect, of course, but there is at least a
recourse on the market for the Maxines of the world.
Maxine's problem will not therefore lead the parties to the constitutional convention to reject the
market. Their third concern will have been satisfactorily answered.

The parties would agree, then, that the free
market is at least as likely to provide adequate
domestic defense, and therefore domestic peace, as
is government. Some concerns might remain, however, about how *just* the peace would be on the market. This question will be addressed in some
detail in the next chapter. For now, it need only
be agreed that domestic peace could reasonably be
expected to be provided on the market.

"Domestic peace," it will be recalled, was the
phrase adopted early in the chapter as a convenient
device for talking about those defensive services
which seem most clearly to be "private goods,"
rather than "public goods." At the time, it may
have seemed like an odd equation: given the way in
which domestic peace is customarily provided in
governed societies, it may have seemed that such a
"good" was more like a public good, than like a
private good.

The discussion of the free market alternative
to government in this area should by now have made
the aptness of the equation more apparent, however.
A public good is defined as any good such that, if
any person x_i in a group $x_1, \ldots, x_i, \ldots, x_n$
consumes it, it cannot feasibly be withheld from
the others in that group. Where domestic peace is
regarded as a situation in which an individual is
reasonably assured that he and his property are
safe from attacks by his neighbors, then domestic
peace is a private good, not a public good; the
free market model shows that it *could* be provided to
Friedman but not to Joe (for example) if Joe decided
not to purchase it (or obtain it through a coopera-

tive venture). In this case, it is possible to take the fifth Olsonian option in defending the free market. Where domestic peace is regarded as something more than this--it might be argued, for example, that it is perfectly consistent to say that an individual might have managed to make himself safe even in the absence of domestic peace-- then it would seem to be a public good, rather than a private good. But in this case it is still likely to be provided in a free market system, albeit indirectly; the market provides defensive services to individuals, and does so in such a way that the services are at least as widely available, and with at least as many "checks and balances," as similar services are under government. Domestic peace is a result of the operations of the market, but is not one of the goods provided directly to "consumers" on the market, when it is viewed in this way. In this case, the argument seems to take the fourth Olsonian option. In either case, it is apt to say that domestic peace is provided *by* the market through the provision of private goods *on* the market.[12]

The term "domestic peace," however, is borrowed from the terminology of nation-states. It suggests a political boundary between groups of people that would not obtain on the free market. If all the world were organized along the lines suggested by the market model, then there would be no point in separating "domestic" issues from "international" issues. The same, of course, would be true if all the world were a single state.

If all the world were on the free market system, then no other defensive goods than the ones discussed already need be provided. On one interpretation of the constitutional convention, therefore, the parties would have heard enough already to decide in favor of the market as regards the provision of peace. If the parties were viewed as deciding for the whole world, that is, then they

---

[12]See David Friedman, *Machinery of Freedom* [31], especially Chapter 39, for a brief but interesting discussion of what he calls the "public good trap."

would reject government as a peace-maker on the
basis of what has already been said. They would
reach this conclusion because in this situation
domestic peace would be the only peace they would
be concerned about, because the free market can be
expected to provide domestic peace at least as well
as--and probably better than--government, and
because they would have chosen government only if
there were no less coercive way of achieving comparable domestic peace.

    It is also possible, however, that the parties
to the constitutional convention are deciding not
for the whole world, but for an isolated part of
it. It might be, therefore, that they must concern
themselves with the possibility that there will
still be other nation-states to deal with once the
free market is established. If the free market
cannot be expected to survive in such an environment, at least as well as a government could, then
this might give the parties grounds for rejecting
the market.

    Murray Rothbard has stated the matter well:

> . . . it is obvious that the larger an area in
> which [the free market] is first established the
> *better* its chances for survival, and the better
> its chance to resist any violent overthrow that
> may be attempted. If [the market] is established
> instantaneously throughout the world, then there
> will of course be *no* problem of 'national
> defense.' *All* problems will be local police
> problems. If, however, only Deep Falls, Wyoming,
> becomes [a free market society] while the rest
> of America and the world remain statist, its
> chances for survival will be very slim. If Deep
> Falls, Wyoming, declares its secession from the
> United States government and establishes a free
> society, the chances are great that the United
> States--given its historical ferocity toward
> secessionists--would quickly invade and crush
> the new free society, and there is little that
> *any* Deep Falls police force could do about it.
> Between these two polar cases, there is an infi-
> nite continuum of degrees, and obviously, the
> larger the area of freedom, the better it could

withstand any outside threat. (*For a New Liberty* [120], pp. 249-50)

Although it is not necessary, in a theoretical
discussion of the comparative virtues of state and
market, to do more than treat the "whole world"
case, limiting the discussion in this way is somewhat unsatisfying. It would be a point in favor of
the free market if it could be argued that it would
be adopted even by a constitutional convention
deciding for less than the whole world. It would
be a point against the free market if it required
universal adoption if it were to be workable. For
this reason, it is important to discuss the issue
of "national defense," even though this term is not
really appropriate for a free market society. The
parties will concern themselves with the ability of
the free market to defend people against the attacks
of nation-states.

Now, as Rothbard suggests, the survivability
of a free market society seems to depend, in part
at least, upon its size. But the matter is considerably more complex than such an observation would
seem to suggest. An analogy might help to demonstrate this complexity.

Imagine that the parties to the constitutional
convention, instead of considering the free market,
are weighing arguments in behalf of and against a
particular kind of state. They are considering a
state in which neutrality is to be scrupulously
observed in international relations, even to the
extent of avoiding alliances with potential protectors. It will be a small state, with an area of
approximately 16,000 square miles, and with a cor-
respondingly small population. The parties will
recognize that these specifications leave the proposed nation extraordinarily vulnerable to attack.
They will see that it cannot plausibly be expected
that it would be able to withstand an all-out
attempt on the part of larger neighbors to conquer
the territory.

If there were no reason for a neighboring
country to wish to attack, then that might offset
the vulnerability. But there is an additional con-

sideration that compounds the problem: the state
being considered is to be a wealthy state, with
great natural beauty and bountiful resources. It
will also lie smack in the middle of a region often
torn by wars of conquest. The question before the
convention: should they opt for the neutrality
position, or should they be more flexible, perhaps
binding the state to powerful protectors?

It is not unreasonable to suppose that the
parties would, after heady deliberation, reject the
neutrality stance. They would see that as noble as
the ideal might be, it is unreasonable to expect
that the neutral state in question would survive
for very long. The danger of conquest would be
much too great. That is, the parties would opt
against the stance taken by Switzerland, which has
managed to maintain its neutrality for 465 years,
since 1515.[13]

The analogy illustrates the problems with
which the parties are faced in the present case,
where they are to decide upon the workability of a
free market society in a world full of nation-states
It shows that the problem is not a matter of mere
size, even though it is clear that size ought to
make a difference.

In order to proceed, though, some assumption
must here be made about the size of the proposed
free market society. Deep Falls, Wyoming, is
clearly too small. But it seems reasonable to
expect that it would not be necessary for the
entire world to be involved in the project. It
will here be assumed that the area envisioned is
approximately the size of present-day super-powers,
such as the United States, the Soviet Union, and
the People's Republic of China. If a free market
of that size would fail, then it would seem that
special assumptions would have to be made about the
international environment if the free market were
to be defended for any territory smaller than the
entire planet. Choosing territories of super-power
size has the advantage of raising certain defense

---

[13]See "World Nations" [157], pp. 626-27.

questions that might not arise for smaller territories, as well as the advantage of providing a
plausible foundation for expansion of the free market: a large free market society would be noticeable, and could serve as a model for people elsewhere, if it survived.

But can it survive?

Once again it will be helpful, in order to see
what the free market must be able to do if it is to
be chosen over government in the constitutional
convention, to examine governmental provision of
national defense in the light of the three principles of tool design.

Government, again, is not a *perfect* tool for
providing defense against foreign states. For the
most part, national defense is a bluff game: a
good defense can only be provided by convincing
potential enemies that attack is extremely costly--
that even if an incursion might be momentarily successful, it will be more than offset by the subsequent retaliation. There are, of course, some ways
of providing a more direct form of defense, such as
anti-aircraft guns, anti-missile missiles, coast
guard and naval patrols, troops stationed along the
borders, etc. But these are necessarily imperfect
forms of defense. It is not economically possible
to defend the borders of a large country in such a
way as to really stop a full-scale attack should it
come. The biggest part of a nation's defense is
the threat of retaliation. At best, this would
defend *most* of the citizenry, in the event of a
real attack. The free market need do no better
than this, if it is to be chosen.

Furthermore, government remains a somewhat
utopian tool, whether one views it as a tool to be
used directly by the governed, or by certain people
who wield it in *behalf* of the governed. This point
about government does not depend upon what the
"tool" is being used for, so it need not be elabo-
rated again. The parties to the constitutional
convention would merely remind themselves that
anti-utopian arguments against the free market must
be examined very closely to see if they do not work

just as well against governments.

Finally, there are some rather serious dangers
involved with utilizing government in national
defense. Governments initiate aggression precisely
as often as other governments defend against
aggression. People are not well served by protectors who start fights, and then mount a defense
against the subsequent retaliation. This is especially true when this defense involves conscripting
those who are to be defended into the defending
forces. It is often very difficult to tell whether
governments actually do defend the citizenry, or
whether perhaps it is the citizenry who defend governments. Most importantly, the governmental
method of providing for defense against foreign
aggression has led, in the current era, to a situation in which it is possible that incalculable damage might be done to the earth and its inhabitants
through the recklessness, poor judgment, or malice
of the handful of people who are now in a position
to start a nuclear war: the leaders of the world's
governments. Some even believe that a nuclear war
would extinguish the human species. These are
rather serious dangers, and the parties to the constitutional convention would keep them in mind. If
the free market could avoid these dangers, that
might be a point in its favor. But at the very
least, any argument to the effect that the free
market would be more dangerous than government
would have to be a powerful one indeed.

Now, the problem of "national" defense is more
difficult than the problem of "domestic" defense,
largely because of the form that foreign aggression
may be expected to take. Such aggression is massive in scope, and it is hard to see how defense
against such aggression can be provided as a private good. Indeed, defense against nuclear attack
was the example used in Chapter VI to illustrate
the idea of a "public good." If national defense
is a public good, then the free market will have
only those few options mentioned in the last chapter from which to choose, if it is successfully to
provide this kind of defense. It will become clear
that although the issue is not cut-and-dried, and
although the free market would clearly be superior

to government in providing national defense if it
ever *can* be made a purely private good, the problem
of providing public goods on the market cannot here
be ignored. There is simply no plausible way of
providing an adequate defense against foreign
aggression to one person without providing it to
others as well.

There are a variety of considerations, however,
that make it reasonable to expect that the need for
a national defense would be much reduced for a free
market society.

For one thing, the costs of foreign "adventures" are likely to make them prohibitive to
profit-seeking defense agencies. It is extremely
unlikely that any one agency would be large enough
to aggress on a foreign nation-state, but even if
several agencies were to get together in such a
venture, it is hard to see how they could expect to
gain. Wars are expensive, after all, and waging
one means that costs have to be passed on to clients.[14] But when Tannahelp and Dawn raise their
rates to cover costs, Murbard rushes in and snatches
away the business. The parties to the constitutional convention can expect that there will be
little or no foreign aggression, less imperialism,
little in the way of "foreign policy," and little
that corresponds to "national interest" that must
be defended on foreign soil.

---

[14]David Henderson has suggested to me that defense agencies
might engage in aggression as an independent venture,
expecting gains from the war that would justify early
"investment" costs. Thus, service to the "domestic" clients might be considered a totally separate undertaking,
and the pricing decision for them might be made separately.
If this is a plausible scenario, then in order to evaluate
the prospects of aggression, one would have to calculate
the chances of competition from other defense agencies in
this new "market," both in its present state and at a later
date, assuming initial success. At any rate, the profit
motive should place relatively severe restrictions upon the
decision to engage in aggression—restrictions that do not
apply to governments.

This should have at least two important effects.
For one thing, the cost of "national defense" can
be expected to be reduced dramatically from what
citizens of the United States, for example, are
used to, since a large chunk of what is presently
called the "defense budget" is devoted to precisely
the kinds of foreign adventures that would be ruled
out in a free market society.[15]   But secondly, the
fact that foreign states are not systematically
being provoked by the activity of the defenders of
the free market society should lower the risk of
foreign attack considerably.   This lowered probability of attack, like the elimination of adventurism,
can be expected to cut drastically the cost of
national defense.

Secondly, it seems reasonable to expect that
national defense would be somewhat decentralized on
the market.   Although it is likely that there will
be a considerable amount of sympathy between the
free marketeers in Bangor, Maine and those in San
Diego, California, it is not too likely that the
residents of Maine would go out of their way to
help to provide a defense network for the Califor-
nians, and vice versa.   Complications arise in the
event of an actual attack, but the present problem
involves providing a defense system designed to
prevent attack.   It seems reasonable to expect that
whatever "national defense" would exist on the market, it would not be a single, continental system.
After all, even a nuclear attack on San Diego is
unlikely to affect most residents of Maine.

If San Diego does get bombed, however, it is
difficult to say how others would react.   In Bangor,
it is very possible that people would be up in
arms, calling out the militia, if not just out of

---

[15]"A study by the Brookings Institute reports that the United
States has used its armed forces 'to influence the behavior
of another nation' short of war no less than 215 times
since the end of World War II.   American strategic nuclear
forces were deployed (e.g. put on alert for effect) on 33
occasions.   The study also reveals that during the same
period the Soviet Union resorted to force 115 times . . . "
("Quickies" [109]).

sympathy for fellow free marketeers, then out of
apprehensions that an attack on them might be imma-
nent. These are the "complications" that arise in
the event of an actual attack. They need to be
taken into consideration, but they do not at all
lessen the probability that defense against foreign
attack would be decentralized on the market.

Now, decentralization need not affect the cost
of national defense, summed over the entire free
market society. But it would affect the size of
the groups of people to whom the "public good" is
to be provided. This could prove important in considering whether the parties to the constitutional
convention can reasonably expect that defense
against foreign aggression would be provided on the
market.

Finally, there may be some features of the
free market system that would tend to deter aggres-
sion--features not typically found among governed
societies.

For one thing, potential aggressors might be
put off by the fact that there will be no government to conquer in the free market society. Murray
Rothbard argues the point in this way:

> The main reason a conquering country can rule a
> defeated country is that the latter has an
> existing State apparatus to transmit and enforce
> the victor's orders onto a subject population.
> Britain, though far smaller in area and popula-
> tion, was able to rule India for centuries
> because it could transmit British orders to the
> ruling Indian princes, who in turn could enforce
> them on the subject population. But in those
> cases in history where the conquered *had* no gov-
> ernment, the conquerors found rule over the con-
> quered extremely difficult. When the British
> conquered West Africa, for example, they found
> it extremely difficult to govern the Ibo tribe
> (later to [try to] form Biafra) because that
> tribe was essentially anarchistic, and had no
> ruling government of tribal chiefs to transmit
> orders to the natives. And perhaps the major
> reason it took the English centuries to conquer

ancient Ireland is that the Irish had no State, and that there was therefore no ruling governmental structure to keep treaties, transmit orders, etc. It is for this reason that the English kept denouncing the 'wild' and 'uncivilized' Irish as 'faithless,' because they would not keep treaties with the English conquerors. The English could never understand that, lacking any sort of State, the Irish warriors who concluded treaties with the English could *only* speak for themselves; they could never commit any other group of the Irish population. (*For a New Liberty* [120], pp. 250-51)

In the second place, potential aggressors would have to consider the possibility of a protracted guerrilla war if it attacked a free market society. Rothbard again:

It is surely a lesson of the twentieth century-- a lesson first driven home by the successful American revolutionaries against the mighty British Empire--that no occupying force can long keep down a native population determined to resist. If the giant United States, armed with far greater productivity and firepower, could not succeed against a tiny and relatively unarmed Vietnamese population, how in the world could [an aggressor] succeed in keeping down the American people? No . . . occupation soldier's life would be safe from the wrath of a resisting American populace. Guerilla warfare has proved to be an irresistible force precisely because it stems, not from a dictatorial central government, but from the people themselves, fighting for their liberty and independence against a foreign State. And surely the anticipation of this sea of troubles, of the enormous costs and losses that would inevitably follow, would stop well in advance even a hypothetical . . . government bent on military conquest. (pp. 251-52)

The parties to the constitutional convention might feel that the Rothbardian point is made much too strongly, at least as regards some arbitrary free market society. Rothbard seems to think that the difficulty of conquering such a society, both

because of the lack of a convenient transmitter of
orders and because of the risk of protracted guerrilla war, would deter potential aggressors. Surely
these considerations would weigh against an attack
in the plans of an aggressor, but they did not deter
the British in West Africa or the Americans in Viet-
nam, both of whom had had an opportunity to learn
from history.

   The parties would agree that the Rothbardian
considerations would have some deterrent effect,
but they are likely to conclude that the real importance of these considerations is that they suggest
that there are some "natural" defenses available to
a free market society that are not nearly so available to a governed society, should an attack actually occur.

   It is reasonable to suppose, then, that in a
free market society 1) the risks of war will be
substantially reduced, since the market is less
likely to provoke wars, and since conquest of a
free market society would be rather difficult;
2) the costs of defense would be markedly reduced,
since the risk of war is less, and since "adventurism" costs would be eliminated; and 3) defensive services are likely to be demanded by--and
provided to--smaller groups than must be served
under super-power governments. These things would
be considered by the parties to the constitutional
convention in the course of determining what the
market would need to provide in the way of national
defense.

   As was noted earlier, however, the most important part of a nation's defense is the threat of
retaliation. So far, the only plausible free market threat has been the threat of guerrilla warfare.
That bomb shelters and personal weapons are private
goods--and as such would surely be provided on the
free market--makes this threat somewhat more substantial, since a potential aggressor would have to
consider the possibility that even a nuclear war
would be extremely expensive, in terms of equipment
and personnel, to win. Indeed, the parties to the
constitutional convention might be very much
impressed by this defensive threat of a free market

society as large as present super-powers, since
this sort of threat seems to have been very effective in defending the People's Republic of China
before it became a nuclear power. It is true that
such things as bomb shelters and guns will sell
well on the market only when the threat of attack
is perceived by people as a genuine threat, but
this seems to be an advantage of the market, rather
than a liability: production of bomb shelters, for
example, is a waste of effort in the absence of a
real threat, and the people who are to be protected
by them might as well be the judges of when such
protection is worth spending money and effort on.

In addition, it seems reasonable to expect
that any new modes of "personal" protection against
foreign attack--radiation medication is a conceivable example--are more likely to develop on the free
market than elsewhere. Such novel goods are likely
to be more profitable than otherwise whenever the
risks of war seem substantial.

Such considerations seem to have some bearing
on the question of whether defense against foreign
aggression could be provided on the market. It is
possible that they would be enough to convince the
parties to the constitutional convention that government is not necessary in this area, but one has
the uncomfortable feeling that more needs to be
done. It is true that even governments can do little more than try to convince enemies that an attack
would be too costly to risk, and the potential of
free market guerrilla warfare has this tendency.
But it is clear that the kinds of defenses discussed
up to this point seem much less effective than the
kind available to governments: in this connection
such devices as anti-missile missiles and large
forces protecting the border spring to mind: these
would seem to be public goods, as is that defensive
"device" which seems most effective of all, the
"nuclear umbrella." [16]

---

[16]The parties to the convention will, of course, recognize
that there is something exceedingly objectionable about the
nuclear umbrella. Its effectiveness stems from the risk to
a potential aggressor that, in the event that the protected

Now, it will be recalled that a non-coercive society, like the free market society, has only a limited number of options available if it is to be able to provide public goods. If the free market must be able to provide such goods if it is to be chosen, then it must take one or more of these options, if it can. Few of them appear to be particularly promising, however.

Consider, for example, the "privileged group" option. If the size of the group that can be expected to make a "demand" for national defense were small enough such that at least one member would be willing to bear the whole cost if he had to, then there would be a presumption that national defense would be provided. It is clear that the costs to the whole continental area would be diminished, for the reasons outlined above. It is further likely that the costs would be split among several areas that are smaller than the entire continental area, thus reducing the group size. But even in such groups, and even with such diminished costs, it is hardly reasonable to expect that one person would be willing or able to bear the whole cost. It is just too much.

The "intermediate group" option appears to be no more promising. It might be thought that the groups of people demanding national defense would be small enough that one member's failure to pay his share would be noticeable to other members, and would lead to bargaining among them. It might be that defensive services are important enough that one could reasonably expect the bargaining procedure to result in provision of the public good on the market. Ayn Rand has taken something like this approach to the problem, suggesting that most of the costs of national defense would be born by the people who benefit in the most obvious way from the

---

nation is attacked, the aggressing nation's population will be decimated. Since there is no reason to assume that the aggressor's civilian population is responsible for the attack, such a "defensive" device seems rather aggressive. This problem is really quite a serious one, but it will not be considered here. The problem seems enormously complex.

existence of the free market society--the most successful sellers of goods and services.[17] Olson's arguments show that it is much less clear than Rand imagines that agreement could be reached voluntarily regarding the proper shares to be paid by each "man of greater ability" (as she calls the successful producer). Since it is reasonable to suppose that those contributing would try to pass the costs of national defense on to the consumers of their products, there would seem to be an economic motivation for some producers to avoid such costs, thereby enabling them to sell products at a lower price than their "responsible" competitors, and drive these latter out of business.

Considerations of this kind show that the Randian version of an intermediate group solution bears a striking resemblance to that option wherein non-public goods are provided as an incentive for paying the costs of public goods. But they also show that this option may not work either. Morris and Linda Tannehill have explicitly advanced this option as the solution to the national defense problem (*The Market for Liberty* [139], pp. 128-32). They imagine that insurance companies might take on the job of providing a national defense, as a necessary part of their business in selling war-loss policies, which are also projected by the Tannehills But they fail to account for competing insurance companies which elect to sell such insurance at a lower price without paying for defense. After all, if company *A* knows that companies *B* and *C* are providing an adequate national defense, it will have no reason to bear such extra costs. It will thus be able to sell insurance at a lower price, win customers away from *B* and *C*, and mess up the whole defensive network. It is not at all obvious that, with a large number of agencies on the market, an agreement could be reached that would prevent this from happening.[18]

---

[17]"Government Financing in a Free Society," in *The Virtue of Selfishness* [113], pp. 116-20.

[18]It is hard to see why such writers as Rand and the Tannehills, who insist that economic incentives must always be

The least promising option of all seems to be the "private goods" option. It is true that some defensive goods are private goods: bomb shelters, guns, and radiation medication would be provided on the market. But missiles and bombs are public goods, it seems, and it is hard to see how they could ever be provided as private goods.

There is only one option left. Perhaps people *could* be expected to contribute toward a national defense, even in a latent group. That is, even though a person's contribution would make only an infinitesimal difference in providing the good, perhaps people would make such contributions anyway.

When the risk of war is real, this is much more likely than when it is not. People do volunteer support for large communal efforts in such situations: they offer their time, their efforts, and their cash. Sometimes they even risk their lives. There is no need to argue with Olson's contention that such behavior is "irrational"--all that is necessary is that it be plausible that people would behave in this way, when threatened with foreign aggression. It does not seem unreasonable to suppose that, so long as there still remain some states with nuclear power, a free market society would at least maintain its own arsenal, employing, perhaps, a relatively small cadre of social servants to keep the weaponry in shape. In the event of war, it is not unreasonable to suppose that people would increase their contributions, even volunteering for a defensive military force, thus laying their lives on the line.

Such things have happened in governed societies, of course. It might be thought that governments are required to enforce the sort of social atmosphere in which such voluntary contributions

---

kept in mind in any analysis of the provision of goods and services to society, have ignored the obvious incentives to welshers in the provision of public goods. They, of all people, should realize that goods are not provided simply because people want them.

may be expected. There seems to be no good reason
to think this, however. What is required is no
more than a willingness to "do one's bit" in an
effort that requires everyone to do his bit.

David Friedman has called national defense the
"hard problem" for a free market society. He is
right. But Friedman notes that sometimes people do
behave in the requisite manner, especially when
there is a wide-spread feeling that they ought to
do so. Friedman suggests that tipping is a good
example. People leave tips even when they have no
intention of ever again taking advantage of the
good service thus rewarded. It is an obligation
that people feel. In the United States, income in
tips totals about two billion dollars annually. As
Friedman notes,

> Such figures suggest that individual feelings of
> obligation, reinforced by social pressure, might
> provide a substantial fraction of the cost of
> defending against foreign enemies--a service
> most of us regard as somewhat more important
> than keeping up the quality of restaurant ser-
> vice. (Friedman [31], p. 195)

A more obviously relevant example is the vast sum
raised for Israel in North America within the first
few months after the 1973 war.[19]

In summary, then, the parties to the constitutional convention will agree that it would be difficult to predict that the free market would be
able to provide the large national defense arrangements commonly provided to the bigger nation-states
of the present era. They will recognize, however,
that the risk of war is less for the free market
society, that the cost of defense is less, and that
the groups demanding the good will be smaller.
They will see that defensive goods that can be made
available as private goods are likely to be more

---

[19]David Henderson has suggested to me that as much as two
billion dollars may have been raised within the first five
months. I have been unable to track down a more precise
figure.

readily available on the market, and that novel
variations on private defenses against foreign
attack are more likely to evolve. They will see
that it will be extraordinarily difficult for a
free market society to maintain huge standing
armies, enormous bomber fleets, and big nuclear
arsenals. This will be virtually impossible when
there is no real threat of war, but somewhat more
likely when there are rumblings of invasion. In
the event of actual war, guerrilla warfare and some
provision of public defensive goods may be expected.

The parties will weigh these considerations
against the dangers of governmental defense. There
is no reason to be sure that they would reject the
free market. The comparison between the market and
the state is a very complex one. National defense
is the hard problem for the free market, but if the
parties view the dangers of the governmental situation as severe enough--dangers which include the
possibility of anihilation of a large part of the
human species--they will conclude that government
is not necessary for providing a national defense.
They may even conclude that it subverts the national
defense.

The parties to the Hobbesian constitutional
convention, then, would opt for the free market if
they were deciding for the whole world. Even in
the event that they were deciding for only one part
of the world, they would choose the free market if
they thought the risk of attack were sufficiently
small, or if they thought the dangers of government
were sufficiently great. Since there is no reason
to be sure that they would not think these things,
it is not unreasonable to suggest that they would
reject government. After all, even if the considerations against government were balanced by considerations for it, it would be rejected. The third
postulate would rule it out.

The greatest part of the job of defending the
free market as a better alternative to government
has been done. This first part of the argument
required that several basic points be made in some
detail--points that will be helpful later, and will
not need to be reproduced in full. Even if the

argument that government is necessary to preserve
peace fails, however, it remains to be seen whether
the arguments represented by Locke and Marx might
not convince the parties to *their* constitutional
conventions that there are good reasons for government. Discussing this possibility is the task of
the next two chapters.

Chapter VIII

Justice on the Market

In one of the few passages in *The Second Treatise of Government* that seem clearly to make reference to the Hobbesian argument, Locke seeks to show how the positions of the two philosophers differ:

> . . . the *State of Nature, and the State of War* . . . however some Men have confounded [them], are as far distant, as a State of Peace, Good Will, Mutual Assistance, and Preservation, and a State of Enmity, Malice, Violence, and Mutual Destruction are one from another. (p. 321)

For Hobbes, human nature is such that, in the absence of government, relations between people can be expected to degenerate to universal war of all against all. This is not the case for Locke.

Nevertheless, the Lockeian argument concludes that government is necessary in human society. It is the "proper remedy" for certain inconveniences of the state of nature which, although not as severe as universal war, are sufficiently serious to justify the utilization of a coercive tool. The inconveniences envisioned by Locke are 1) the fact that in the state of nature some people refuse to make the Law of Nature their rule, and 2) the fact that in the state of nature, where each person is executor of the Law of Nature, this Law is likely to be imperfectly applied, because of the corruptive influences of self-interest and ignorance of the Law (p. 396).

Now, it might seem unfair to the Lockeian position to identify government as a *coercive* remedy to the ills of the state of nature. Locke insisted, after all, that " . . . no one can be . . . subjected to the Political Power of another, without his own *Consent*" (p. 374). If Lockeian "government" were no more than a voluntary agency which people commissioned to protect them from violations of the Law of Nature, it would bear a striking resemblance to the private protection agencies and associations discussed in the last chapter. If this were the case, then Lockeian "government" would represent a kind of institution that might very well meet the ethical requirements of the third postulate. If government is not coercive, then it would seem that the third postulate would be irrelevent in deciding whether or not to adopt government in the constitutional convention. Locke's argument could be handled very quickly in the present context, in such a case, by simply discussing the appropriateness of referring to voluntary protection associations as "governments."

There is more than this at stake, however, in the Lockeian defense of government. This is due to the fact that Locke feels that a person gives tacit consent to being governed even if he does no more than travel freely on the highway (p. 392). This is because " . . . every Man, that hath any Possession, or Enjoyment, of any part of the Dominions of any Government, doth thereby give his *tacit Consent*, and is as far forth obliged to Obedience to the Laws of that Government, during such Enjoyment, as any one under it" (p. 392). As Locke points out, this means, effectively, that everyone within the territory dominated by a given government consents, at least tacitly, to that government. Such an understanding of "tacit consent" implies that everyone living in Franco's Spain (for example) consented to his government, which is somewhat surprising, given the periodic reports of resistance there.

Surely there is such a thing as tacit consent. But it is just as certain that Locke's characterization of it is far too broad to make any sense of what it means to *refuse* to consent. It is simply nonsensical to say that anyone who freely walks the streets of Spain gives tacit consent, by doing so, to the government of Spain.[1]

---

[1]For a generally very good discussion of these matters, see A. John Simmons, "Tacit Consent and Political Obligation" [129]. See also Harry Beran, "In Defense of the Consent Theory of Political Obligation and Authority" [10]. One of

If Locke's understanding of "tacit consent" suggests that governments may rule people who, in fact, do *not* consent to being ruled, then it seems that Lockeian government is coercive. Locke does say that giving one's tacit consent to government obliges one to do what the government says; or, more accurately, he says that the tacit consenter has as much an obligation to obey as anyone. Thus if a government has the right to rule *anyone*, on the Lockeian view, it has the right to rule everyone in the territory, whether they really consent or not. Lockeian government is therefore coercive: it claims the right to coerce its own "clients."

The issue before the Lockeian constitutional convention is the problem as to whether government is necessary to preserve or protect certain fundamental human rights. This issue needs to be dealt with even if government is not necessary to preserve peace, since it is conceivable that peace could be preserved even in a society that systematically violated human rights.

Now, there are a pair of things that need to be said about human rights, in the present context, in order to avoid certain misconceptions that might otherwise obscure the later discussion.

First, the term "right" will not be used here as an abbreviation for "natural right." Neither

---

the most intriguing articles in recent Locke literature suggests that Locke may have intended consent to play a much smaller role in his theory than has previously been thought; see John Dunn, "Consent in the Political Theory of John Locke" [28]. Attempting to understand what really *does* play the role that others have thought consent to play in Locke has led Iain W. Hampsher-Monk to suggest that it may be patriarchalism, the very theory which Locke takes such pains to refute in the *First Treatise*; see Hampsher-Monk's "Tacit Concept of Consent in Locke's Two Treatises of Government: A Note on Citizens, Travellers, and Patriarchalism" [45]. Whatever the verdict on these questions of textual interpretation, it seems clear that Lockeian government is not wholly "voluntary" in the sense required by the present discussion.

will any other particular theory of the *basis* or *foundation* of human rights be presupposed. Rather, the "rights" terminology is here understood as no more than a convenient device for talking about social justice. No more is assumed about rights than that if a person has his rights violated, he has been done wrong. The question as to whether rights could be preserved or protected without government amounts, then, to the question as to whether an ungoverned society would be a just one. It is hoped that appealing to the relatively unanalyzed conception of "rights" in this way will allow the discussion to proceed, without having to become embroiled in such complex questions as: "Just what, exactly, *is* a right?", and "How does one come to have rights?" There is no doubt that these questions are important and interesting; they simply cannot be dealt with adequately in the present work.

Second, although the question before the constitutional convention will be whether government is necessary to preserve or protect certain fundamental human rights, no effort will here be devoted to trying to draw up a list of such rights. It is assumed that people have rights: that there is a distinction to be drawn between just and unjust treatment of people. Drawing up a list of rights that would include all the necessary qualifications, however, and which would adequately cover the precedence that one right might take over another in a given situation, and which would, in general, give a reliable procedure for determining whether any given act was right or wrong, is a rather mammoth task. It is certainly not the task of the present essay.

Thus no objection will be made here to theories that imply that whether a person has a right to some particular thing may depend at least partially upon what culture he is in, or upon the material conditions of production of his society. It is only assumed that for *any* culture--or for *any* set of material conditions of production--there will be some rights that people have, and some distinction between justice and injustice. The main question will be, then, whether governments are necessary *in general* to preserve rights or to maintain justice.

The parties to the constitutional convention, in examining this question, will once again be interested in evaluating the job that government may be expected to do in protecting the rights of its citizens.[2]

They will note, first, that no government is likely to render justice in a perfect way, if only because of the uncertainties that necessarily arise in individual cases. Furthermore, they will note that governments of large societies, especially, may be forced to ignore some of the more subtle factors that go into determining whether a person's rights have been violated. This is because, in the first place, governmental provision of justice in large societies will have to rely, if it is to be consistent (and therefore just), upon some given procedure of determining what is right and what is wrong. There are reasons to expect that any parti- cular procedure--or any particular list of human rights--will have to be incomplete, given the com- plexity of human rights. In the second place, gov- ernments are likely to be less than perfectly responsive to changing circumstances that require new interpretations or revisions of the existing code. It is perfectly reasonable to expect that evaluations of the justice or injustice of particu- lar acts will depend, in part at least, upon the circumstances in which they occur. To acknowledge that this is the case need not imply ethical rela- tivism, since even absolutists tend to recognize that evaluation of individual cases requires the weighing of many complex considerations. The par- ties to the constitutional convention will note that governmental response to changing circum- stances is likely to be somewhat sluggish, given the basic conservatism of government, and that gov- ernmental response, when it comes, must necessarily favor only one of the new interpretations or revi- sions that might be made. At best, government can

---

[2]For a straight-forward evaluation of Locke's particular argument, from an anarchic perspective, see David B. Suits, "On Locke's Argument for Government" [138].

be expected to be able to do no more than to provide a system that minimizes injustice in society.
It can hardly eliminate it.

The parties will, of course, remind themselves
that there is a utopian element in the ideal of
government--that government is less than perfectly
suited to the known characteristics of people.

Finally, the parties will recognize that there
are certain significant dangers involved in utilizing government as a means of preserving justice.
To adopt government is to adopt an institution
extremely well suited, because of the powers it is
given, to ignore or violate the rights of individuals. If the rulers decide to suspend human
rights for some reason, there is little that those
whose rights are suspended can do about it. Indeed,
it might be argued that the very establishment of
government jeopardizes not only a human right, but
an obligation: the obligation to do what is right
and avoid what is wrong, and to make this evaluation
oneself. If one delegates part of the responsibility to distinguish between right and wrong to governmental authority, one might very well be placing
oneself in a situation in which one will be forced
to do something that seems (at least) to be wrong.
This tension between "human autonomy" and authority
has led Robert Paul Wolff to suggest that "just
government" might be a self-contradictory notion:
" . . . the just state must be consigned the category of the round square, the married bachelor, and
the unsensed sense-datum" (Wolff [158], p. 71).
Even if the parties find Wolff's suggestion a bit
too strong, they will recognize the dangers in
adopting government.

Recognizing the various limitations of government as a protector of human rights, the parties to
the constitutional convention will have given themselves a good idea of what a non-coercive social
tool--like the free market--must be able to do if
it is to be chosen over government.

There are, of course, a variety of systems of
justice that have been offered in the history of
ethical and political thought. In the modern era,

the world has become the stage for ideological competition between several such systems, all of which
claim to be most conducive to the wellbeing and
progress of human society.

Under governments, the question as to which
system of justice one lives by is determined, for
the most part, by *where* one lives. The particular
rights that a person can expect to have protected--
as well as the *extent* to which these rights are
actually protected--depend in a major way upon such
factors as which side of a particular wall in
Europe he lives on, upon whether he lives in Havana
or Miami, etc. Smaller differences depend upon
whether he resides in New York, Phoenix, Boston, or
Deep Falls.

The fact that ideology varies with geography
tends to obscure the ideological competition
between different systems of justice in at least
two ways.

For one thing, it is extremely difficult to
separate defense of the ideology under which one
lives from defense of one's homeland. Under a geographic distribution of ideologies, that is, patriotic inclinations can confound ideological competition in such a way as to preserve particular systems of justice even when they are inadequate, and
even when they are recognized as inadequate by the
people who must live under them.

But in addition, the contemporary geographic
distribution makes it difficult for people to regis-
ter dissatisfaction with the system under which
they live. If a person doesn't like the way justice is administered in his country, and if he sees
no prospect of changing the system from within, he
must move elsewhere. This might require great sac-
rifices, and is made yet more difficult by immigra-
tion restrictions in countries to which he might
like to move, and by the possibility that his own
government might make it very difficult to leave.
In such an environment, the competition between
different ideological systems gets bogged down, and
becomes dependent upon factors extraneous to the
issue as to which system is most conducive to the

progress--or the wellbeing--of human society.

Things would be quite different, of course, if
people had no "patriotic" attachments to their
homelands, and if people were perfectly mobile. If
a person became unsatisfied with the system of justice that prevailed in one country, he could simply
move to another. As populations shifted, one can
imagine that governments would "compete" with each
other for citizens, by adjusting their systems of
justice in such a way as to attract immigrants.

One of the virtues of the free market model of
social organization is that it seems to capture the
idea of competition among various systems of justice, without requiring perfect universal mobility.
Private protection agencies and associations may be
expected to differ among themselves with respect to
the particular sets of "rights" that they protect,
as well as with respect to the degree of efficiency
with which they protect people. If a person
becomes dissatisfied with the way in which one
agency protects him, he can switch agencies, or
join an association. The free market breaks the
ties between societal organization and geography.[3]

---

[3]Karen Johnson, in "Political Obligation and the Voluntary
Association Model of the State" [61], agrees with the present contention that the state is *not* a voluntary association, yet she argues that it would be foolish to make it
voluntary if we could. Further, she argues that the state
gives rise to obligations "morally more serious" than those
incurred through voluntary association (p. 17). The argument proceeds in two main steps. In the first step, she
tries to argue against a voluntary scheme by contending
(rather than arguing) that governments would relax their
attempts to meet people's needs once they were no longer
pressed by coerced citizens to mend their ways. This, of
course, simply contradicts the contention of this essay that
"governments" would have to compete to maintain clientele
and would have an interest in doing so by trying to offer
better service, but Johnson gives no account of why this
seems unlikely to her. The second step of her argument
assumes the foolishness of "competing governments," and
assumes the general unavailability of exit from governed
society. The political obligations incurred by citizens are

The parties to the Lockeian constitutional
convention will recognize all of this, and they
will also see, by virtue of arguments similar to
those presented in the Hobbesian constitutional
convention, that domestic peace is as likely to
prevail on the market as it is in governed societies. They will be concerned, however, over the
possibility that the mechanism that makes peace
likely on the market may do so by sacrificing justice.

The parties will recall that peace is made
likely by the unprofitability of war. In the case
of Friedman and Joe, their two defense agencies
decided to resort to third party arbitration,
rather than do battle. Private arbitrators, then,
are the free market substitute for governmental
courts.

The parties will wonder, however, how these
arbitrators are to make their decisions. Doesn't
the notion of private arbitration smuggle into the
free market model a requirement that there be some
standardized code of justice that the arbitrators
must refer to? If this were the case, then the
free market's claim to being able to provide alternative systems of justice might become suspect.

David Friedman discusses this problem in
Machinery of Freedom :

> In [a free market] society, who would make the
> laws? On what basis would the private arbitra-
> tor decide what acts were criminal and what
> their punishments should be? The answer is that
> systems of law would be produced for profit on
> the open market . . . There could be competition
> among different brands of law, just as there is
> competition among different brands of cars. (p.
> 159)

---

the result of their all being in the same boat--coerced by
the state with no way out, and with no recourse but to participate or to be forced to participate by others who have
better sense. The argument does not seem to be particularly
strong.

In such a society there might be many courts and
even many legal systems. Each pair of protection agencies agree in advance on which court
they will use in case of conflict. Thus the
laws under which a particular case is decided
are determined implicitly by advance agreement
between the protection agencies whose customers
are involved. In principle, there could be a
different court and a different set of laws for
every pair of protection agencies. In practice,
many agencies would probably find it convenient
to patronize the same courts, and many courts
might find it convenient to adopt identical, or
nearly identical, systems of law in order to
simplify matters for their customers. (p. 159)

Not only would it be reasonable to expect a
variety of different protection agencies, differing
among themselves to a greater or lesser degree with
respect to the particular rights they protect, and
with respect to their efficiency in protecting people, it would also be reasonable to expect a similar variety of arbitrators:

In such a society law is produced on the market.
A court supports itself by charging for the service of arbitrating disputes. Its success
depends on its reputation for honesty, reliability, and promptness and also on the desirability
to potential customers of the particular set of
laws it judges by. The immediate customers are
protection agencies. But the protection agency
is itself selling a product to its customers.
Part of that product is the legal system, or
systems, of the courts it patronizes and under
which its customers will consequently be judged.
Each protection agency will try to patronize
those courts under whose legal system its customers would like to live. (pp. 159-60)

Now, although Friedman seems to expect that
private arbitrators will make their living by selling "legal systems" on the market, this may not be
the most appropriate way of describing the situation. Arbitrators would be able to make a living
on the market because they provide a service that
is in demand. What is demanded, however, is not

necessarily an elaborate legal code, but rather the
skill to settle disputes in a manner acceptable to
the parties involved. When two agencies find that
the commitments they have made to their respective
clients may lead to a confrontation between the
agencies, they will search for a means of avoiding
costly battle, while at the same time maintaining
the confidence of their clients. Arbitration suggests itself, but not just any arbitrator will do.
The "demand" for arbitrators is a demand for people
who can weigh the needs of disputing agencies and
arrive at a solution to which both would agree.
Arbitrators will be evaluated, therefore, more on
the basis of the results they have achieved in past
arbitrations than on the basis of the principles
that guide their decisions. They sell performance,
rather than law. This being the case, it might
even be a liability for an arbitrator to commit
himself, in doing business, to any particular code
of laws.

The parties to the constitutional convention
might become concerned that such free market arbitrators would tend to "sell" justice by deciding in
favor of the highest bidder. This is not particularly likely in the free market, since, as Friedman
notes, such a procedure would be suicidal: an
arbitrator could hardly expect to stay in business
for very long, once having established a corrupt
reputation (p. 163). Agencies looking for arbitrators would fear the results of being on the wrong
side of a bribed decision, since their needs might
be ignored altogether; clients looking for agencies
would steer clear of those that chose corrupt arbitrators, unless they could be sure that their
agency would always make the highest bid. Even
then, they would fear (as would the agencies) that
inter-agency war might break out when it was dis-
covered that decisions were being bought. The
demand for arbitrators is a demand for honest solutions that are agreeable to the disputing parties.
The demand for dishonest arbitrators is small and
unstable.[4]

---

[4]It is interesting to note that the situation is quite different in governed societies. It is commonly the case, in

It is reasonable to suspect, then, that a variety of "systems of justice" would be available on the market, through the provision of defensive services by private agencies and associations, and that this variety would not be significantly diminished by the necessity of arbitrating disputes between agencies. Such disputes are likely to be settled by arbitrators who are skilled in finding solutions that are based on the particular needs of each pair (or group) of disputants.

There would be *some* systems of "justice" that are likely to be excluded, however. Wherever a particular system of justice is both extremely idiosyncratic with respect to what most people think of as just, and also extremely threatening to the bulk of society, it is to be expected that it will either never be represented by an agency or association, or that, once represented, it will quickly be extinguished. Friedman considers the extreme case of a system of "justice" that was committed to defending the "right" to murder:

> There would hardly be enough murderers at any one time to support their own protective agency, one with a policy of patronizing courts that did not regard murder as a crime. Even if there were, no other protective agency would accept such courts. The murderers' agency would either accept a reasonable court or fight a hopeless war against the rest of society. (p. 164)

It is clear, however, that for any system of justice to be excluded, it must meet both requirements: it must be idiosyncratic, for otherwise the cost of suppressing the system would be prohibitive, and would not willingly be borne by clients of other agencies; and it must be threatening, for otherwise no other agency would have any reason to incur the cost of suppressing it, since clients may choose to do business with a less imperialistic

---

such societies, that judges have a guaranteed clientele. Typically, judges can expect to maintain their positions indefinitely, unless they commit a "serious" crime. This helps to stabilize the demand for corruption.

agency, if it costs less. What is important, the
parties to the constitutional convention would realize, is that no realistically proposed system of
justice is likely to meet both requirements. Reasonable alternative systems would be able to compete on the market, and they would stand or fall
depending upon how well they meet the needs of
their clientele.

The parties would agree, then, that there is
no reason to expect that anyone would have to go
unprotected on the free market. They would also
agree that there is little or no danger of monopolization of the defense industry. They would be
satisfied on these points for the same reasons that
satisfied their colleagues in the Hobbesian constitutional convention--reasons that were outlined in
the last chapter.

In addition, the parties will conclude that
people living in a market society will have a variety of options to choose from in deciding how they
wish to be protected. This means not only that
people would be free to avoid systems which appear
to them to be unjust or inefficient, but also that
the options that are available to them are likely
to be more carefully tailored to their needs. Systems of justice that make life miserable for people
are not likely to last long, since people will be
free to choose others. Finally, the parties will
see that the variety of options available on the
market is likely to be preserved, even when conflicts arise between agencies; only the most radical alternatives, ones that are both unpopular and
threatening, can reasonably be expected to be sup-
pressed. Thus, it is only if one of the alternatives *does* prove to be most conducive of the well-
being of human society that it will become dominant, and even then it can be expected that a variety of agencies will strive to provide the system
of justice thus chosen. Justice can be provided on
the free market, and there is no reason to expect
that it would not be provided.

The public goods problem can thus be by-passed,
in a way, just as it was in the discussion of domestic peace. On the one hand, justice can be pro-

vided directly to people as a private, rather than
as a public good, through protection of their
"rights." Given the free market model, it is not
plausible to contend that protection of rights is
the kind of good that, if it is provided to one
person in a given group, it must be provided to the
others as well. On the other hand, just *societies*
are *public* goods. But they are provided through the
protection of individual rights. In either case,
justice is provided on the market through the provision of private goods.[5]

Finally, it is not the least of the virtues of
the free market model that it relieves the tension
between the necessity that people cooperate to make
their lives more comfortable, on the one hand, and
the obligation to make one's own evaluation of
right and wrong, on the other. This can be seen
through a comparison of the market with the political ideal of unanimous direct democracy.

Unanimous direct democracies are non-coercive.
If such societies are to take action on any matter
at all, they require that every society member give
his consent. If even one member fails to consent,
then nothing is done. Unanimous direct democracies
are almost universally held to be hopelessly imprac-
tical. As Robert Paul Wolff argues, such democracies seem to present " . . . a genuine solution to
the problem of autonomy and authority" (Wolff [158],
p. 27), but they require " . . . the imposition of
impossibly restrictive conditions which make [them]
applicable only to a rather bizarre variety of
actual situations" (p. 23).

Private protection agencies, too, are non-
coercive in the relevant sense. If an individual
is dissatisfied with the actions taken by his
agency, he need not continue to support them. But
where unanimous direct democracies collapse when
one member fails to consent, private protection
agencies may very well survive: they simply undergo
a shift in "membership."

---

[5]See David Friedman, *Machinery of Freedom* [31], Chapter 39.

On the free market, "societies" are common
interest groups, more or less on the Aristotelian
model. Since there is no requirement that free
market societies establish unanimous consent within
a given geographic area, they are not subject to
the same restrictions that govern unanimous direct
democracies. They serve as focal points for societal organization, but they do not violate the
demands of human "autonomy." The free market
resolves what Wolff has called "the fundamental
problem of political philosophy" (p. vii) by questioning the need for "authority" in providing the
social services that governments have tried to provide, and it does this by breaking the conceptual
links between societies and geography.[6] The human
need for social cooperation, discussed in the first
chapter of this essay, is met by the free market,
and human autonomy is not sacrificed. The market
thus resolves an ancient political dilemma by going
between its horns.

The parties to the Lockeian constitutional convention will see that under government *and* the free
market, any particular system of justice is likely
to be less than perfectly adequate in taking into
consideration the more subtle factors that go into
determining whether a person's rights have been
violated. They will expect, however, that the free
market would provide alternatives from which people
could choose the *most* adequate, from their point of
view. The parties will also anticipate that the
free market is more likely to be responsive to
changing circumstances and to changing human needs
than is government.

The parties will agree, further, that the mar-

---

[6]It is the Aristotelian ideal of community which inspires
this distinction, of course. Aristotle emphasizes that a
state (in his sense) is determined *not only* by geographic
characteristics, but also by common views regarding the good
life. Wilhelm Hennis has agonized over this problem in his
"Ende der Politik? Zur Krisis der Politik in der Neuzeit"
[54] (see especially p. 516). The free market model of
social organization tries to ease the problem by questioning
the importance of the geographic considerations.

ket gives people a considerably greater chance of avoiding the dangers of inefficient or unjust systems, and that it provides a resolution of the conflict between the need for human cooperation and the obligation to remain "autonomous." The parties will conclude that the free market can be expected to do at least as good a job of providing justice as does government, and they will have some reason to expect that it might even do a better job. They will see, therefore, that government is not necessary to protect or preserve human rights, and that the third postulate rules it out.

The parties to the Lockeian constitutional convention would reject government, in favor of the free market.

Chapter IX

Transition on the Market

No mode of social organization, including the
free market, can reasonably be expected to be perfectly responsive to the need for social change.
As people find solutions to problems that have been
plaguing them, new problems arise. As people
achieve the goals they have been working towards,
new goals present themselves. There is no reason
to expect this dynamic character of human life,
both individual and social, to change in the fore-
seeable future. It is unreasonable to demand of
any form of social organization that it end once
and for all the progression of human problems and
the need for creativity. Even if some organizational form could do these things, it is not at all
clear that it should be adopted. Life without
change would be a bore.

Nevertheless, there is probably no particular
human problem that ought to go unresolved. What is
needed from a social theory is a means of facilitating the solution of particular human problems,
and thus a means of smoothing the path for social
progress. The arguments of the last two chapters
should have provided support for the thesis that
the free market mode of social organization can be
expected to be superior to the governmental mode in
this important respect. The demand for inovative
solutions to most human problems seems more likely
to be met on the market than under government,
since private protection agencies, like other busi-
nesses providing goods and services on the market,
would be forced to compete for clientele, and since
the ability to solve human problems and meet human
needs is likely to be the dominant criterion of
success on the market.

It might be argued, however, that the free
market itself requires, if it is to survive, certain background social conditions that are not met
in existing societies, and that government is necessary at least during a transition period, in
which the conditions for the market are created.

It is this problem, above all others, that will concern the parties to the Marxian constitutional convention.

Of the three arguments in defense of government, the Marxian argument is clearly the most sympathetic to anarchism. It is true, of course, that Hobbes and Locke can be read in such a way as to emphasize certain anti-governmental features; but in neither of these two authors is there to be found the open hostility to government that is repeatedly stressed in Marx's works. Governments are characterized as the means that one class uses to dominate another. They are essentially oppressive in nature. The state must be overthrown, with an eye toward eventually creating the conditions in which states would no longer be necessary.

Marx is not, however, an anarchist. States, he argued, are the products of class conflict. Class conflict, in turn, is the result of competition among different groups or classes of people for scarce goods—for the products of human effort, as well as for natural resources. The particular form that class conflict will take in any given era depends to a great extent upon the material conditions of production of that era. So long as the material conditions of production are such that material goods are relatively scarce, class conflict may be expected to continue. So long as class conflict continues, dominant classes will continue to utilize governments to consolidate their own favorable position and to prevent other classes from making gains. As the proletariat takes power, the state can be used as an instrument for improving the material conditions of production to such an extent that scarcity no longer dominates human society, that class conflict therefore no longer need arise, and that governments no longer have a role to play in society. The proletarian state becomes a tool for achieving the conditions that will lead to the demise of the state.

In evaluating government as a tool for achieving the ends described in the Marxian argument, the parties to the constitutional convention will be most concerned over the potential dangers of tool

- 194 -

use. They will, of course, recognize that government is a less than perfect means for achieving the
goals intended for it: they will recognize, that
is, that there are certain problems involved with
trying to liberate people through use of a tool
that has evolved as a means of dominating people.
They will also recognize, as did the parties to the
Hobbesian and Lockeian constitutional conventions,
that governmental tools are less than perfectly
suited to the known characteristics of people. But
such considerations will only serve, in the long
run, to make more urgent their concern that government might be ideally suited to actually *subvert* the
progress in conditions of production that they hope
to achieve.

The transitional government is supposed to
utilize its power in directing production toward
the elimination of the kind of scarcity that leads
to class conflict. This will require that the government have rather enormous powers, and that these
powers be used in pursuit of the true interest,
rather than the perceived interests, of the governed. The whole project will fail dismally if
either 1) those who govern are not able to perceive the true interest of the governed, or
2) those who govern do not have the power to rule
in the true interest of the governed, or 3) those
who govern rule in the perceived interest of particular groups, rather than in the true interest of
the governed as a whole.

The dangers of using government as a tool for
ending the class conflict are made all the more
urgent by the fact that, even in a proletarian
society, there are likely to arise differences
among groups of people as regards the ways in which
they *perceive* their own interest. It is for this
reason that the government must be given the power
to overrule those perceptions that are wrong, in
favor of the right perceptions. But it is also for
this reason that governing becomes so difficult:
if the *governors* make a mistake, and guide the whole
of society down the wrong path, then it is quite
possible that the social situation might be made
worse, rather than better.

Furthermore, if it is true that class conflict arises most especially from attempts by those who control the means of production to maintain their privileged position, it is not at all clear why such conflict would not be preserved in the transitional state. After all, there will still be a class of people, different from the class of "producers," who will have broad control over production: the class of governors.[1]

It is true, of course, that Marx sometimes envisioned a more or less syndicalist form for the transitional state--something along the lines of the Paris Commune. But it is just as true that Marx at other times saw the necessity of a stronger, more centralized structure than that provided by the Commune ideal. As Elizabeth Rapaport has suggested, the Marxian argument in behalf of the transitional state seems to envision a temporary division of labor, which alots to some the job of governing the transition. This division will become less and less necessary--and less appropriate, as well--as the transitional state approaches its objective: the fully constituted society. But in the meantime, "Those who can best discern and implement the genuine interests of the producers should be in authority."[2]

If this is the case, then more power must be given to those who govern than is suggested by the syndicalist model:

> . . . for Marx what distinguishes an antagonistic conflict is that it is an irreconcilable conflict of interest whose resolution requires the sacrifice of the genuine interest of one class to that of another. A non-antagonistic conflict is either a reconcilable or a merely apparent conflict of interest resulting from a partial or distorted view of genuine interest.

---

[1]See Milovan Djilas, *The New Class: An Analysis of the Communist System* [27].

[2]"Anarchism and Authority in Marx's Socialist Politics" [114], p. 343.

The conflicting interests of classes are antagonistic precisely because they are irreconcilable while the divergent interests or conceptions of legitimate interests of the producers
in socialist society are not irreconcilable.
Diverging interests or conceptions of interest
within socialist society result from sectoral,
sectional and other divisions among the producers . . .

. . . syndicalist political organization is
incapable of resolving such conflict except by
imposing the partial interests of the majority
on the minority or those in a strong position on
those in a weak position. The representatives
of local units cannot fail to represent a partial point of view, since their constituencies
are inherently parochial. The solution to
socialist political conflict cannot therefore be
pure syndicalist democracy. Some means must be
found for resolving political conflict in ways
that reflect and further the genuine interests
of all the producers. This requires first that
there be authority relations in socialist society, and that those in authority have the legit-
imated power to impose decisions which serve the
universal interests of the producers. It also
requires that those in authority should not
merely be representatives but leaders . . . Everyone will not be equally capable of providing
leadership. Those who can best do so must be so
employed as long as the social and material
bases of the division of labor endure. (Rapaport [114], pp. 342-43)

It seems, therefore, that the governors would
have to have broad control over production in the
transitional state. Thus the risk of new, class-
like divisions of society--or, at least, of mistaken choices that guide the entire society down
the wrong path--are quite real. The danger of tyranny rises from within the Marxian argument:

The problem of socialist authority is
double-edged. Appropriate institutions must be
devised which enable effective leadership and
which legitimize its authority. But as much as

effective authority is essential to the development of socialism, the wrong kind of authority relations are inimical to it. On grounds integral to the theory of historical materialism, Bakunin's prophetic warning that socialist authority could (for Bakunin read would) become tyrannical can be reproduced. For if the most fundamental political relations in any society are the political relations within production, then the most critical political relations in socialist society are between the producers and their leadership. Because of the nature of socialist society, the integration of the erstwhile distinct political and economic spheres makes it possible to concentrate a truly awesome power in the hands of those responsible for planning and directing the economy. So said Bakunin. Marx could have said the same. (p. 343)

The parties to the Marxian constitutional convention will be very much concerned, therefore, over the possible dangers of choosing government as the tool for making the transition to a classless society.

Now, it does seem correct to say that the free market requires, if it is to succeed, certain background conditions that are not met in existing societies. The market will stand a chance of getting off the ground only if people have some expectation that it will be able to perform in accordance with their needs. At present, most people have no such expectation, and it will take a lot of discussion and a lot of experimentation to change this situation.

To make this concession, however, is not to concede anything to the defenders of government. It does not follow, from the thesis that people do not now have enough confidence in the market to choose it over government, that they *should* not choose the market, or that it is reasonable for them to continue their support of government. At most, it may be concluded that people *will* not choose the market in the near future: that the free market society may not be realized for some

time. To acknowledge this is not to support the
claim that governments are necessary, or even that
they are acceptable. If the confidence issue comes
before the Marxian constitutional convention, therefore, the parties will recognize that certain edu-
cational steps may need to be taken, if the free
market is adopted. But the confidence issue will
not cause the parties to reject the market.

The Marxian argument suggests, however, that
the confidence issue pales beside another "background" problem which confronts the free market.
Marx argued that there were extremely close links
between the phenomenon of political domination, on
the one hand, and the material conditions of production, on the other. Until radical changes are
made in the material conditions of production, it
will be impossible to put an end to political domination, and therefore to the state. But unless a
particular kind of government comes to be, it will
be impossible to make the necessary changes in the
material conditions of production. Both of these
points are vital elements in the Marxian argument,
and it will pay to examine them separately, as they
are presented to the parties to the constitutional
convention as reasons for rejecting the free market.

The first claim, that governments cannot be
eliminated until the material conditions of production are improved to such an extent that classes
need no longer compete for the fruits of production, seems to assume that any non-coercive alternative to government implies an absence of such
competition. The free market, it is clear, implies
no such thing. Indeed, the fact that the free market model simply *accepts* competition, and seems even
to *rely* upon it, is, in the minds of many people,
one of the most scandalous things about it. The
free market society does not require that individuals and classes no longer compete for the fruits of
production.

But would it not happen that this kind of competition would lead to political domination of one
class over another? Doesn't the free market assume
that competition would be peaceful and friendly--a

rather unlikely assumption, given the stakes of the
competition? It was the burden of Chapters VII and
VIII to argue that the free market makes no such
assumption, and that both peace and justice are at
least as available on the market, even under conditions of social competition for the fruits of production, as they are under governments. It is not
likely that such competition would lead, on the
market, to political domination of one class over
another. This is largely because the market makes
it possible for those who provide the necessary
social services in a safe and efficient way to make
gains in the competition for the fruits of human
production.

Given the free market model, and the arguments
of the last two chapters, it seems incorrect to say
that governments cannot be dispensed with until the
material conditions of production are dramatically
improved. It might very well be true that *most*
anarchistic schemes would be doomed by imperfect
material conditions, but the parties to the Marxian
constitutional convention would see, by virtue of
arguments similar to those presented to the other
conventions, that this is one of the ways in which
the free market differs from traditional anarchic
visions. It presupposes neither that competition
would end, and that people would simply begin to
love one another, nor that the danger of aggression
would fade away. It merely suggests that competition can be directed more productively on the free
market, and that adequate protection from the dangers could be provided.

It remains to be seen, however, whether some
kind of state might not be required in order to *end*
class conflict, and the general competitive environment which goes along with it. The second element
of the Marxian argument supports the claim that
this is the case: only a certain kind of state--
the proletarian state--can bring about those changes
in the material conditions of production that would
eliminate scarcity, and thus end class conflict.[3]

---

[3]It seems obvious to me that this, for Marx, is the most crucial feature of the proletarian state. Nevertheless, I have

If this were the case, the parties to the Marxian constitutional convention .might choose to adopt the proletarian state, and to reject the free market alternative. Since an essential part of the Marxian argument is the contention that what is needed to end class conflict is a quick and efficient means of improving the conditions of production, the question that would most concern the parties is this: Is the required improvement of the material conditions of production more likely to be achieved by the proletarian state than on the free market?

Marx clearly thought that it was. On his view, although the capitalist mode of production was nothing short of astounding in its ability to mobilize the forces of labor in the creation of more and more goods, and to make dramatic steps in improving the material conditions of production with respect to the conditions produced by preceding modes of production, it was, nevertheless, fatally flawed. That is, although the "bourgeois" system was " . . . the first to show what man's activity can bring about," although it " . . . accomplished wonders far surpassing Egyptian pyramids, Roman aqueducts, and Gothic cathedrals" (*Manifesto* [86], p. 83), and although it " . . . created more massive and more colossal productive forces than have all preceding generations together" (p. 85), its accomplishments must necessarily fall short of those necessary to put an end to scarcity, and thus to class conflict: it has " . . . forged the weapons that bring death to itself" (p. 87) in creating the proletarian class.

The reasons that Marx thought this are complex, but two main lines of reasoning may be isolated, which seem to capture the essentials.

For one thing, Marx was committed to an economic theory which had as one of its implications

---

found that some readers of Marx object to my assigning such importance to this business about the elimination (perhaps I should say "radical reduction"?) of scarcity. For support for my understanding of Marx, see Allen Buchanan, "The Marxian Critique of Justice and Rights" [18].

the thesis that under capitalism, the means of production would be concentrated in fewer and fewer
hands, in such a way as 1) to promote the growth
of an ever larger "Industrial Reserve Army" of
unemployed workers and displaced former capitalists, 2) to provide capitalists with a weapon--
namely, the threat of displacing uncooperative
workers with members of the reserve pool--in conflicts with their employees, thus ensuring that
labor is kept in its place (*Capital* [82], vol. I,
pp. 691-93), and 3) to thereby create a class of
people--the proletarians--who are not able to par-
take in the increased bounties produced by the system (pp. 701-02). Although the accomplishments of
capitalism are indeed monumental, they serve the
interests of an increasingly smaller number of ben-
eficiaries, and set the stage for renewed class
conflict by actually creating a deprived class.

As Gabriel Kolko has observed, however, it has
not been the tendency of the capitalist system,
unaided by coercive governmental support, to concentrate capital in fewer and fewer hands. Much to
the chagrin of would-be monopolists, the tendency
of the marketplace seemed to be quite the opposite:

> Despite the large number of mergers, and the
> growth in the absolute size of many corporations,
> the dominant tendency in the American economy at
> the beginning of this century was toward growing
> competition. Competition was unacceptable to
> many key business and financial interests, and
> the merger movement was to a large extent a
> reflection of voluntary, unsuccessful business
> efforts to bring irresistible competitive trends
> under control. Although profit was always a
> consideration, rationalization of the market was
> frequently a necessary prerequisite for main-
> taining long-term profits. As new competitors
> sprang up, and as economic power was diffused
> throughout an expanding nation, it became appar-
> ent to many important businessmen that only the
> national government could rationalize the econ-
> omy. Although specific conditions varied from
> industry to industry, internal problems that
> could be solved only by political means were the
> common denominator in those industries whose

leaders advocated greater federal regulation.
Ironically, contrary to the consensus of historians, it was not the existence of monopoly that
caused the federal government to intervene in
the economy, but the lack of it. (*Triumph of
Conservatism* [64], pp. 4-5)

That this sort of phenomenon was accompanied
by almost universal improvement in the standard of
living, and that it was not a uniquely American
phenomenon, is documented impressively by T.S. Ashton, in "The Standard of Life of the Workers in
England, 1790-1830."[4] Ashton's summary of the
data:

> During the period 1790-1830 factory production
> increased rapidly. A greater proportion of the
> people came to benefit from it both as producers
> and as consumers. The fall in the price of tex-
> tiles reduced the price of clothing. Government
> contracts for uniforms and army boots called
> into being new industries, and after the war the
> products of these found a market among the
> better-paid artisans. Boots began to take the
> place of clogs, and hats replaced shawls, at
> least for wear on Sundays. Miscellaneous com-
> modities, ranging from clocks to pocket handker-
> chiefs, began to enter into the scheme of expen-
> diture, and after 1820 such things as tea and
> coffee and sugar fell in price substantially.
> The growth of trade-unions, friendly societies,
> savings banks, popular newspapers and pamphlets,
> schools, and nonconformist chapels--all give
> evidence of the existence of a large class
> raised well above the level of mere subsistence.
> (Ashton [47], p. 154)

Ashton's work also documents the existence of a
class of people "shut out" from the benefits of
economic progress, but even by 1830, it seems that
this class was in the minority.

In general, recent historical work has been so
harsh on the once popular thesis that capitalism

---

[4]In *Capitalism and the Historians* [47], pp. 123-55.

made life miserable for people in the early nineteenth century, that even such prominent advocates
of the thesis as J.L. and Barbara Hammond finally
came to recant:

> . . . statisticians tell us that when they have
> put in order such data as they can find, they
> are satisfied that earnings increased and that
> most men and women were less poor when this dis-
> content was loud and active than they were when
> the eighteenth century was beginning to grow old
> in a silence like that of autumn. The evidence,
> of course, is scanty, and its interpretation not
> too simple, but this general view is probably
> more or less correct.[5]

So it seems that Marx was wrong in thinking
that a market economy necessarily leads to a con-
centration of wealth in fewer and fewer hands, and
a consequent impoverishment of a growing proletarian class. On the market, the rich get richer and
the poor get richer. It would not be fair to be
too severe with Marx for misconstruing the effects
of the market, however, since his analysis was not
unique in its mistaken predictions. There is a
sense in which Marx may be regarded as the last of
the great classical economists, since his work
shared many of the assumptions made by his predecessors. Nevertheless, the results produced by the
market during the nineteenth century ultimately
caused a major revolution in economic theory, a
revolution that is not yet complete. Marx's mistakes are understandable.

The Marxian economic theory seems to be only
part of the story, however. One can imagine that
even if Marx were to concede that free market capitalism might be well suited to improving the material conditions of production indefinitely, he might
nevertheless still advocate rejection of the market
in favor of a proletarian state. After all, it is
unreasonable to assume that capitalists would simply
ignore the disappointing effects of the marketplace,
especially when theorists had promised them rather

---

[5]*The Bleak Age* [44], p. 15.

enormous power on the market. When these prophe-
cies fail to materialize, wouldn't capitalists
attempt to insure domination of the market by coercive means? On Marx's view, it is precisely this
sort of motivation that accounts for states in
human society.

The reasons for thinking that the market provides safeguards against such siezures of power
were presented in earlier chapters. It is not
denied that disappointed capitalists might try to
win dominance--it is contended, instead, that they
will not be able to do so, try as they might. The
Marxian analysis of state vs. anarchy assumes a
"soft" version of anarchy, wherein people are
expected to be a great deal more considerate of one
another, and a great deal more altruistic, than
they can reasonably be expected to be, so long as
there remains some degree of scarcity in desired
goods. The free market is a "hard" anarchy: it
does not ignore human failings, but, instead, it
tries to minimize their undesirable effects; where
it is possible, the free market tries to bring even
the failings into the service of society.

If it is at all possible to eliminate (or radically reduce) scarcity in the world, therefore,
and thus to eliminate class conflict, the parties
to the Marxian constitutional convention will have
no reason to expect that the free market is not
well suited to doing so. Where capitalists have
recourse to an existing government, it is possible
that they will use that government to consolidate
their own gains, and thus to thwart general progress. On the free market, however, they have no
such recourse: and as it was argued in earlier
chapters, it would be difficult--if not impos-
sible--for them to *establish* government once the
free market has been accepted.

The parties to the constitutional convention
will have still better reasons for rejecting the
Marxian state, however. Not only does it seem that
the free market would be as capable as any system
of making the required improvements in material
conditions of production, there are strong reasons
for expecting that the proletarian state could *not*

- 205 -

do so.

In 1920, the Austrian economist Ludwig von Mises published "Die Wirtschaftsrechnung im sozialistischen Gemeinwesen" [98], in which he advanced the thesis that economic calculation of the kind necessary to support a growing economy would be impossible under socialism. This rather bold thesis created quite a stir among European socialists at the time, and led, ultimately, to an attempted refutation, advanced by the Polish economist, Oskar Lange.[6]

The Misesian argument is summarized in the following quotation from Mises' *Socialism: An Economic and Sociological Analysis* [97], a work that reproduces and elaborates upon the earlier, influential essay:

> Let us try to imagine the position of a socialist community. There will be hundreds and thousands of establishments in which work is going on. A minority of these will produce goods ready for use. The majority will produce capital goods and semi-manufactures. All these establishments will be closely connected. Each commodity produced will pass through a whole series of such establishments before it is ready for consumption. Yet in the incessant press of all these processes the economic administration will have no real sense of direction. It will have no means of ascertaining whether a given piece of work is really necessary, whether labour and material are not being wasted in completing it. How would it discover which of two processes was the more satisfactory? At best, it could compare the quantity of ultimate pro-

---

[6]See, for example, Oskar Lange and Fred M. Taylor, *On the Economic Theory of Socialism* [71]. Although it was von Mises' analysis that brought about the controversy, similar critiques of socialism were advanced independently by Boris Brutzkus, "The Doctrines of Marxism in the Light of the Russian Revolution" (Part I of *Economic Planning in Soviet Russia* [16]), a work first published in the Soviet Union in 1921, and by Max Weber, *Wirtschaft und Gesellschaft*, Vol. III of *Grundriss der Sozialökonomik* [155], pp. 55-56.

ducts. But only rarely could it compare the
expenditure incurred in their production. It
would know exactly--or it would imagine it
knew--what it wanted to produce. It ought
therefore to set about obtaining the desired
results with the smallest possible expenditure.
But to do this it would have to be able to make
calculations. And such calculations must be
calculations of value. They could not be merely
'technical,' they could not be calculations of
the objective use-value of goods and services . . .

Under a system based upon private ownership
in the means of production, the scale of values
is the outcome of the actions of every independent member of society. Everyone plays a
two-fold part in its establishment first as a
consumer, secondly as a producer. As consumer,
he establishes the valuation of goods ready for
consumption. As producer, he guides
production-goods into those uses in which they
yield the highest product. In this way all
goods of higher orders also are graded in the
way appropriate to them under the existing conditions of production and the demands of society.
The interplay of these two processes ensures
that the economic principle is observed in both
consumption and production. And, in this way,
arises the exactly graded system of prices which
enables everyone to frame his demand on economic
lines.

Under Socialism, all this must necessarily
be lacking. The economic administration may
indeed know exactly what commodities are needed
most urgently. But this is only half the problem. The other half, the valuation of the means
of production, it cannot solve. It can ascertain the value of the totality of such instruments. That is obviously equal to the value of
the satisfactions they afford. If it calculates
the loss that would be incurred by withdrawing
them, it can also ascertain the value of single
instruments of production. But it cannot assim-
ilate them to a common price denominator, as can
be done under a system of economic freedom and

money prices.

It is not necessary that Socialism should dispense altogether with money. It is possible to conceive arrangements permitting the use of money for the exchange of consumers goods. But since the prices of the various factors of production (including labour) could not be expressed in money, money could play no part in economic calculations.

Suppose, for instance, that the socialist commonwealth was contemplating a new railway line. Would a new railway line be a good thing? If so, which of many possible routes should it cover? Under a system of private ownership we could use money calculations to decide these questions. The new line would cheapen the transportation of certain articles, and, on this basis, we could estimate whether the reduction in transport charges would be great enough to counter-weigh the expenditure which the building and running of the line would involve. Such a calculation could be made only in money. We could not do it by comparing various classes of expenditure and savings in kind. If it is out of the question to reduce to a common unit the quantities of various kinds of skilled and unskilled labour, iron, coal, building materials of different kinds, machinery and the other things which the building and upkeep of railways necessitate, then it is impossible to make them the subject of economic calculation. We can make systematic economic plans only when all the commodities which we have to take into account can be assimilated to money. True, money calculations are incomplete. True, they have profound deficiencies. But we have nothing better to put in their place. And under sound monetary conditions they suffice for practical purposes. If we abandon them, economic calculation becomes absolutely impossible.

This is not to say that the socialist community would be entirely at a loss. It would decide for or against the proposed undertaking and issue an edict. But, at best, such a deci-

sion would be based on vague valuations. It
could not be based on exact calculations of
value.

A stationary society could, indeed, dispense with these calculations. For there, economic operations merely repeat themselves. So
that, if we assume that the socialist system of
production were based upon the last state of the
system of economic freedom which it superseded,
and that no changes were to take place in the
future, we could indeed conceive a rational and
economic Socialism. But only in theory. A stationary economic system can never exist. Things
are continually changing, and the stationary
state, although necessary as an aid to specula-
tion, is a theoretical assumption to which there
is no counterpart in reality. And, quite apart
from this, the maintenance of such a connection
with the last state of the exchange economy
would be out of the question, since the transition to Socialism with its equalization of
incomes would necessarily transform the whole
'set' of consumption and production. And then
we have a socialist community which must cross
the whole ocean of possible and imaginable economic permutations without the compass of economic calculation.

All economic change, therefore, would
involve operations the value of which could neither be predicted beforehand nor ascertained
after they had taken place. Everything would be
a leap in the dark. Socialism is the renuncia-
tion of rational economy. (*Socialism* [97], pp.
120-22)

The only sustained effort to answer von Mises'
criticism of socialism--Oskar Lange's--led ultimately to a position which is almost universally
regarded as a retreat from Marxism, and an acceptance of the main lines of the critique.[7] In his

---

[7]Lange's most characteristic strategy was to argue that
market-like mechanisms could be designed to function as
information processors even in a socialist state. For a

final statement on the issue, in the posthumously
published *Political Economy* [70], Lange accepts the
"praxeological" approach that led to von Mises'
conclusions. Although Lange himself thought that
he had countered the anti-socialist argument by
showing how there was still room in a progressive
society for a general Marxian approach, both free
market advocates and orthodox Marxists agreed that
his "counter-argument" conceded all the important
points to von Mises. Ronald Meek, who liked Lange's
work, noted that " . . . significantly, the references to Marx' work become purely incidental."[8]
Ben Brewster, a more orthodox Marxist, argued that
both Meek and Lange had fallen for " . . . the most
bourgeois ideology of them all, von Mises' 'Praxio-
logy' . . .".[9] Murray Rothbard, a student of von
Mises' and an advocate of the free market mode of
social organization, discussed in great detail (and
with obvious relish) the " . . . retreat from Marxist economic theory in Oskar Lange's last years."[10]

Since the Misesian critique was widely known
among European socialists during a time when socialism was quite popular, and when several socialist
societies were being formed, and since the only
sustained effort to counter the critique resulted
in a position which critics on all sides agree is a
retreat from Marxian principles, the parties to the
Marxian constitutional convention will be very much
concerned over the possibility that socialist soci-

---

recent discussion of "market socialism," see David Miller,
"Socialism and the Market" [91].

[8]*Economics and Ideology and Other Essays* [90], p. 216.

[9]Brewster [15], p. 90.

[10]"Lange, Mises and Praxeology: The Retreat from Marxism," in
Toward Liberty [146], vol. II, p. 307. For a considerably
more sympathetic assessment of Lange's work, see G.R. Fei-
wel, "Lange's Contribution to Economics" [30]. For further
discussion of the controversy, see Lionel Robbins, *The
Great Depression* [119]; F.A. Hayek (ed.), *Collectivist
Economic Planning* [48]; Abram Bergson, *Essays in Normative
Economics* [11], and "Market Socialism Revisited" [12].

eties--or proletarian states--would be unable to
make the kind of economic progress that is required
if the class conflict is ever to end. Since they
have no reason to expect that the free market would
be unable to sustain such progress, they would
surely reject the proletarian state, and choose the
market.

In general, then, the parties would agree that
government is not necessary to make a transition to
the free market, and that the free market is likely
to do at least as good a job in providing an environment for economic progress as is government. If
class conflict is to be ended, therefore, there
seems to be no good reason to expect that the free
market could not provide the appropriate conditions.

Since the Marxian argument fares no better as
a defense of the thesis that government is necessary than did the Hobbesian and Lockeian arguments,
and since that thesis is an essential part of all
three arguments in behalf of government, the defense
of the free market seems to have been successful.
The three main defenses of government, represented
by the arguments of Hobbes, Locke, and Marx, fail.
They fail because the third postulate rules them
out in favor of the free market alternative.

Chapter X

Some Proposed Problems of the Model

The main argument against the moral acceptability of government is now complete.

There still remain to be discussed, however,
two recently advanced objections to the model of
social organization here proposed. These objections suggest that the model may be self-defeating,
in at least two different ways. The problems about
to be discussed have been raised by Robert Nozick,
in his *Anarchy, State, and Utopia* [102], and have been
used by him to argue against the model, and in
behalf of what he calls the "minimal state."

The two objections are these: first, that the
model is unstable--that it will inevitably lead
back to the state; second, that without a certain
"redistributive" proviso, the model is unjust. If
either of these things is the case, the model
defeats itself, for its justification purports to
be that it provides a morally acceptable *alternative*
to government (and therefore to the state).

Nozick's arguments represent the only serious
attention that has been paid the free market model
of societal organization in recent mainstream philosophy, and it is clear that Nozick knows the model
well. His arguments are tough and somewhat complex.
If the model can survive the criticisms of a thinker
of Nozick's calibre, it will have passed a crucial
test.[1]

Nozick does not consider himself to be a stat-
ist. He does not believe that governments have any
rights that individuals, singly or in combination,

_____

[1]For a generally good recent assessment of Nozick's contribution to political philosophy, as well as some interesting
criticisms, see Peter Danielson, "Taking Anarchism Seriously" [26].

have not explicitly granted them.[2]   In economics,
for example, the government ought to keep its hands
off the affairs of its citizens.   In general,
Nozick is a firm opponent of paternalism.   His concern with the free market model has to do only with
the business of protecting the rights of individuals.

Attention is focused, therefore, upon the
arrangement of private protection associations (or
agencies) described earlier.   Nozick begins by outlining the arrangement, and then sketches the *apparent* differences between such a scheme, on the one
hand, and a state, on the other.   Since this contrast gives a fairly clear picture of what Nozick
conceives to be at least *necessary* conditions for a
state, it is worthwhile to quote him at some considerable length:

> There are at least two ways in which the scheme
> of private protective associations might be
> thought to differ from a minimal state, might
> fail to satisfy a minimal conception of a state:
> (1) it appears to allow some people to enforce
> their own rights, and   (2) it appears not to
> protect all individuals within its domain.
> (*Anarchy, State, and Utopia* [102], pp. 22-23)

> For our purposes here we need focus only upon a
> necessary condition that the system of private
> protective agencies (or any component agency
> within it) apparently does not satisfy.   A
> state claims a monopoly on deciding who may use
> force when;   it says that only it may decide who
> may use force and under what conditions;   it
> reserves to itself the sole right to pass on the
> legitimacy and permissibility of any use of
> force within its boundaries;   furthermore it

---

[2]Although "A combination of individuals may have the right to
do some action C, which no individual alone had the right to
do, if C is identical to D and E, and persons who individually have the right to do D and the right to do E combine"
(p. 89).   " . . . the legitimate powers of a protective
association are merely the *sum* of the individual rights that
its members or clients transfer to the association" (p. 89).

claims the right to punish all those who violate
its claimed monopoly. (p. 23)

We may proceed, for our purposes, by saying that
a necessary condition for the existence of a
state is that it (some person or organization)
announce that, to the best of its ability (taking into account costs of doing so, the feasi-
bility, the more important alternative things it
should be doing, and so forth), it will punish
everyone whom it discovers to have used force
without its express permission. (This permission may be a particular permission or may be
granted via some general regulation or authori-
zation.) This still won't quite do: the state
may reserve the right to forgive someone, *ex
post facto*; in order to punish they may have
not only to discover the 'unauthorized' use of
force but also prove via a certain specified
procedure of proof that it occurred, and so
forth. But it enables us to proceed. The protective agencies, it seems, do not make such an
announcement, either individually or collectively.
*Nor does it seem morally legitimate for them to
do so.* So the system of private protective
associations, if they perform no morally illegitimate action, appears to lack any monopoly
element and so appears not to constitute or contain a state. (p. 24)

The second reason for thinking the system
described is not a state is that, under it
(apart from spillover effects) only those paying
for protection get protected; furthermore, differing degrees of protection may be purchased.
External economies again to the side, no one
pays for the protection of others except as they
choose to; no one is required to purchase or
contribute to the purchasing of protection for
others. Protection and enforcement of people's
rights is treated as an economic good to be provided by the market, as are other important
goods such as food and clothing. However, under
the usual conception of a state, each person
living within (or even sometimes traveling outside) its geographical boundaries gets (or at
least, is entitled to get) its protection.

Unless some private party donated sufficient
funds to cover the costs of such protection (to
pay for detectives, police to bring criminals
into custody, courts, and prisons), or unless
the state found some service it could charge for
that would cover these costs, one would expect
that a state which offered protection so broadly
would be redistributive. It would be a state in
which some persons paid more so that others
could be protected. And indeed the most minimal
state seriously discussed by the mainstream of
political theorists, the night-watchman state of
classical liberal theory, appears to be redistributive in this fashion. Yet how can a protection agency, a business, charge some to provide its product to others? (pp. 24-25)

Thus it appears that [even] the dominant protective agency in a territory not only lacks the
requisite monopoly over the use of force, but
also fails to provide protection for all in its
territory; and so the dominant agency appears
to fall short of being a state. But these
appearances are deceptive. (p. 25)

It might appear, from these passages, that
Nozick's specification of the necessary condition
for the existence of a state includes *both* a claim
by some person or organization of a monopoly over
the use of force in a specified geographic area *and*
a provision of protection, by that person or organization, to all in that area. If this were so, then
his necessary condition would be compatible with,
but stronger than, the necessary condition utilized
in the present discussion. Postulate (B) of the
introductory chapter defined "state" in terms of
"government," and Postulate (A) suggested, as the
only necessary condition of government to be discussed here, that for a person or organization to
be a government, it must assume the right to coerce
its own clients (or subjects). It would seem that
Nozick's monopoly condition is roughly equivalent
to Postulate (A), and that his redistribution condition, if it is to be included among the necessary
conditions for states, is an *additional* necessary
condition.

It would be a peculiar addition, however. It would make it inappropriate to call any organization that satisfied the monopoly condition, but failed to redistribute protective services, a state. A ruling clique that claimed (and had) a monopoly on the use of force, but which protected only its own members (against, perhaps, the unprotected and exploited masses) would fail to constitute a government, and the entire community, including the clique, would not be a state. That seems to exclude far too much. It is likely that the clique would be an *unjust* government, and the state an *unjust* state, but that is clearly quite different.

Nozick seems to be aware of this. In spite of appearances, it seems that the monopoly condition is the only necessary condition for the existence of a state that he discusses. He therefore seems to be in general agreement with definitional Postulates (A) and (B), and has nothing to add to them. His language is therefore in conformity with that of the present essay. The redistribution condition is, at most, a necessary condition for a *just* state (in his view), rather than for a state.

This becomes clear in the course of Nozick's discussion of the distinction between what he calls the "minimal state" and the "ultraminimal state." The former satisfies both the monopoly condition and the redistribution condition, while the latter satisfies only the monopoly condition (pp. 26-28). He regards both as states, although they differ in that the ultraminimal state is unjust, while the minimal state is just (as will become clear). *Since* he thinks of both as states, it is apparent that the redistribution condition is not a necessary condition for the existence of a state.

The passages quoted above, at the beginning of this chapter, do a pretty complete job of outlining the entire program for the first section of *Anarchy, State, and Utopia*. Nozick begins with private protection agencies, notes how they *seem* to differ from states (the passages are loaded with carefully placed qualifications like "might be thought," "appears," "apparently," and the like), and thereby

- 217 -

specifies a necessary condition for a state. He
goes through all of this in some detail, but warns
his reader, at the end, that "these appearances are
deceptive." It is clear how the argument that follows is supposed to go. Nozick intends to show
that the "scheme of private protective associations"
does not really differ from states in the ways they
may at first "seem" to.

In particular, Nozick will argue that an "invisible-hand" process (one which shows " . . . how
some overall pattern or design, which one would
have thought had to be produced by an individual's
or group's successful attempt to realize the pattern, instead was produced and maintained by a process that in no way had the overall pattern 'in
mind'" (p. 18)) might (and perhaps would) lead to a
smooth transition from a private protection scheme
to the ultraminimal state, without violating anyone's rights. Thus the private protection scheme
is unstable.

But since the ultraminimal state will turn out
to be (in Nozick's view) unjust, it will be *morally
obligatory* to make the transition from the ultraminimal to the minimal state.

The free market scheme, as envisioned earlier,
is unstable, and tends toward equilibrium at the
ultraminimal state. The process by which the transition is made violates no one's rights, and is in
that respect morally unobjectionable. But that
rest state is morally objectionable for independent
reasons, and an ideal equilibrium is achievable by
making a further transition (which, of course, must
itself violate no one's rights) to the minimal
state.

It is now possible to proceed to an examination of the details of Nozick's argument.

Nozick begins with a Lockeian "State of
Nature"; at the outset, he imagines that each individual person is responsible for protecting himself
and his property against violations by others.

There are certain problems that seem likely to

arise, however, from such a situation. For one
thing, a system of private and personal protection
and enforcement is likely to be biased: " . . . men
who judge in their own case will always give themselves the benefit of the doubt and assume [in conflicts with others] that they are in the right.
They will overestimate the amount of harm or damage
they have suffered, and passions will lead them to
attempt to punish others more than proportionately
and to exact excessive compensation" (p. 11). Thus
the dictates of "calm reason and conscience" are
abandoned, and long-standing feuds seem to be the
likely result.

Furthermore, there are likely to be differences in "station" between different people, and
these may be great enough to make it practically
impossible for some people adequately to protect
themselves.

Especially in the light of this last possibility, but perhaps also because of the first, *groups*
of people may get together to form mutual-protection
associations, wherein all members commit themselves
to answering the distress calls of any single member.

There are at least two obvious inconveniences
to this solution of the problem. In the first
place, everyone is always on call to come to the
aid of members in distress, and this may make
excessive demands on the time of members (especially if the group is a large one). Some arrangement must be made for rotating responsibilities,
perhaps, such that appropriate, rather than excessive, responses are made. Perhaps the *modus operandi*
of contemporary volunteer fire departments might
provide some clues about how to overcome this incon-
venience.

In the second place, however, there is a danger that *some* members might cry "wolf," dragging
everybody out of bed at odd hours on false alarms.
Or others may wish to use the association in aggressing on non-members, making false claims against
their prospective victims. Or some members may get
into squabbles with one another, *both* calling out

the guard, raising some rather difficult problems
for the protectors (rather like NATO's problem in
the conflict between Greece and Turkey over Cyprus).

Either of these inconveniences may lead the
members to decide to hire specialists to take
charge of the protective function--might lead, that
is, to the formation of private protection *agencies*
(p. 13).

Nozick then asks "What will occur when there
is a conflict between clients of different agencies?" (p. 15). There really is no problem if the
two agencies happen to come to the same conclusion
about the proper disposition of the case. But what
if they differ? Nozick suggests three alternate
possibilities:

1) The two agencies do battle. One agency
always wins. This leads to a general tendency for clients to abandon the losing
agency, and to take their business to the
winner.

2) Each agency has a geographic power center.
Each wins battles fought close to its own
center. People living in the hazy border
areas move closer to one or another of the
centers.

3) The two agencies are well balanced. Either
battles often occur, or battles are avoided
(because of the cost of battling) and some
principle of arbitration is agreed to by the
agencies. This yields a sort of unified
"federal system" under which clients of *both*
agencies now live. Such a federation agreement is a likely end state for any type (3)
situation.

In all three cases, Nozick argues, people wind
up with a single common system within their geographic area. This system makes judgments about
whom to protect and when, and it enforces its judgments (pp. 15-16). Especially in the light of
Nozick's third alternative, it may be crucial to
re-evaluate the issue that occupied much of Chapter

VII: what happens on the free market in the event
of a potential "monopolization" of the defense
industry?

Now, it is not clear that Nozick has managed
to list all of the reasonable possibilities. He
thinks that only these three are worth considering
(p. 16), but it is difficult to see why. It may be
that Nozick has limited the likely possibilities by
envisioning only a *pair* of agencies in competition
with one another, withing the geographic area in
question. It is not obvious that he has done this,
but why doesn't he consider:

> 4) Agencies A, B, and C frequently squabble.
> Each agency has customers spread out fairly
> evenly throughout the area. A always beats
> B, B always beats C, and C always beats A
> (something like this was going on among
> Muhammed Ali, George Forman, and Joe Frazier
> a few years ago)?

Will the three agencies make some sort of mutual
arrangement about adjudicating disputes? Or will
they keep on battling? If they decide to submit to
some arbitration principle or another, will it be a
single principle that all agree to? Or will A make
one deal with B, and another with C? Why should A
deal with B at all? Or B with C? Even if some
complex arrangement is agreed to by all, why should
it be thought of as a single unified judicial system, much less a single unified *federal* judicial system? These problems may be compounded considerably
if the number of agencies is large.

The answers to these questions do not just
flow smoothly from the mere consideration of (4).
And if there is a possibility that some relatively
stable arrangement could result that could *not*
plausibly be described as a single common system
within the given geographic area, then the
invisible-hand argument that Nozick is in the process of sketching will be somewhat weaker than it
might otherwise be. It will not show that a state
must arise from the anarchic situation--only that it
could thus arise. Not that the free market model *is*
unstable--only that it *might* be.

This is not a particularly damaging point against Nozick, however, since all that is necessary, to overcome anarchist moral objections to the state, is to show that the state *could* arise from anarchy without violating anyone's rights.

It is necessary, therefore, to follow the argument further.

Nozick's contention is that a representative geographic area would (or could) wind up with a single common system which has clear superiority in settling disputes. For simplicity, he calls this common system the "Dominant Protective Association," or DPA, of the area. It must be kept in mind, however, that the system *may* be a "federation" (or aggregate) of several protection agencies.

The DPA is not yet a state. Or at least, Nozick has not yet shown that it satisfies his monopoly criterion. For that criterion was stated in this way: "a necessary condition for the existence of a state is that it (some perosn or organization) announce that, to the best of its ability . . . it will punish everyone whom it discovers to have used force without its express permission" (p. 24). All that Nozick has so far is a system that has evolved through *ad hoc* enforcements of claims in two-party disputes. No "announcement" of the kind needed to satisfy the monopoly requirement has been made by the DPA, "*Nor does it seem morally legitimate for [it] to do so.*"[3]

---

[3]Nor is it obvious even that it *could* do so. Under Nozick's third alternative, the DPA may very well be a rather elaborate network of agencies, linked by agreements regarding decision procedures for settling disputes. It is not at all clear that such a situation would involve *any* policy, whether it be one of making announcements or one of enforcing "rights," that would be common throughout the DPA. This complicates matters somewhat, since 1) the third alternative is the most likely one, given the arguments of Chapter VII, above; 2) it is not clear that the DPA would not suffer from internal jockeying for position among component agencies, which might make any agreements among them quite unstable; and 3) Nozick's argument seems to depend upon

Now Nozick begins to argue that this is mere appearance.

Under the scheme as outlined so far, every individual retains the right to protect person and property from violations by others. Some people have hired professional agencies to take care of this matter for them. In the course of time, one system, the DPA, comes to dominate the territory. But there still may remain a number of "independents," who have never contracted with the DPA. There may also be small mutual-protection associations, and possibly a few tiny agencies here and there, too small to attract the wrath of the DPA. For simplicity, call every person or group not affiliated with the DPA an "independent."

These independents live within the area of the DPA. They defend themselves, jointly or individually, against everyone else, *including* clients of the DPA. "The geographical territory covered by the protection association then might resemble a slice of Swiss cheese, with internal as well as external boundaries" (p. 54).

Given any "violation," every protector, whether individual, association, or agency, will have some procedure that it uses to determine who has committed the violation, and to determine what action should be taken. Consider, as an example, a case of stolen property.

Joe Bock comes home one day to discover that his valuable porcelain rocking chair has been stolen. Either Joe sets out to recover it himself, or he turns the matter over to his protection agency.

Assume that Joe is an independent. He has what he takes to be a perfectly reliable procedure for discovering who it was that stole the rocker: he reads tea leaves. Other people (or agencies)

---

some common DPA policy. In spite of these problems, it will be fruitful to evaluate Nozick's argument without raising them in the text. It is assumed, then, that the DPA can and will have some common policy toward others.

have different procedures that they take to be
reliable--the Robert Nozick Agency, down the street
from Joe, goes through all kinds of painful inves-
tigation, lengthy court procedures, and even then
gives the accused the benefit of the doubt. Joe
takes the Nozickian system to be quite pathetic.
All that work to support a superstition! True,
Nozick's clients really do believe in the Nozickian
procedure, but it's obvious to Joe that tea leaves
know.

Now, Joe would be perfectly content to leave
the Nozick agency and its clients to its own silly
procedure, if it weren't for the danger that it
might, by chance, someday pick Joe out as being
guilty of some crime or another. That is a risk,
after all: several times Joe has, just for the fun
of it, checked the findings of the Nozick procedure
against the tea leaves, and most of the time the
agency procedure was way off. It is really quite a
dangerous business, living around people who use
such an unreliable procedure for determining guilt.

Consider, now, the DPA. It, like all protectors, has its procedures. And for it, as for all
protectors and protectees, there are *some* possible
procedures--other than its own, of course--which
pose serious risks of punishing the wrong person.
This may pose risks, in particular, upon the clients of the DPA. How might the agency and its clients deal with independents who use unreliable procedures of justice?

The DPA, like any protection agency, has the
obligation to protect its clients from harm, where
it can. It may not violate the rights of independents to make the world safer for its clients, but
short of that, it will try to *prevent* harm to clients rather than mop up after a violation has been
committed. It would be bad for business to let too
many clients get hurt.

What about independents who use unreliable
procedures for determining guilt? May the DPA (or
any agency) prevent these independents from using
their unreliable procedures upon the clients of the
agency?

- 224 -

Nozick argues that they may. He has two arguments to support his conclusion,[4] and is not sure
which is the one that is correct, but one of them,
he *is* sure, does the job (p. 107).

Either people have "procedural rights"--the
right that, before they are punished for some
alleged violation, their guilt be determined by
some just procedure--or they do not. If they have
such rights, then the DPA is acting within *its*
rights (these are nothing more, after all, than the
rights of the clients transferred) in defending its
clients against those trying to violate this procedural right.

But even if people don't have procedural rights
(they're awfully difficult to spell out adequately,
whether people have them or not (p. 96)), then
Nozick argues that the DPA may *still* stop independents who use unreliable procedures against its
clients. It is true, he says, that *anyone* has a
right to punish a wrongdoer--including independents.
This is not some right reserved only to the DPA.
But it is also true that anyone who punishes another
without knowing that that other person is guilty of
doing wrong, himself does wrong. For example, if *A*
doesn't know that *B* is a thief, and *A* steals from
B, or otherwise "punishes" *B*, it would appear that
A has done wrong (assuming that *A* is not punishing
B for something else *B* has done wrong). Now, users
of unreliable procedures do not know that the people their procedures pick out as guilty have really
done wrong (since the procedures are unreliable).
Thus they, like *A*, have themselves done wrong (if
they punish those picked out by their procedures),
although they, like everyone else, have a *right* to
punish.[5]

---

[4]There are other arguments, such as an argument from fear,
that lend partial support to the same conclusion. These
others are not sufficient, however, to establish the ultraminimal state. The main line of argument from state of
nature (private protection agency scheme) to ultraminimal
state is the one traced in the text.

[5]There seem to be reasons to have doubts about *both* of Nozick'

It is thus wrong, according to Nozick, to use unreliable procedures of justice, independently of whether, in some particular case, they happen to come up with the correct result, and it is permissable to punish users of such procedures.

So the conclusion is the same, whether people have procedural rights or not, says Nozick: in either case, " . . . a protective agency [like anyone else] may punish a wielder of unreliable or unfair procedure who (against the client's will) has punished one of its clients, independently of whether or not its client actually is guilty and therefore even if its client is guilty" (pp. 107-08).

What is more, anyone--and therefore the DPA, too--has a right to *resist* someone who is applying an unknown procedure against him. That is, if it is not known whether the procedure is unreliable or not, anyone has a right to resist the use of the procedure, at least until information about its reliability is provided (p. 102).

Now, since the DPA has the right to stop an independent from applying an unknown procedure, and to punish an independent who uses a procedure known to be unreliable, on any client of the DPA, it may announce that it *will* do these things if the occa-

---

arguments for the permissability of punishing users of unreliable procedures. Procedural rights seem to be hopelessly vague, and it is not at all clear that the second argument is on the right track. If A thinks that B has done wrong, and is right, and he punishes B for doing wrong without over-doing it, it doesn't seem obvious that A should later be punished himself if it turns out that his procedure for determining guilt was faulty. Is it possible that distinguishing, among cases where B has done wrong, but A doesn't know it, between cases where A *thinks* that B has done wrong, on the one hand, and cases where A is simply aggressing, on the other, might clear up this source of confusion in Nozick's argument? If so, then what makes A culpable in some cases, innocent in others, may *not* have anything to do with his ignorance, and Nozick's case for punishing users of unreliable procedures may be spoiled.

sion arises. Anyone could. But since the DPA is
dominant in the territory, it can do what no other
protector, whether individual or agency, can do:
it can act without fear of *itself* being punished by
someone else for using an unreliable procedure.
The DPA

> will act freely on its own understanding of the
> situation, whereas no one else will be able to
> do so with impunity . . . But when it sees
> itself as acting against actually defective pro-
> cedures, others may see it as acting against
> what it thinks are defective procedures. It
> alone will act freely against what it thinks are
> defective procedures, whatever anyone else
> thinks. As the most powerful applier of princi-
> ples which it grants everyone the right to apply
> *correctly*, it enforces its will, which from the
> inside, it thinks *is* correct. From its strength
> stems its actual position as the ultimate
> enforcer and the ultimate judge with regard to
> its own clients. Claiming only the universal
> right to act correctly, it acts correctly by its
> own lights. It alone is in a position to act
> solely by its own lights. (pp. 108-09)

The DPA constitutes a *de facto* monopoly on the exercise of the right to stop others from using unreliable procedures against its clients. Or so Nozick
says (p. 109).

But in fact, that's not quite correct. Not
only is it true that *not* only the DPA has the right
in question (for everyone has this right, as the
DPA admits), it is also the case that *not* only the
DPA can (practically) exercise that right.

Nozick says "It is not merely that it *happens*
to be the only exerciser of the right it grants
that all possess; the nature of the right is such
that once a dominant power emerges, it alone will
actually exercise that right. For the right includes
the right to stop others from wrongfully exercising
the right, and only the dominant power will be able
to exercise this right against all others" (p. 109).

This is a rather odd argument. Just because

a DPA would be the only power that could exercise
the right in question against *all* others, it doesn't
follow that it alone will actually exercise the
right. In fact, it doesn't even *happen* that the DPA
will be the only exerciser of the right. Independents, in conflicts among themselves, can and (one
would think) would exercise the right upon occasion.

The rights of the DPA extend only to conflicts
in which its clients are involved (with the exception of the right that everyone has to intervene to
aid an unwilling victim whose rights are threatened
-- *if* the unwilling victim is willing to accept the
aid). The DPA must allow people to enforce their
own rights, if either 1) the conflict does not
involve a client of the DPA, or 2) the people in
question use a procedure that the DPA knows to be
reliable (that is, an independent who uses the
same procedure as the DPA must be allowed to wreak
his vengence *even on a client* , if it is known to the
DPA that the procedure is the same).[6] So the DPA
does not even have a *de facto* monopoly on the exercise of the right to defend against unreliable procedures, let alone a monopoly on the use of force.

Nozick notes that "Since no claim is made that
there is some right which it and only it has [and
it would be illegitimate for the DPA to make such a
claim], no monopoly is claimed" (p. 108). The DPA
does *not* say that only it may decide who may use
force and under what conditions; it does *not*
reserve to itself the sole right to pass on the
legitimacy and permissibility of any use of force

---

[6]Roy A. Childs, in "The Invisible Hand Strikes Back" [20],
has suggested, on the basis of this point, that the Nozickian state is highly unstable. Childs argues that the clients of the DPA will be financially motivated to take their
business to agencies which use precisely the same procedure
as the DPA, but which are *not* obliged to cover certain costs
that only the DPA will have to bear. These special costs
are related to Nozick's contention, to be discussed later in
this chapter, that the DPA has an obligation to finance protection for non-clients. But if Childs is correct, then no
DPA will be able to maintain dominance for long. It will
lose business simply *because* it is the DPA.

within its boundaries; it does *not* claim the right to punish all those who violate its claimed monopoly. It does *none* of these things because, as Nozick sees, "The dominant protective agency's domain does *not* extend to quarrels of non-clients *among themselves* " (p. 109). The DPA *claims* no monopoly, and it *has* no monopoly, as was argued in the preceding paragraph.

Yet that means that Nozick's own "necessary condition" for the existence of a state, quoted early in the present chapter, is not met. That condition was: to be a state, some person or organization must announce that, to the best of its ability, it will punish everyone whom it discovers to have used force without its express permission. The DPA may not legitimately do that. If it did, it would be threatening to violate the rights of others, and acting upon the threat would be a violation. And Nozick's intent is clearly to establish that the transition from anarchy to ultraminimal state can be made without violating anyone's rights.

If the DPA makes such an announcement, and acts upon it, it violates rights. If it stays within its rights, it fails to meet Nozick's own necessary condition for statehood. So earlier appearances were not so deceiving after all: state and protective agencies seemed to be different--and they are.

So even if one can agree with Nozick's entire argument regarding the rights that the DPA in fact has,[7] one will be disappointed in the end. For things still "seem" the same as when Nozick began his argument: he has not justified even an ultra-

---

[7]Three possible sources of controversy have been noted above: 1) it is still not clear that there is no relatively stable arrangement for dealing with inter-agency disputes that could *not* plausibly be described as a single common system within the given geographic area; 2) neither of Nozick's arguments for the permissability of punishing users of unreliable procedures seems adequate; and 3) it is not obvious that the DPA would be able to have *any* unified and stable policy.

minimal *state* by his "invisible-hand" argument from
voluntary protection associations. The only thing
that a DPA has a "monopoly" on--even on Nozick's
terms--is the ability to exercise the right of punishing (or resisting) unreliable punishers, against
all who use unreliable procedures of justice (or
threaten to use them) *against its own clients*. Which
is merely to say that it's the DPA.

Nozick recognizes most of this, apparently,
and it seems that he is unsure as to what he should
do about it. What he finally decides to do is
somewhat peculiar. He abandons the "necessary"
condition that he so carefully set out at the beginning of the argument. Thus he fails to do what he
set out to do, and tacitly admits this failure.

Nozick abandons the necessary condition in
favor of a comparison between anthropological
descriptions of the state, on the one hand, and the
characteristics of the territory we have been
exploring, with its DPA, on the other.[8] He reveals
his mixed feelings about the result in the following passage:

> We therefore conclude that the protective assoc-
> iation dominant in a territory, as described, *is*
> a state. However, to remind the reader of our
> slight weakening of the [earlier] condition, we
> occasionally shall refer to the dominant protec-
> tive agency as 'a statelike entity,' instead of
> simply as 'a state'." (p. 118)

So the argument that the state can evolve from
the state of nature, without violating the rights
of anyone, by an invisible-hand process, does not
hurt the thesis of the present essay, since it turns
out that the Nozickian argument survives only if
the term "state" is used in a sense different from
'that set out at the beginning of his argument. It
was necessary to discuss Nozick's argument, however, since it seemed at first that he was going to

----

[8]In fact, it's not at all clear that the DPA is any more similar to a state on the anthropological condition than it was
on the earlier one.

try to make his case using roughly the same characterization of the state that has been used throughout this discussion. Even if Nozick's (final) usage is preferred, therefore, then the main argument of the present essay goes through, once a translation of the sort suggested in the Introduction is made. But it is clear that Nozick's argument is no serious threat to the main thesis; the purely contractual free market society is *not* unstable, in the sense of leading ultimately to what it was designed to replace. It doesn't (and can't) do that, without violating people's "rights." That such an evolution is not likely in any case--even ignoring rights--was argued in earlier chapters.

But is the situation so far portrayed, in which a dominant protection association evolves, with a right to punish independents who use unreliable procedures of justice against the association's clients, a *just* one? It was the task of Chapter VIII, above, to make it plausible that justice would be at least as well provided on the free market as under government, but here it is necessary to face what may be quite a different argument. It may be that the DPA, while not being a state in the present sense, is unjust in its own special way. Nozick's second objection may still work against the free market model, even though his first one didn't.

The second objection corresponds to the second feature of what Nozick thinks of as the illusion that the scheme of private protective associations differs from a minimal state. That is, it appears that the DPA would not protect all individuals within its domain. It was noted earlier that Nozick is probably not making the claim that "redistribution" of justice is a necessary condition for a state, but rather that justice demands that such redistribution be made. It is now possible to understand his argument for that conclusion.

The DPA prohibits the use, by independents, of unreliable procedures of justice *against its clients*. The determination that a given procedure is unreliable, in such cases, will be made by the DPA itself. What the independent thinks of the procedure does

- 231 -

not make any difference.

So what happens if a client of the DPA commits some offense against an independent? The independent has his own procedure of determining guilt and deciding what to do about it, but if the DPA regards his procedure as unreliable, he will not be able to use it. For even if his procedure happens, in this case, to make the same determination that the DPA's own procedure makes, he is punishable, according to the DPA, simply because he uses the procedure.

So he won't use the procedure. Or if he tries, he will be stopped. Or even if he manages to punish the client, he will himself be punished by the DPA.

How, then, is the independent to defend himself, or to see that justice is done if someone violates his rights? He has the right to seek justice from those who have done him wrong, but the DPA seems to be standing in the way of his exercising that right. This situation seems to be unjust, for it appears to leave independents (at least those who are inclined to use procedures deemed unreliable by the DPA) effectively helpless against offenses committed by clients of the DPA:

> Since the prohibition makes it impossible for the independents credibly to threaten to punish clients who violate their rights, it makes them unable to protect themselves from harm and seriously disadvantages the independents in their daily activities and life. Yet it is perfectly possible that the independents' activities including self-help enforcement could proceed without anyone's rights being violated (leaving aside the question of procedural rights). (p. 110)

Nozick argues that the resolution of this dilemma is to be found in his "Principle of Compensation":

> . . . those who are *disadvantaged* by being forbidden to do actions that only *might* harm others must be compensated for these disadvantages

- 232 -

foisted upon them in order to provide security
for the others. (pp. 82-83)

The principle relies itself upon Nozick's contention that "the dilemma, 'either you have a right to
forbid it so you needn't compensate, or you don't
have a right to forbid it so you should stop,' is
too short" (p. 83). There is a middle ground,
which allows us to go between the horns of the
dilemma; there are *some* actions which people have a
right to forbid, provided that they compensate
those to whom the actions are forbidden. The use
of unreliable procedures of justice by independents
falls into this category, and a likely form of
"compensation" in this case would be the provision,
by the DPA, of protection services to those prohibited from protecting themselves.

It would appear that Nozick is correct at
least in thinking that dealing with risk provides
important problems for the model presently under
discussion, just as it does for any proposed social
system which hopes to preserve justice. It is not
so clear, however, that Nozick's own solution is
the right one.

One possible source of doubt is his emphasis,
in the argument that leads up to the Principle of
Compensation, upon response-policies--policies that
guide the response of a protector *after* a violation
has occurred--rather than upon prevention-policies
--policies that guide the behavior of a protector
in advance of violations. It is not that Nozick
ignores prevention-policies; in fact, the Principle
of Compensation itself evolves as a prevention policy. But the trend of the discussion seems to play
down the possibility that the DPA, for example,
might efficiently protect its clients by way of
armed guards, strong locks, and the like. It is
not clear that *this* sort of prevention policy might
not lower the risk of violations enough to avoid
the necessity of forbidding the *risky* actions of
others, since it keeps its attention focused on
actual violations. It ought at least to have been
more fully discussed.

Another possible problem is the link that

Nozick seems to see between prohibition of an act, on the one hand, and punishment above and beyond mere restitution if the act is performed, on the other. It might be thought that restitution is all that it is *ever* legitimate to require of someone who has violated the rights of another. This is a complicated issue in its own right, of course, but Nozick should have addressed it more squarely, given the role it plays in his argument.

Finally, there is the problem, which Nozick notes, of spelling out just what sorts of things constitute the relevant sorts of "disadvantages." In particular, there is a rather nasty problem of definite description involved with deciding which actions, if prohibited, would disadvantage people (p. 82). There is also, of course, the problem of specifying what "disadvantage" amounts to. Nozick doesn't have a theory of disadvantage, and the lack of it is a source of trouble for the Principle of Compensation (pp. 81-83).

It is not necessary for present purposes, however, to quarrel with Nozick about these points. What is important to note here is that, even if the whole argument for the Principle of Compensation goes through, the Principle does not have quite the effect one might think.

The present problem is the possibility that the protection agency scheme might be unjust. In the first place, if the Principle of Compensation is correct, then it may require a "redistribution" of protection services that would make the DPA resemble, anyway, a state.

There are two points to be made here.

First, the compensation required is not redistributive, as Nozick himself points out:

> We . . . see that such provision need not be
> redistributive since it can be justified on
> other than redistributive grounds, namely, those
> provided in the principle of compensation. (p.
> 114)

The point is that to call an institution or practice "redistributive" implies something about the
reasons for establishing the institution or prac-
tice--reasons different from those Nozick uses in
arguing for an obligation on the part of those who
prohibit unreliable procedures of justice to compensate those who are prohibited.

Second, and most important, the provision of
protective services by the DPA is far from universal in the area it dominates. Once again, attention is directed to the passages quoted at the
beginning of the chapter: " . . . under the usual
conception of a state, each person living within
(or even sometimes traveling outside) its geographical boundaries gets (or at least, is entitled to
get) its protection" (pp. 24-25). The Principle of
Compensation requires nowhere near such broad cov-
erage. It requires only that *those independents* who
are inclined to use unreliable procedures of justice, and who are therefore prohibited from using
them *against clients of the DPA* , must be themselves
provided protection services by the DPA in squabbles
with clients. The DPA need not provide protection to
independents in disputes with other independents.
Neither must it provide protection to independents
who use reliable procedures. The only people protected by the DPA are its own clients and a certain
class *among* the independents, and this latter only in
certain situations.

So the redistributive condition for statehood
is not met by the DPA any more than the monopoly
condition is. Even if every point in Nozick's
chain of arguments be granted him, therefore, it
still appears

> that the dominant protective agency in a terri-
> tory not only lacks the requisite monopoly over
> the use of force, but also fails to provide pro-
> tection for all in its territory; and so the
> dominant agency appears to fall short of being a
> state. (p. 25)

Neither instability nor injustice lead to the collapse of the free market model of social organization. It has survived Nozick's criticisms.

Conclusion

The ethical argument against government under-
mines the thesis that it is morally acceptable to
create or maintain governments. Typical arguments
in behalf of government rely on the idea that govo-
ernment is necessary if certain important social
values are to be obtained, and this idea seems not
to be well founded. Since government is a coercive
tool, and since coercive tools are morally acceptable only if their ends cannot be reached by
non-coercive means, government would be acceptable
only if there were no non-coercive alternatives to
it. The ethical argument against government suggests that there is at least one non-coercive model
for social organization--the free market model--
which is at least as likely as government to provide the things for which government is thought to
be necessary, and which thereby rules out government as an acceptable social tool.

In the first three chapters of this essay, the
prima facie case for government was outlined. The
basis for this case is the obvious necessity that
people cooperate with one another in order to
achieve survival and a reasonably comfortable life.
Three influential arguments in behalf of government
were then isolated--arguments which proceed from
this necessity--and were outlined in the form given
them by their most powerful exponents, Thomas Hobbes,
John Locke, and Karl Marx.

The next three chapters were devoted to giving
a common structure to these three arguments, and to
placing them in a methodological framework that
makes it easier to determine whether they succeed
or fail. This framework--the Rawlsian framework--
provides a locus for arguments for and against government, and it is from within this framework that
the free market model of social organization could
be introduced and compared with the governmental
model. Certain constraining factors having to do
with the provision of "public goods"--factors which
must be taken into consideration by any non-coercive
model for social organization--were acknowledged
and a preliminary sketch of the free market model

was then given.

The first six chapters, then, amounted to a
structuring of the argument; the first three chapters sketched the case for government, and the next
three chapters cast this case in a form in which
the arguments could be critically discussed. Chapters VII-IX compared the free market model to government, and government came out the loser in this
comparison. It appeared that there were no reasons
to think that government was necessary to achieve
the ends for which it is thought to be necessary in
the three core arguments in its defense, and that
the free market is therefore preferable as a means
for organizing society. Government was deemed morally unacceptable because of the availability of a
non-coercive means of achieving its ends.

The last chapter, Chapter X, concerned itself
with answering a pair of objections to the model
that have recently been advanced by Robert Nozick.

It is not the present contention that the free
market society is perfect. It is clear that even
if such a society were to be able to shake free
from the historical human obsession with government, and thus be given a chance to demonstrate its
virtues, it would still emerge fully equipped with
many ancient human problems. There would still be
conflicts between people; there would still be
murders, thefts, and breaches of promise. Some
people would be richer than others, and some would
have to struggle even to live. Some people would
still hunger for power, and the ingenious ones
among them would be likely to find some success in
gaining it. Decisions would not always be made
rationally, and some people would make disastrous
mistakes.

These are the problems of every human society,
however. Here, no more has been argued than that
the purely contractual free market society would be
at least as capable of dealing with these problems
as is governed society. There is, in fact, good
reason to believe that the market society would be
better able to deal with them. In addition to the
obvious advantage of avoiding institutions designed

explicitly to interfere with individual human rights,
it seems likely that the kinds of conflict prevalent in all societies would be dramatically reduced
in scale in the market society.

Furthermore, many sources of conflict common
to governed societies are likely to be absent in a
fully voluntaristic social arrangement; solutions
to *any* problems are likely to be relatively more
accessible in the contractual society, since its
"institutions" could probably respond more rapidly
to success or failure in accomplishing what they
were designed to do; the market is likely to provide alternative means of satisfying most needs,
and the producers of these means will be in competition with one another; finally, the market is
ideally suited to provide new ideas and new services, as the need arises.

It is important to reaffirm, however, two
things that were noted in the Introduction.

First, the content of the present argument
rests mainly on the third postulate. The first two
postulates serve primarily as guides to the usage
of terms throughout this essay.

Second, the postulates are not defended here.
Significant controversy might arise over their ten-
ability.

If the third postulate is untenable, therefore, the whole argument is endangered. It seems,
however, that it is at least as uncontroversial as
may be expected of any ethical postulate, and there
are no obvious grounds for being suspicious of it.
It says, after all, no more than that in the absence
of good reasons to the contrary, people should not
be coerced.

If the first or second postulates are found to
be untenable, the consequences are not nearly so
grave. This is fortunate, since they may be somewhat more controversial than the third postulate.
If they are deemed unacceptable, then the argument
presented here still goes through, with a thorough-
going term-for-term substitution of the kind suggested in the Introduction.

If such substitution is necessary, however, this book will have supported not the abandonment of government, but rather the abandonment of a certain kind of government: *coercive* government. That is in keeping with the basic intent of the project.

In other words, even if it could be shown that coercion is *not* an "essential character" of government--that the free market model of social organization represents merely a special kind of governmental model, rather than a special brand of anarchy --it would still not be necessary to abandon the free market model. It is not the main purpose of this project to contest such a possibility, although the terminology used throughout this discussion does clearly reflect a bias against it. But if it appeared that coercion were not a necessary condition of government, then it would be necessary to change the terminology of this essay and accept the contention that it is only the most pervasive *kind* of government that is here being criticized, and that what is proposed here is merely the adoption of another. It is the free market model of social organization, whether it is really anarchic or not, which has outlasted its competitors in the deliberations of the constitutional conventions. If the arguments for it are accepted, then the book will have achieved the ends for which it was intended.

In the absence of good arguments against the three initial postulates, however, the conclusion of this book may be stated in its boldest form: government is morally unacceptable; it should be abandoned.

Works Cited

1. Anscombe, Elizabeth. "On the Source of the Authority of the State." *Ratio*, 20 (1978), 1-28.

2. Aristotle. *The Politics*, trans. T.A. Sinclair. 1962; rpt. Harmondsworth, England: Penguin Books, 1970.

3. Arrow, Kenneth J. "Some Ordinalist-Utilitarian Notes on Rawls' Theory of Justice." *Journal of Philosophy*, 70 (1973), pp. 245-63.

4. Bakunin, Michael. "Gossudarstwennost i Anarchija." Quoted extensively in Karl Marx, "Konspekt von Bakunins Buch 'Staatlichkeit und Anarchie'." Karl Marx and Friedrich Engels. *Werke*. Berlin: Dietz Verlag, 1962. XVIII.

5. _____. *Marxism, Freedom, and the State*, trans. and ed. K.J. Kenafisk. London: Freedom Press, 1950.

6. Bastiat, Frédéric. *Essays on Political Economy*, trans. rev. David A. Wells. New York: G.P. Putnam's Sons, 1877.

7. Beackon, Steve and Andrew Reeve. "The Benefits of Reasonable Conduct: The *Leviathan* Theory of Obligation." *Political Theory*, 4 (1976), 423-38.

8. Becker, Lawrence C. "The Labor Theory of Property Acquisition." *Journal of Philosophy*, 73 (1976), 653-64.

9. _____. *Property Rights: Philosophic Foundations*. London: Routledge and Kegan Paul, 1977.

10. Beran, Harry. "In Defense of the Consent Theory of Political Obligation and Authority." *Ethics*, 87 (1976/77), 260-71.

11. Bergson, Abram. *Essays in Normative Economics*. Cambridge: Harvard University Press, 1966.

12. _____. "Market Socialism Revisited." *Journal of Political Economy*, 75 (1967), 655-73.

13. Böhm-Bawerk, Eugen von. *Capital and Interest: A Critical History of Economical Theory*, trans. William Smart. 1890; rpt. New York: Kelly and Millman, 1957.

14. _____. *Karl Marx and the Close of His System*, ed. Paul M. Sweezy. 1949; rpt. New York: A.M. Kelley, 1966.

15. Brewster, Ben. Review of *Economics and Ideology and Other Essays* by Ronald L. Meek. *New Left Review*, November–December, 1967.

16. Brutzkus, Boris. *Economic Planning in Soviet Russia*. London: George Routledge and Sons, 1935.

17. Buchanan, Allen. "Exploitation, Alienation, and Injustice." *Canadian Journal of Philosophy*, 9 (1979), 121–39.

18. _____. "The Marxian Critique of Justice and Rights." Forthcoming, *Canadian Journal of Philosophy*, 1980 or 1981 (?).

19. Buchanan, James M. "Ethical Rules, Expected Values, and Large Numbers." *Ethics*, 76 (1965/66), 1–13.

20. Childs, Roy A. "The Invisible Hand Strikes Back." *Journal of Libertarian Studies*, 1 (1977), 23–34.

21. Chkhikvadze, V.M. "Human Rights and the Ideological Struggle." *Soviet Studies in Philosophy*, 16 (1977/78), No. 3, 3–18.

22. Cornuelle, Richard C. *Reclaiming the American Dream*. New York: Random House, 1965.

23. Dacey, Raymond. "The Role of Economic Theory in Supporting Counterfactual Arguments." *Philosophy and Phenomenological Research*, 35 (1974/75), 402–10.

24. Dalgarno, M.T. "Analysing Hobbes's Contract." *Proceedings of the Aristotelean Society*, 76 (1975/76), 209–26.

25. Daniels, Norman. "Wide Reflective Equilibrium and Theory Acceptance in Ethics." *Journal of Philosophy*, 76 (1979), 256–82.

26. Danielson, Peter. "Taking Anarchism Seriously." *Philosophy of the Social Sciences*, 8 (1978), 135-52.

27. Djilas, Milovan. *The New Class: An Analysis of the Communist System*. 1957; rpt. New York: Praeger, 1958.

28. Dunn, John. "Consent in the Political Theory of John Locke." *Historical Journal*, 10 (1967), 153-82.

29. Elzinga, Kenneth G. "Predatory Pricing: The Case of the Gunpowder Trust." *Journal of Law and Economics*, 13 (1970), 223-40.

30. Feiwel, G.R. "Lange's Contribution to Economics." *Scientia*, 108 (1973), 331-56.

31. Friedman, David. *The Machinery of Freedom: Guide to a Radical Capitalism*. New York: Harper and Row, 1973.

32. Friedman, Milton. *Capitalism and Freedom*. 1962; rpt. Chicago: University of Chicago Press, 1970.

33. Gauthier, David. "Justice and Natural Endowment: Toward a Critique of Rawls' Ideological Framework." *Social Theory and Practice*, 3 (1974), 3-26.

34. _____. "Rational Cooperation." *Noûs*, 8 (1974), 53-65.

35. Gerth, Hans (ed.). *The First International: Minutes of the Hague Congress of 1872*. Madison, Wisc.: University of Wisconsin Press, 1958.

36. Godwin, William. *Enquiry Concerning Political Justice and its Influence on Morals and Happiness*, ed. F.E.L. Priestley. Toronto: University of Toronto Press, 1946.

37. Goehlert, Robert. "Anarchism: A Bibliography of Articles, 1900-1975." *Political Theory*, 4 (1976), 113-27.

38. Goldman, Emma. *Anarchism and Other Essays*. New York: Mother Earth, 1910.

39. _____. *My Further Disillusionment in Russia*. Garden City, N.Y.: Doubleday, Page and Co., 1924.

40. Goodman, Paul. *Communitas: Means of Livelihood and Ways of Life*, with Percival Goodman. Chicago: University of Chicago Press, 1947.

41. _____. *Growing Up Absurd: Problems of Youth in the Organized System*. New York: Random House, 1960.

42. _____. *People or Personnel: Decentralizing and the Mixed System*. New York: Random House, 1965.

43. _____. *Utopian Essays and Practical Proposals*. 1962; rpt. New York: Vintage Books, 1970.

44. Hammond, J.L. and Barbara. *The Bleak Age*. Rev. ed. London: Pelican Books, 1947.

45. Hampsher-Monk, Iain W. "Tacit Concept of Consent in Locke's Two Treatises of Government: A Note on Citizens, Travellers, and Patriarchalism." *Journal of the History of Ideas*, 60 (1979), 135-39.

46. Hancey, James O. "John Locke and the Law of Nature." *Political Theory*, 4 (1976), 439-54.

47. Hayek, Friedrich A. (ed.). *Capitalism and the Historians*. 1954; rpt. Chicago: University of Chicago Press, 1967.

48. _____ (ed.). *Collectivist Economic Planning*. 1935; rpt. London: George Routledge and Sons, 1938.

49. _____. *The Constitution of Liberty*. 1960; rpt. Chicago: Henry Regnery, 1972.

50. _____. *Individualism and Economic Order*. 1948; rpt. Chicago: Henry Regnery, 1972.

51. Hazlitt, Henry. *Economics in One Lesson*. 1946; rpt. New York: Manor Books, 1973.

52. _____. *Failure of the "New Economics": An Analysis of the Keynesian Fallacies*. Princeton: Van Nostrand, 1959.

53. _____. *Man vs. the Welfare State*. 1969; rpt. New Rochelle, N.Y.: Arlington House, 1970.

54. Hennis, Wilhelm. "Ende der Politik? Zur Krisis der Politik in der Neuzeit." *Merkur*, 25 (1971), 509-26.

55. Hobbes, Thomas. *Leviathan*. Ed. C.B. Macpherson. 1651; rpt. Harmondsworth, England: Penguin Books, 1972.

56. Holmstrom, Nancy. "Exploitation." *Canadian Journal of Philosophy*, 7 (1977), 353-69.

57. Hospers, John. *Libertarianism: A Political Philosophy Whose Time Has Come*. Special ed. Santa Barbara, Calif.: Reason Press, n.d.

58. _____. "The Nature of the State." *Personalist*, 59 (1978), 398-404.

59. Jefferson, Thomas. *Basic Writings of Thomas Jefferson*, ed. Philip S. Foner. New York: Wiley, 1944.

60. Johnson, Karen. "A Note on the Inapplicability of Olson's Logic of Collective Action to the State." *Ethics*, 85 (1974/75), 170-74.

61. _____. "Political Obligation and the Voluntary Association Model of the State." *Ethics*, 86 (1975/76), 17-29.

62. Keyt, David. "The Social Contract as an Analytic, Justificatory, and Polemic Device." *Canadian Journal of Philosophy*, 4 (1974/75), 241-52.

63. Kolko, Gabriel. *Railroads and Regulation: 1877-1916*. Princeton: Princeton University Press, 1965.

64. _____. *The Triumph of Conservatism: A Reinterpretation of American History, 1900-1916*. 1963; rpt. Chicago: Quadrangle Books, n.d.

65. Kropotkin, Peter. *The Conquest of Bread*, ed. Paul Avrich. New York: New York University Press, 1972.

66. _____. *Ethics: Origin and Development*, trans. Louis S. Friedland and Joseph R. Piroshnikoff. 1924; rpt. New York: Dial, 1936.

67. _____. *Kropotkin's Revolutionary Pamphlets*, ed. Roger N. Baldwin. New York: Dover Publications, 1970.

68. _____. *Memoirs of a Revolutionist*. Boston: Houghton Mifflin, 1930.

69. _____. *Mutual Aid: A Factor of Revolution*, ed. Paul Avrich. New York: New York University Press, 1972.

70. Lange, Oskar. *Political Economy*. New York: Macmillan, 1963.

71. _____ and Fred M. Taylor. *On the Economic Theory of Socialism*. New York: McGraw-Hill, 1964.

72. Locke, John. *An Essay Concerning Human Understanding*, ed. A.C. Fraser, 2 vols. Oxford: Clarendon Press, 1894.

73. _____. *Two Treatises of Government*, ed. Peter Laslett. Rev. ed. 1960; rpt. New York: New American Library, n.d.

74. McBride, William Leon. "The Concept of Justice in Marx, Engels, and Others." *Ethics*, 85 (1974/75), 204-18.

75. McClennan, Edward F. Review of *The Liberal Theory of Justice* by Brian Barry. *Social Theory and Practice*, 3 (1974), 117-22.

76. McGee, John S. "Predatory Price Cutting: The Standard Oil (N.J.) Case." *Journal of Law and Economics*, 1 (1958), 137-69.

77. McKenzie, Richard B. "The Economic Dimensions of Ethical Behavior." *Ethics*, 87 (1976/77), 208-21.

78. Madison, James. *The Complete Madison*, ed. Saul K. Padover. New York: Harper, 1953.

79. Margolis, Joseph. "Justice as Fairness." *Humanist*, 33, No. 3 (1973), 36-37.

80. Martin, Rex. "Two Models for Justifying Political Authority." *Ethics*, 86 (1975/76), 70-75.

81. _____. "Wolff's Defence of Philosophical Anarchism." *Philosophical Quarterly*, 24 (1974), 140-49.

82. Marx, Karl. *Capital: A Critique of Political Economy*. 3 vols. 1967; rpt. New York: International Publishers, 1974.

83. _____. *A Contribution to the Critique of Political Economy*, ed. Maurice Dobb. 1970; rpt. New York: International Publishers, 1972.

84. _____. *Karl Marx: Early Writings*, ed. and trans. T.B. Bottomore. New York: McGraw-Hill, 1964.

85. _____. *The Poverty of Philosophy*. 1963; rpt. New York: International Publishers, 1973.

86. _____ and Friedrich Engels. *The Communist Manifesto*. 1888; rpt. Harmondsworth, England: Penguin Books, 1972.

87. _____ and Frederick Engels. *The German Ideology*, ed. C.J. Arthur. 1970; rpt. New York: International Publishers, 1973.

88. _____ and Frederick Engels. *Selected Works*. 3 vols. 1969; rpt. Moscow: Progress Publishers, 1973.

89. _____ and Friedrich Engels. *Werke*. 41 vols. in 44. Berlin: Dietz Verlag, 1962.

90. Meek, Ronald L. *Economics and Ideology and Other Essays*. London: Chapman and Hall, 1967.

91. Miller, David. "Socialism and the Market." *Political Theory*, 5 (1977), 473-90.

92. Miller, Fred D., Jr. "The State and the Community in Aristotle's *Politics*." *Reason Papers*, No. 1 (Fall, 1974), 61-69.

93. Miller, Richard. "Rawls and Marxism." *Philosophy and Public Affairs*, 3 (1973/74), 167-91.

94. Mises, Ludwig von. *Human Action*. 3rd rev. ed. Chicago: Henry Regnery, 1966.

95. _____. *Kritik des Interventionismus*. Jena: Gustav Fischer, 1929.

96. _____. *Omnipotent Government: The Rise of the Total State and Total War*. 1944; rpt. New Rochelle, N.Y.: Arlington House, 1969.

97. _____. *Socialism: An Economic and Sociological Analysis*, trans. J. Kahane. Rev. ed. 1951; rpt. London: Jonathan Cape, 1972.

98. _____. "Die Wirtschaftsrechnung im sozialistischen Gemeinwesen." *Archiv für Sozialwissenschaft und Sozialpolitik*, 47, No. 1 (1920), 86-121.

99. Murphy, J. "Marxism and Retribution." *Philosophy and Public Affairs*, 2 (1973), 217-43.

100. Nielsen, Kai. "Distrusting Reason." *Ethics*, 87 (1976/77), 49-60.

101. _____. "On Philosophic Method." *International Philosophical Quarterly*, 16 (1976), 349-68.

102. Nozick, Robert. *Anarchy, State, and Utopia*. New York: Basic Books, 1974.

103. _____. "Coercion." *Philosophy, Science, and Method*, ed. S. Morgenbesser, P. Suppes, M. White. New York: St. Martin's Press, 1969.

104. Olson, Mancur. *The Logic of Collective Action: Public Goods and the Theory of Groups*. Cambridge, Mass.: Harvard University Press, 1965.

105. Oppenheimer, Franz. *The State*. Indianapolis: Bobbs-Merrill, 1914.

106. Proudhon, Pierre Joseph. *General Idea of Revolution in the Nineteenth Century*, trans. John Beverley Robinson. London: Freedom Press, 1923.

107. _____. *What is Property? An Inquiry into the Principle of Right and of Government*, trans. Benjamin R. Tucker. 1890; rpt. New York: Dover, 1970.

108. Punzo, Vincent C. "The Modern State and the Search for Community: The Anarchist Critique of Kropotkin." *International Philosophical Quarterly*, 16 (1976), 3-32.

109. "Quickies." *Reason*, 8, No. 12 (1977), 11.

110. Rand, Ayn. *Atlas Shrugged*. 1957; rpt. New York: New American Library, n.d.

111. _____. *Capitalism: The Unknown Ideal*. 1967; rpt. New York: New American Library, n.d.

112. _____. *The Fountainhead*. 1943; rpt. New York: New American Library, n.d.

113. _____. *The Virtue of Selfishness: A New Concept of Egoism*. 1964; rpt. New York: New American Library, n.d.

114. Rapaport, Elizabeth. "Anarchism and Authority in Marx's Socialist Politics." *Archives européennes de sociologie*, 17 (1976), 333-43.

115. Rasmussen, Douglas B. "A Critique of Rawls' *Theory of Justice*." *Personalist*, 55 (1974), 303-18.

116. Rawls, John. *A Theory of Justice*. 1971; rpt. Cambridge, Mass.: Belknap Press, 1973.

117. Reiman, Jeffrey H. "Anarchism and Nominalism: Wolff's Latest Obituary for Political Philosophy." *Ethics*, 89 (1978/79), 95-110.

118. Riker, William H. and Peter C. Ordeshook. *An Introduction to Positive Political Theory*. Englewood Cliffs: Prentice-Hall, 1973.

119. Robbins, Lionel. *The Great Depression*. New York: Macmillan, 1936.

120. Rothbard, Murray N. *For a New Liberty*. New York: Macmillan, 1973.

121. _____. *Man, Economy, and State*. Los Angeles: Nash, n.d.

122. _____. *Power and Market: Government and the Economy*. 1970; rpt. Menlo Park, Calif.: Institute for Humane Studies, n.d.

123. Rousseau, Jean Jacques. *The Social Contract*, trans. Willmoore Kendall. 1964; rpt. Chicago: Henry Regnery, n.d.

124. Russell, Bertrand. *History of Western Philosophy and its Connection with Political and Social Circumstances from the Earliest Times to the Present Day*. 1946; rpt. London: George Allen and Unwin, 1962.

125. Sanders, John T. "The Free Market Model Versus Government: A Reply to Nozick." *Journal of Libertarian Studies*, 1 (1977), 35-44.

126. Schwartz, Adina. "Moral Neutrality and Primary Goods." *Ethics*, 83 (1972/73), 294-307.

127. Schaefer, David Lewis. "The 'Sense' and Nonsense of Justice." *Political Science Reviewer*, 3 (1973), 1-41.

128. Schedler, George. "Hobbes on the Basis of Political Obligation." *Journal of the History of Philosophy*, 15 (1977), 165-70.

129. Simmons, A. John. "Tacit Consent and Political Obligation." *Philosophy and Public Affairs*, 5 (1975/76) 274-91.

130. Singer, Marcus G. "Justice, Theory, and a Theory of Justice." *Philosophy of Science*, 44 (1977), 594-618.

131. Singer, Peter. "Philosophers Are Back on the Job." *New York Times Magazine*, 7 July 1974, 6-7 and 17-20.

132. Slote, Michael. "Morality and Ignorance." *Journal of Philosophy*, 74 (1977), 745-67.

33. Smith, Adam. *An Inquiry into the Nature and Causes of the Wealth of Nations.* 1776; rpt. New Rochelle, N.Y.: Arlington House, n.d.

34. Spooner, Lysander. *No Treason.* Boston: Lysander Spooner, 1870.

35. _____. *The Unconstitutionality of Slavery.* Boston: B. Marsh, 1860.

36. Stekloff, G.M. *History of the First International,* trans. Eden and Cedar Paul. London: Martin Lawrence, 1928.

37. Suits, David B. "On Hobbes's Argument for Government." *Reason Papers,* No. 4 (Winter, 1978), 1-16.

38. _____. "On Locke's Argument for Government." *Journal of Libertarian Studies,* 1 (1977), 195-203.

39. Tannehill, Morris and Linda. *The Market for Liberty.* Lansing, Mich.: Morris and Linda Tannehill, 1970.

40. Taylor, Richard. *Freedom, Anarchy, and the Law: An Introduction to Political Philosophy.* Englewood Cliffs, N.J.: Prentice-Hall, 1973.

41. Telser, Lester G. "Abusive Trade Practices: An Economic Analysis." *Law and Contemporary Problems,* 30 (1965).

42. _____. "Cutthroat Competition and the Long Purse." *Journal of Law and Economics,* 9 (1966).

43. Thomson, Judith Jarvis. "Property Acquisition." *Journal of Philosophy,* 73 (1976), 664-66.

44. Thoreau, Henry David. "On the Duty of Civil Disobedience." 1849; rpt. with omissions, *Toward Liberal Education,* ed. Louis G. Locke, William M. Gibson, and George Arms. 4th ed. New York: Holt, Rinehart and Winston, 1962, 608-21.

45. _____. *Walden.* 1854; rpt. New York: Time Incorporated, 1962.

146. *Toward Liberty*. 2 vols. 1971; rpt. Menlo Park, Calif.
     Institute for Humane Studies, 1973.

147. "Trends." *Reason*, 7, No. 10 (1976), 58.

148. Tuccille, Jerome. *Radical Libertarianism: A Right
     Wing Alternative*. Indianapolis: Bobbs-Merrill,
     1970.

149. Tucker, Benjamin. *Individual Liberty*. New York: Van-
     guard Press, 1926.

150. _____. *Instead of a Book*. 2nd ed. New York: B.R.
     Tucker, 1897.

151. Tucker, Robert. *The Marxian Revolutionary Idea*. New
     York: Norton and Co., 1969.

152. Tur, Richard H.S. "Anarchy versus Authority: Towards a
     Democratic Theory of Law." *Archiv für Rechts- und
     Sozialphilosophie*, 63 (1977), 305-26.

153. Turgot, Anne Robert Jacques. *Reflections on the Forma-
     tion and Distribution of Riches*. 1770; rpt. New
     York: Macmillan, 1922.

154. Wagner, Richard E. "Pressure Groups and Political
     Entrepreneurs: A Review Article." *Papers on
     Non-Market Decision Making*, 1 (1966).

155. Weber, Max. *Grundriss der Sozialökonomik*. Tübingen:
     J.C.B. Mohr, 1921.

156. Wei-Hsun Fu, Charles. "Marxism-Leninism-Maoism as an
     Ethical Theory." *Journal of Chinese Philosophy*,
     5 (1978), 343-62.

157. "World Nations." *The Official Associated Press Almanac
     1974*. Maplewood, N.J.: Hammon Almanac, 1973.

158. Wolff, Robert Paul. *In Defense of Anarchism*. New
     York: Harper and Row, 1970.

159. Wood, Allen. "The Marxian Critique of Justice." *Phi-
     losophy and Public Affairs*, 1 (1972).